ISABELLA

AND THE STRANGE DEATH OF
EDWARD II

by the same author

The Mysterious Death of Tutankhamun

ISABELLA

AND THE STRANGE DEATH OF
EDWARD II

Paul Doherty

CARROLL & GRAF PUBLISHERS
New York

Carroll & Graf Publishers
An imprint of Avalon Publishing Group, Inc.
161 William Street
NY 10038–2607
www.carrollandgraf.com

First published in the UK by Constable,
an imprint of Constable & Robinson Ltd 2003

First Carroll & Graf edition 2003

ISBN 0–7867–1193–0

Printed and bound in the EU

Contents

Prologue: England under Edward I   1

1 A Fitting Marriage . . .   11

2 Isabella and the King's Favourite   35

3 The New Favourite and Isabella's Disgrace   69

4 The She-Wolf Triumphant   105

5 The Burial of a King   133

6 The Downfall of the She-Wolf   155

7 The Immortal King   183

8 The King is Dead, Long Live the King   217

Notes   241

Bibliography   251

Index   257

To Carla, my wife,
with all my love

England under Edward I

Oh day of wrath, oh day of mourning!
See fulfilled Heaven's warning.
Heaven and Earth in ashes burning!
See what fear man's bosom rendeth,
When from Heaven the judge descendeth,
On whose sentence all dependeth.

Dies irae, the opening words of the medieval hymn-writer, Thomas de Celano, chill the soul and concentrate the mind, not only on an individual death but the end of all things. Such verses characterize the most significant difference between medieval and modern consciousness. We regarded the millennium as something to look forward to, an exciting time of change. The medieval mind viewed 'The Millennium' as that moment in history when the sky would melt, the earth would catch fire, the sun darken, the moon turn to blood and the stars fall from heaven. The very fabric of creation would be ripped apart to reveal Christ coming in judgement at the end of the world. Thus in 1300, people were ever-conscious of the imminent dissolution of all things, when the human and divine would finally merge.

To the medieval mind these two realities co-existed: the Visible – the fabric of life – and the Invisible. The two were not totally distinct but intermingled. The fourteenth century developed such an attitude even further, manifesting itself not only in the glorious cathedrals of Salisbury and Gloucester but in the constant pilgrimages to Becket's tomb at Canterbury and the Virgin's statue at Walsingham, whilst for braver souls there were always the attraction of St James Compostella, St Peter's in Rome or, the greatest prize of all, Jerusalem.

The people of the fourteenth century were only too aware of the spiritual realities which framed their everyday existence. They were highly sensitive to the powers of darkness, to the air being peopled with demons, to Lucifer, the Fallen Angel, wandering God's creation, 'roaring like a lion seeking whom it may devour'. At the same time they were acutely conscious of the powers of light: of Christ and 'His sweet Mother', of ministering angels and mediating saints. Every village church had its altar and those that were large enough, their Lady Chapel, statues, shrines, and exuberant wall paintings which depicted the truth of man's spiritual destiny. Chaucer's *Canterbury Tales* reflects these realities perfectly, describing a pilgrimage to Becket's shrine, which included the good, the noble, the bad and the indifferent of fourteenth-century England. Chaucer's poetry exudes a spring-time freshness as well as the energy and bustle of his era with all its idiosyncrasies, strengths and failings, virtues and vices.

The fourteenth century can be described as the high point of the Middle Ages and yet it also contained within it the very seeds of its own destruction. Nowhere is this more apparent than in the lives and careers of the

'Anointed Ones' of Westminster, who did so much to shape and influence the lives of their subjects. In 1300, England was ruled by Edward I (1272–1307), the greatest of the Plantaganet line, a born warrior, statesman and general. Edward I could be viewed as either a visionary or a fanatic. He dreamed of uniting England, Wales, Ireland and Scotland under one rule from Westminster: the beginning of the notion of 'Empire' which, even today, England still struggles to break free from. Edward I had no such doubts. He wanted his writ to run as far north as the Highlands of Scotland, across Wales to the western coast of Ireland: his England would be replicated and extended. Edward's barons, or great Earls, would lead his armies of mailed, mounted knights, leather-garbed footmen and archers, to subjugate all opposition. Castles would be built and narrow-laned towns, with their market places, churches and plaster-and-wood houses, founded to promote commerce. Harbours and ports would be developed to receive his warships and merchantmen, those sturdy, one-masted, fat-bellied cogs on which England so depended for protection and commerce. The power of the English Church, owing an uneasy allegiance to the Popes in exile at Avignon, would make itself felt; the primacy of Canterbury would be accepted by all. The great religious orders, the Benedictines, Franciscans and Dominicans, would be encouraged to found monasteries and priories, till the land and remind the people that, if there was one Christ, one Pope, one Church, there was also only one King: the Anointed One, who wore the Confessor's crown and sat enthroned in splendour at Westminster. Yet many of these dreams soon turned into nightmares; the seeds of hideous war, betrayal and bloodshed were planted deep.

Edward I had a strong sense of *Communitas Regni* – Community of the Realm. He possessed the wit to realize that his world was changing. Some peasants no longer tilled the land but allowed it to grass over to graze sheep whose wool was avidly sought by the merchants of the Low Countries, that collection of warring states on France's northern border, Hainault, Brabant and Flanders.

This newly found wealth led to the rapid expansion of cities such as York, Bristol and, above all, London. A city, dominated by the Tower, London comprised a cramped acreage of narrow streets, jostling houses and countless churches. A busy, prosperous place, the centre of royal government and its system of law and order, London was proving to be one of the leading cities of western Europe. It housed the emerging Inns of Court and, above all, the great departments of state: the Exchequer, or treasury, where sheriffs from the shires would have to deliver their accounts four times a year; and the Chancery, or great 'Writing Office', where clerks, trained at the universities of Oxford and Cambridge, ran the civil service. The city was also the hub of royal justice with its Courts of King's Bench and Common Pleas held in Westminster Hall. London of the early fourteenth century represented the growing wealth and complexity of English society and housed the guilds and fraternities, like those of Corpus Christi in Bread Street, the Grocers of Soper Lane or the Brewers at All Hallows near London Wall.

The powerful burgesses and merchants of London and other commercial centres had used their newly found wealth to build churches, market places, stately mansions and warehouses as well as to promote their own interests. They had formed guilds, powerful trading organizations, and had sent their sons to cathedral schools and on to the Halls of Oxford or Cambridge. Afterwards they would follow a career in the Church or the expanding civil service, which supported the Crown and its policies, both at home and abroad. These burgesses advanced the interests of their own cities, particularly London, and demanded a say in national government. Politics, they argued, was too important to be left to the King and his great Council of nobles and bishops.

England was thus a thriving melting-pot of many conflicting worlds: the great lords, the merchants, the ever-busy civic burgesses, the prosperous peasants and, of course, the poor, who were always with them. Two mighty organizations cut across this energetic, jostling society. First was the Crown – the all-powerful King, surrounded by his lawyers and councillors. Even here change had begun. The King swore a great oath to rule justly and, in return, received the obedience of his subjects. This basic pledge of mutual solidarity had been put under scrutiny by lawyers, who had evolved a philosophy of interdependence. The King was there to rule but he must do so wisely. He must take the advice of his Council, which must include the Great Lords of the Soil. Others, like the lawyer Bracton, developed this even further, proclaiming '*Quod omnes tangit ab omnibus approbetur*' – 'What affects all must be approved by all'.

Edward I had implemented this theory in a more practical way for his own uses by summoning his Parliaments, where he could meet the community of the realm to discuss matters of mutual interest, be it finance, military defence, war or law. Naturally, the different stratas of such a hierarchical society did not intermingle. The Lords met together in one session, representatives of the Commons assembled in another. The latter were evolving a system of 'redress before supply': the King needed their consent to levy effective taxes; they, in turn, could respond by submitting petitions for royal redress, or at least an answer, to their general or particular grievances. It was a finely balanced system. On the one hand, the King could act the autocrat, but on the other he had to be aware of the advice and opinion of other sections of the community he ruled.

Edward I of England was the embodiment of such a balance: king and warrior, Edward had developed 'Parliaments' to aid good government, not necessarily realizing that the system he patronized might one day limit his own power. He used Parliament not only to gain the consensus of the community but also to enact statute law which had the full consent of that community.

The second organization which cut across and dominated all aspects of medieval society was the Church. Aristotle called man a political animal; the fourteenth century Church defined him as religious. Every human being, it preached, had an eternal destiny and the Church was there to ensure this destiny was fulfilled. The Catholic Church was a power to be reckoned with. It stretched across borders, it proclaimed a philosophy completely free of national aspirations. The power of the Pope, the Bishop of Rome, was all-pervasive and each kingdom, England included, had to respond to this power. The English Church was part of an international organization. Its leaders, the Archbishops of Canterbury and York, the bishops in their different dioceses, all had to acquire papal approval before they could assume office. In turn, these bishops ruled large sprawling dioceses where the Church was represented in towns and villages by a vicar, priest or religious. The local manifestation of the Church's power was the parish chapel and the organization which grew up around it.

Of course there were tensions. The Catholic Church was an international power but national aspirations did surface. The popes had to fight a continuing battle with the kings of England over the control of the national Church and the comprehensive social message it preached. Edward I, and his son Edward II, were both drawn into this conflict as they strove to keep united, under their own personal rule, the disparate, and often conflicting, sectional interests of their kingdom.

Edward I strove for uniformity and union and had the personality and strength of character to carry this through. He launched a devastating war on Wales to bring the principality under the direct rule of the English Crown and to establish his borders on the edge of the Irish Sea. The Welsh princes, including the principal chieftain, Llewellyn, were caught and executed, their tribes crushed and a string of powerful castles, controlled by Marcher (or border) barons such as the de Spencers and Mortimers, would keep the country in subjection.

Edward now turned to Scotland where conflicting rival claims to the crown allowed him to intervene, first as the 'honest broker' and then as the powerful prince and conquering king. In 1286, King Alexander III of Scotland had taken a mortal fall whilst riding through a storm to visit his new queen. His only heir was his granddaughter Margaret, whose father was the King of Norway. Edward immediately suggested that his son, Edward II, and the Maid of Norway be betrothed and marry. He got his way but in October 1290, the young girl, en route to Scotland, died on board ship and her corpse was taken back to Bergen. The death of the Maid of Norway thus dragged the English Crown into a savage, bloody war with Scotland. Edward supported a number of claimants to the Scottish throne but his long-term goal was the annexation of that kingdom and its absorption under the English Crown, just as he had achieved in Wales.

In the end Scotland proved a hard nut to crack. A group of astute war leaders, William Wallace, Archbishop Wishart of Glasgow and finally Robert the Bruce, reduced the Plantaganet's ambitions to nothing. The recent film *Braveheart* vividly describes the bloody savagery of Edward's war in Scotland: in that sense the film is accurate. Scotland was turned into a battlefield, its cities burnt, and its nobles became partisan fighters hiding out in the woods and glens.

Edward's vision remained quite simple: one king ruling over a united realm, whose writ could run in Cornwall, London, North Wales, Dublin or Edinburgh. Naturally such a drive for centralization provoked its own reaction. Wales was conquered but Scotland rejected Edward's vision and fought for its own. Edward was a medieval king, aware of his own fiefdom which, in his view, not only included England, Scotland, Ireland and Wales but also the Duchy of Gascony, that great prosperous wine-growing area centred around the town of Bordeaux in south-west France. Gascony was vital to English interests, not only as a relic of the great Angevin empire of Henry II, but also because of the increasing profits from its rich fertile vineyards.

In France, however, the same beliefs held sway: the Capetian Philip IV, through his council of ministers and different 'Parlements', also tried to impose his autocratic vision of what his kingdom should be. Naturally, two such strong kings clashed over every aspect of influence: the Church, international status and, above all, the English duchy of Gascony. Philip IV dreamed of bringing that prosperous area of south-west France under the direct control of the Capets. At the same time, Philip and Edward had to pay public lip-service to the idea of an international lasting peace brokered by the papacy. Their rivalry, coupled with the desire to be seen as acting as one, led to the idea of an alliance by blood between the two most powerful ruling houses of Europe. The marriage of Princess Isabella, daughter of Philip IV, and Prince Edward I's son, originated from these conflicting ideals. It is hardly surprising that this much-vaunted marriage, far from resolving conflict, only exacerbated it, both in their respective kingdoms and beyond.

ONE

A Fitting Marriage . . .

'. . . We ask you to send our beloved son in Christ,
your son Edward, Prince of Wales with an appropriate
retinue of Prelates and Magnates and prudent men . . .
for contracting the marriage treaty between himself and
the daughter of the aforesaid King of France . . .'

Clement V to Edward I, 25 August 1305

Isabella was a fairy-tale princess. The chroniclers attest to
her loveliness, to her beautiful blonde hair, which she
inherited from her father, Philip Le Bel, and her slightly
arabic features from her mother Johanna of Navarre. We
have no accurate pictorial representation of Isabella; however, her face and striking features are faithfully represented
by a carved statue which decorates John of Eltham's tomb,
her second son, in Westminster Abbey.[1]

Isabella was born in 1296, the only surviving daughter of
Philip IV, nicknamed 'The Beautiful', of France. She was
twelve when she married Edward II and left her father's
court. Little evidence remains about her early life, only
a few fragments concerning grants to the princess and
her dependants, but scarcely enough to build a coherent

picture of her life at the French court, be it the Louvre Palace or the other royal residences in and around the Île de France. She was the youngest of Philip and Johanna's four children and, like her three brothers, Louis, Philip and Charles, Isabella was used as a powerful political pawn by her father in extending his own influence both in France and across Europe.[2]

Philip IV was no nationalist but he had a clear and distinctive view of the power and influence due to his own dynasty, the House of Capet. Philip, flattered by his lawyers, William of Nogaret and Peter Dubois, saw himself as a second Charlemagne, a king who would dominate Europe: the western borders of France would be extended to the Rhine; Philip would bring under his control those small squabbling countries to the north – Flanders and Hainault; the powerful independent fiefs of Burgundy and Brittainy would be annexed. Above all, he would wrest from the English Crown the remains of its great Angevin empire. John of England had lost most of this in the thirteenth century but two strategic areas remained: the counties of Ponthieu and Montreuil in northern France and the wine-rich duchy of Gascony.[3]

Philip IV's great-grandfather was St Louis and, in Philip's eyes, this saintly king made the entire Capetian line sacred, superior to all ruling dynasties, including the papacy. Philip's foreign policy, a mixture of skilful administration and brutal force, met with varying degrees of success. His three sons were married off to powerful, wealthy French heiresses but, when he couldn't achieve diplomatic success through marriage, Philip used both sword and trickery, as he did against the English-held duchy of Gascony. The status of that duchy, and the relationship of its Duke, the

English king, to the French Crown had been defined by the Treaty of Paris in 1259. Essentially, the Treaty caused more problems than solutions, the principal difficulty being that the King of France was, in theory if not practice, the overlord of his Duchy and could insist on treating its Duke, the King of England, as a vassal. In 1292–3 Philip adopted a war-like stance over certain Gascon problems and tricked Edward I of England into surrendering the duchy into French hands pending a resolution of their difficulties. Edward I, more than a match for Philip's wiles, only agreed to this because his military commanders informed him that, if Philip launched an all-out war against the duchy, they would not be able to defend it. Edward, facing serious difficulties in Scotland at the time, agreed to its surrender. Philip, of course, refused to hand it back and both countries drifted into armed confrontation.

Philip's long-term plan was not to hold the duchy for ever; this would inevitably lead to war and he had other matters to settle. In 1297, Philip persuaded Edward to submit their dispute to the arbitration of Pope Boniface VIII. Philip and the papacy had clashed before. The French king put pressure on the Pope and, in 1298, the hapless Boniface VIII issued his arbitration. The duchy of Gascony should be returned to the English Crown; a lasting peace would be signed between England and France, sealed by the marriage of the widowed Edward I to Philip IV's sister Margaret, whilst the French king's two-year-old daughter, Isabella, would be betrothed to the Prince of Wales.[4]

Philip was delighted. He had not only achieved his own ambitions but blocked Edward I's attempt to build up a coalition in northern Europe through his own system of marriage alliances. Edward's daughter, Elizabeth, had married Count Flores I of Holland whilst another daughter, Eleanor, had married the Duke of Bar, who controlled territory on France's northern border. More importantly, Edward had hoped to thwart France's ambitions over the Low Countries by secretly marrying his heir, the Prince of Wales, to Guy of Flanders' daughter. Philip obtained assurances from Edward that he would not accept a Flemish princess for his son but Philip trusted no one; just to make sure, he seized the Flemish princess concerned and incarcerated her until her death. Some claim she died of natural causes, others hint that Philip was not above using more subtle means to eliminate an opponent and the Flemish princess may have died from poisoning. Indeed, Philip IV had won such a reputation for secret intrigue, that the same chronicler even accused him of removing his wife and Queen, Johanna of Navarre, for his own nefarious purposes.[5]

By 1298 Philip believed he had checked not only Edward but other potential opponents. He had also created a power which ensured that Capetian influence was felt in all the courts of Europe, especially England. One day his grandson would sit on Edward the Confessor's throne at Westminster. Another grandson would be created Duke of Gascony, thus detaching that rich province from the English Crown and making its long-term absorption into the Capetian patrimony all the more likely. France's northern borders would be protected from Edward I's meddling whilst the marriage alliances of his sons could eventually extend Philip's power from the Rhine to the Atlantic.

Philip adopted a 'belt and braces' attitude to his daughter's marriage. Edward had only one male living heir. If the young Prince of Wales, or the infant Isabella, died before the marriage took place, Philip had an insurance policy. The marriage of his sister Margaret to the widowed Edward I would ensure some success and guarantee that if a grandson didn't inherit the English throne, a nephew would do just as well: this marriage, too, would be an integral part of any peace process.

Isabella's later conduct as Queen proves how the best-laid plans often go awry. However, in 1298 Edward I probably hoped for the same. He had been forced to accept the papal arbitration. He was facing baronial opposition to his war taxes at home, whilst his attempts to conquer Scotland had dragged England into a bitter guerrilla warfare which was draining the English Crown of men and resources. Edward I's motto was 'Keep Faith' but he never explained to *whom* he should keep faith. Marriages might be made in heaven, the papacy might describe the Anglo-French Treaty as a great, diplomatic, God-ordained triumph, but Edward I resolved that, if the opportunity presented itself, he would keep Gascony and marry his heir to someone else. In the meantime he publicly accepted the papal decree and sent letters full of fraternal greetings to 'his sweet cousin' Philip of France; secretly, Edward spent considerable energy plotting his escape from Philip's trap.

At first Edward met with little success. The papal arbitration was quite explicit: the marriages must go ahead or Philip would keep Gascony. Edward played along. On 12 May 1299 he despatched envoys to complete the arrangements for his marriage to Margaret and that of his heir to Princess Isabella. On the 19 June 1299, under papal auspices, Edward reluctantly put his seal to a marriage treaty. Isabella would marry his son. Edward would assign her dowry lands in England and France and Philip would pay a marriage portion of £18,000. The treaty made it very clear: 'no marriage, no Gascony'. Philip knew what his 'sweet cousin' Edward was plotting so he demanded that prominent members of the Gascon nobility take an oath to renounce allegiance to England if either Edward, or his heir, repudiated Isabella's marriage. Edward, shocked at such open distrust of his promises, committed Philip to paying a fine of £100,000, a veritable fortune, if he in turn reneged on Isabella's marriage. In addition, the English demanded that Isabella's mother Queen Johanna, and others of Philip's family, also took the most solemn oath, promising they would do everything to ensure the marriage took place. However, in 1298 Isabella was only two years old. Time was on Edward's side. Philip, too, realized there was 'many a slip twixt cup and lip'; Gascony was restored piecemeal but Philip kept the powerful castle of Mauleon as an 'open door' should Edward repudiate the treaty.

The two kings now circled one another like experienced swordsmen, each looking for an opening. Philip's dream was to have his young daughter married and Gascony detached from the English Crown. Edward hoped to stifle opposition at home, crush the Scottish rebels under Wallace and extricate himself from his own diplomatic predicament. Ostensibly both kings followed the protocols: charming and affectionate letters were exchanged. They addressed each other as 'sweet kinsmen', 'brothers'. Gifts were despatched, envoys met but little real progress was made on the marriage.[6]

Isabella was only six years old when her mother died in rather mysterious circumstances in 1302. Like many royal children, particularly princesses, she was relegated to the nursery, looked after by servants and kept well away from the main stream of court life. Moreover, although Edward I married Margaret, neither the English king nor his heir showed any interest in young Isabella. There are no records of any letters sent or gifts despatched. Communication between the French and English courts was quite regular but very little reference was made to Isabella, apart from the fact that she had been chosen to marry the Prince of Wales.

The turn of the new century created fresh opportunities for Edward. Philip was drawn into a bitter struggle with Pope Boniface VIII over royal rights in the French Church. The Pope retaliated by opening a secret correspondence with Edward, gently encouraging him to reject both the 1298 settlement and the consequent treaty. Philip responded by sending armed men to assault the Pope in his own house.[7]

More importantly, Philip had grown tired of his lawyers' advice. He may have brought England to heel but Flanders was still proving to be a thorn in his side. In 1302 the tension between the two countries erupted into war. Philip's troops poured across the Flemish border. All of Europe expected Flanders to be crushed in one single campaign. Instead, at Coutrai, the Flemish burgesses, armed with spears and protected by rows of stakes, annihilated the mounted chivalry of France. Edward seized this opportunity to try and secretly repudiate the marriage of his son to Isabella. He opened clandestine negotiations with Flanders for the hand of another Flemish princess and, when this failed, considered a marriage alliance between his heir and the Castilian Infanta: Edward I's first wife, Eleanor, came from Castile and an ally on France's southern border would be useful.[8] Nevertheless, Philip still possessed Mauleon, the gateway to Gascony: his troops could occupy the entire duchy in weeks. Edward, involved in a full-scale war against Scotland, was astute enough to realize he could not fight a war on two fronts. Both countries were exhausted by conflict and eager for a settlement. In May 1303 a lasting peace was sealed and the Prince of Wales despatched envoys to negotiate his solemn betrothal to Isabella.

The nine-year-old Princess met these envoys on the 20 May 1303 and made her solemn commitment to marry Prince Edward in the presence of Gilles, Archbishop of Narbonne.[9] Philip's luck also changed. In November 1305, the pleasure-loving Frenchman, Bertrand de Got, was elected Pope Clement V. Clement, probably at Philip's behest, tried to persuade Edward to send his heir to Lyons for the papal coronation: a fitting occasion, Clement maintained, for the marriage between his son and Isabella.[10] Secretly, Edward was horrified. Time had passed: Isabella was now nine years old and the Pope was ready to grant a dispensation so that, despite her tender years, Isabella could marry the English heir. If Edward I objected to the marriage, Philip could then depict him as repudiating the treaty as well as offering grave insult to the papacy.

The diplomatic machinery of both French and papal courts ground on, despite English reservations. Clement V issued a dispensation for Isabella to marry as she had not reached the canonical age to do so.[11] Clement and Philip also agreed to a solemn meeting of all parties at Lyons, a marvellous occasion and setting for the marriage between an English prince and his French bride.

Edward twisted and turned. He dared not object to the

marriage: his first line of defence was that he could not spare his heir for such a long journey, so the marriage would have to be by proxy. The Prince of Wales gave his father's envoys to Lyons the authority to contract such a marriage on his behalf. Isabella appointed her own proxies.[12] In the end the marriage did not take place. On the back of Clement's dispensation for Isabella to marry, a clerk has scrawled, '*Dispensatio Matrimonii Reginae Angliae Non Valeat*'. In other words this dispensation was never implemented. However, it is interesting to note that, almost three years before the wedding actually took place and Isabella's arrival in England, European courts already regarded her as '*Regina Angliae*', 'Queen of England'.

This marriage by proxy was deliberately frustrated by Edward. His envoys seized on the fact that Philip had not returned the castle of Mauleon so everything went back to square one.[13] The papacy, however, now involved in Philip's secret designs to seize the wealth of the Templar Order, refused to give up. A Spanish cardinal was sent to England, arriving in the spring of 1307. The cardinal gave solemn assurances that all of Edward's territories in France were to be returned. He insisted that the Prince go to France to attend another meeting between the Pope and Philip during April and May 1307.[14] Edward was forced to accept this and his heir dutifully travelled to Dover. The English king even agreed to release 100,000 Marks from the Exchequer but then, abruptly, the Prince was recalled north,[15] and so no money was ever released. He was still playing for time, although, this was beginning to run out.

By 1302 Robert the Bruce had emerged as the new Scottish leader and was intent on a relentless campaign against the English occupying army.[16] Five years later, Edward I, sixty-eight years of age and racked with illness, was determined on one last, all-out invasion to remove this threat. He was on the brink of this campaign when, stricken by sudden illness, he died on the 7 July 1307, leaving the marriage of his son unresolved. In a sense this was a triumph for Edward I: for almost nine years he had endeavoured to extricate his son from a marriage he never intended to let happen. It was now up to this same son to decide what future course these negotiations would take.

At the time of Edward I's death, Isabella was eleven years old. In medieval eyes, she was on the brink of womanhood and had been raised in a tradition, immortalized by the tales of King Arthur and his knights, where princesses were regarded as objects to be worshipped, ladies in the tower, over whose favours gallant knights fought. Isabella would have been aware of these stories as well as the court ritual and code of chivalry surrounding them, and up to her final days, she remained a fervent admirer of the Arthurian legend: she not only collected books on Arthurian tales but lent them to others.[17]

This medieval code of Arthurian chivalry is very clearly reflected in Chaucer's *The Knight's Tale* where the brothers, Arcite and Palemon, fight over their beloved. Taken to extremes, these chivalrous rules reduced women to objects: prizes to be fought over, according to the rules of the tournament, or married in order to secure access to an inheritance. Such attitudes encouraged a broad stream of medieval consciousness to regard women as either objects of desire in themselves or as possessions to be used as bargaining counters for other more mundane reasons, land or inheritance. The tales of La Tour Landry, a string of moralizing stories, emphasize the subservience of women and the necessity for their complete obedience to their husbands. A far-fetched example is La Tour Landry's *The Book of the Knight*, where three merchants wager that each of their wives will do whatever they ask, be it leaping into a basin or dancing on a table.[18]

Another work, *The Menagier of Paris* laid down how the young wife of a Paris merchant existed to please her husband and satisfy his every whim: 'Take pains to cherish the person of your husband and I beg of you to keep him in clean linen . . . I advise you to prepare such comforts for your husband and remember the country folks' proverb how three things drive a good man out of his home: a leaking roof, a smoking chimney and a scolding wife.'[19]

If women broke out of this mould they could expect not only human, but divine retribution. The English chronicler Knighton, a canon of Leicester, described how, in 1348, a group of high-born women began to ape the men in organizing their own tournaments, but finished the story on a high moralizing note, describing how God put 'their frivolity to rout by heavy thunder-storms and diverse extraordinary tempests'.[20]

True, these works were written in the second half of the fourteenth century but they captured a popular trend and public attitude. The subservience of the wife to the husband was seen as part of a divinely ordained plan, a theme which, no doubt, was constantly stressed in Isabella's early education.

Yet there was also another prevalent strain of thought, best represented by Chaucer's brilliant sketch of the Wife of Bath and her tale. The Wife of Bath owned her own business; she went on 'package tours' to the sacred rines of Canterbury, Compostella and Cologne; she saw a number of husbands through the church door for marriage and out again to the graveyard. She is pugnacious, assertive, and not afraid to speak her mind.[21] This is not a caricature or exaggeration. In the towns and cities of both France and England, women often played an important civic role, particuarly in trade and industry; even in medicine, until 1520, a number of physicians in England were women.[22] The Wife of Bath's tale goes further, emphasizing the superiority of women and the need for wives to exercise mastery over their husbands.[23]

Isabella would have been aware of such conflicting attitudes. Her mother had been a queen and ruler in her own right, and Queens of England had also held their own. Eleanor of Aquitaine led her husband, Henry II (1154–89) a merry dance, both in their private as well as their public lives. The Empress Mathilda, for nineteen years, waged a bitter civil war against her cousin Stephen for the English crown whilst, according to rumour, King John's wife took lovers so indiscreetly, her husband retaliated by hanging them from her bedposts.

Isabella progressed through a series of roles: first the princess in the shadows, then the honourable queen, then the dutiful wife. She was only twelve when she married Prince Edward and it took sixteen years of intense provocation, before she emerged as the 'She-Wolf', the 'new Jezebel'. This progression, from the passive to the active, is the most fascinating aspect of Isabella's life and career, not only for her actions but for the true reasons behind those actions.

In all fairness, her prospective husband, Edward of Caernarvon, was, for the greater part of his youth and early

manhood, a similar pawn on the diplomatic chessboard.
Like Isabella, he was brought up well away from the
machinations of the court, only emerging onto the political
scene when his aged father decided to use him for his own
political purposes. Indeed, Edward of Caernarvon proved
to be as big a contradiction as his future wife. In the main,
historians have been unanimous in their condemnation of
a king who lost his crown, his wife and his life. Edward II
spent most of his reign fighting his barons, not on matters
of high principle, but to protect favourites such as Gaveston
and de Spencer. The most scathing judgement on Edward
of Caernarvon is that of T. F. Tout who dismissed him as
'a coward and a trifler'.[24]

The Articles of Deposition which brought Edward II's
reign to an end, begin with the contemptuous remark that
the King 'was not competent to govern for, in all his time,
he had been led and ruled by others who have advised
him badly to his own dishonour to the destruction of the
Church and all his people.'[25]

The key to his character surely lies in his early years. His
father was forty-five years of age when Edward was born
at Caernarvon on 25 April 1284. His mother, Eleanor of
Castile, whom Edward I loved to distraction, died when
the Prince was only six. For most of his early life Edward
was dismissed by his father to the royal manor of Langley
in Hertfordshire with his nurse, Alice Leygrave, his doctor
Robert de Cysterne and his tutor and guardian Sir Guy
Ferre, a former soldier and courtier and one of his father's
henchmen.[26]

Left to his own devices, bereft of a father and a mother-
figure, the young Edward naturally looked for friendship
from others, whether they were ditchers, rowers, sailors

or boatmen. From them he learnt how to gamble at games such as Pitch and Toss. Free of any strictures, young Edward went to bed when he wanted and soon won the reputation of a late sleeper, so much so that, when he decided to reform his ways, the elderly Bishop of Worcester loudly proclaimed the Prince had renounced his bad habits because he was now getting up early in the morning.[27]

Prince Edward appears to have had a lively intellect and to have been interested in hunting, horses and music. A member of his household wrote the first earliest known English treatise on hunting. Another, the minstrel Richard Rhymer, was sent to Gloucester to learn how to play a favourite instrument.[28] The Prince kept a camel at Langley and even took a lion with him on his progresses through the kingdom.[29] He was well educated, although his French proved better than his Latin. He took his coronation oath in the French language, whilst the Pope had to thank the Archbishop of Canterbury for translating his letters for the new King from Latin into French.[30] Edward of Caernarvon was a gossip, a constant letter-writer, communicating with his sisters and foreign princes. These letters depict an easy-going, good-natured young man with a well-developed sense of humour. No wonder he later paid his painter, James of St Albans, the huge sum of fifty shillings 'for dancing on the table before him and causing him to laugh uproariously'.[31] In many ways Edward would have made an excellent country squire; it was his terrible tragedy to be king.

By 1298, the year of the papal arbitration, Edward of Caernarvon was fourteen, being slowly drawn into the politics of the court. He attended council meetings, joined his father at certain festive occasions while being trained for his role as a fighting king.

Nowhere does the young Edward betray any interest in Isabella or his planned marriage. He attended the wedding of Isabella's aunt, the Princess Margaret, to his own father at Canterbury Cathedral in 1299, and soon established cordial relationships with his young step-mother as well as with Isabella's uncle, Louis, Count of Evreux, to whom he despatched affectionate, pleading letters.[32]

It was in 1297 that the young Prince of Wales met the real love of his life. In the autumn of 1297 Edward I returned from Flanders: in his retinue was the young Gascon 'Perrot Gaveston', who was paid for military service in the English forces between August and November 1297 – the first mention of this fateful name in English records. According to the chroniclers, 'As soon as the King's son saw him [Gaveston] he fell so much in love that he entered upon an enduring compact with him.'[33] The young Prince had found his soulmate and, over the next two years, this friendship ripened. His father, busy in Scotland, allowed his heir to continue his happy-go-lucky existence, which he spent boating along the Thames with his barge-master Absalom of Greenwich, dicing and gambling or taking the pilgrims' routes to Canterbury to pray before the 'blissful bones' of Thomas à Becket.[34]

Unsurprisingly, the old King grew suspicious that his heir was more concerned with private pleasure than public duty. In the early summer of 1300 the young Prince was ordered to join his father's great campaign against the Scottish rebels. While the English armies moved slowly north, the King and his son visited the great monastery of Bury St Edmunds and an incident occurred which provides an insight into Edward of Caernarvon's mental development. He was now sixteen years old, able to bear arms and stand in the line of battle. He was regarded as a man and expected to display all the virtues of a warrior. When the King left Bury St Edmunds, the young Prince stayed on a further week, joining the monks in chapter, chapel and recreations. He 'asked to be served with a monk's portion such as the brothers take in refectory'.[35] Now there is no hint that the young Edward was trying to escape his military duties, though he may have been happy to be away from his father's eagle eye. The most probable explanation for this further week's holiday in a monastery was that Edward was lonely. His father was a distant military figure, his mother dead, his sisters either married, abroad, or in convents. Edward's letters to them show a desperate yearning to be liked. The monks of Bury St Edmunds probably provided the serene atmosphere Prince Edward so desperately needed and missed. The comradeship of the refectory, the soul-soothing chant of Divine Office, the harmony of the cloisters and the quiet industry of the library and the scriptorium were attractive for a young prince increasingly under the busy rule of his iron-willed father.

Eventually Prince Edward joined his father's forces, where he acquitted himself well in a short siege before Caerlaverock Castle, one of the many fortresses in Scotland the English needed to seize.[36] His father was pleased and decided it was time for his son to assume more duties. The young Prince later represented the King at the funeral of Edmund, Earl of Cornwall, in January 1301. The following month, he was created Prince of Wales and given all the royal lands in that county, together with the Earldom of

Chester.[37] However, the young Prince was growing older. More importantly, he was now under the influence of his 'sweet brother', Gaveston; the Gascon was a born mimic, a satirist, the perfect foil for a prince growing increasingly resentful, as later events proved, of his father's regime.

By 1305 Edward of Caernarvon was twenty-one years old, a seasoned warrior, with extensive estates. His father was sixty-six, a king of iron will and hard physique. Edward I could be generous and open-handed but his cruelty and his savage temper were well known. He could disguise this, as in 1297 when, to win a rapprochement with his barons over taxation, he appeared on a specially erected stage outside Westminster. The old king publicly cried through his fingers, begged for his opponents' forgiveness and tearfully announced that, if he died in defence of the kingdom, they should remember his good deeds and make his young heir king. Of course, it was pure play-acting but it won the day. Once Edward I had set his mind on something he rarely gave up. Like all successful men of power, he wanted his son to be like him in all ways. When this seemed unlikely, he resorted to bully-boy tactics. The Prince of Wales was understandably frightened of such a father, proclaimed as one of the outstanding warriors of Christendom. At the battle of Falkirk in 1298, the King's horse kicked him, breaking two ribs. Ignoring the pain, he fought a day-long battle and then engaged in a furious pursuit of the defeated Scots. Scottish opponents were hanged, drawn, disembowelled and quartered: Bruce's sister Mary and the Countess of Buchan were placed in cages and slung over the walls of royal castles as a warning to other rebels.[38]

Tensions between such a father and son were bound

to surface; they originated in a deeper antagonism than resulted from Prince Edward's more relaxed lifestyle – and Piers Gaveston may have been partly responsible. Perhaps the King was offended by his son's constant search for a family, be it with Gaveston or others such as the great noblewoman Agnes de Valence: Prince Edward praised her for acting as a 'good mother' to him and promised, in turn, to act as her dutiful 'son'.[39] For his part, the Prince of Wales resented his father's control. Whatever the real reason, this family tension erupted when the Prince clashed with his father's principal minister, Walter Langton, Bishop of Coventry and Lichfield.[40]

Langton was treasurer and in 1305 was under orders to curb public expenditure, including that of the royal households. The Prince of Wales's great passion was hunting. He despatched envoys to Lombardy in northern Italy for horses and mares. He bought the entire stud of a dead earl. He begged his sister Elizabeth to send him her white greyhound to mate with his own: 'for we have a great wish to have puppies from him'. He was keen to buy a sparrow hawk to hunt partridges and gleefully accepted a set of greyhounds from the Earl of Hereford. Langton reined in such spending. The Prince retaliated with mockery, sending a curious letter to Louis Count of Evreux, Philip of France's half-brother and Isabella's uncle, in which he scorned the very gifts he was sending with his letter: 'We are sending you a big trotting palfrey which can hardly carry, it stands still when on one leg. We also send you some mis-shapen greyhounds from Wales which can only catch a hare if they find it asleep.'[41]

The young prince was obviously feeling the economic squeeze, which not only affected his hunting stables but his favourite manor at Langley in Hertfordshire. Edward had set this up as his headquarters, rebuilding the gatehouse known as 'Little London' and leasing it out to his friends. Such frivolity was brought to an abrupt end: the building work and the hangers-on were stopped and his drinking companions were told to leave. However, the Prince retaliated by organizing a deer-poaching expedition in Langton's own park.

In June 1305, Edward of Caernarvon was summoned to the royal court at Midhurst. When Langton reproached the Prince for his poaching, young Edward's reaction was extreme. There is no evidence of physicial violence but, in a stream of invective, the Prince of Wales released the pent-up resentments against his father's principal minister. The Prince of Wales himself wrote an account to the Earl of Lincoln: 'On account of certain words which were reported to him [i.e. the King] as having passed between us and the bishop, he became so enraged with us that he has forbidden us to come into his household. He has forbidden all the officials of his household and of the Exchequer, to give or lend us anything for our keep.'

The Prince was subsequently banished from the King's presence and his income summarily cut off. The incident must have been well publicized. A few months later a hapless nobleman, William de Braose, lost his case in court and cursed the King's judges; this was reported to the royal council and de Braose was imprisoned and publicly humiliated. In passing sentence the council blatantly referred to what had happened to the young Prince, to illustrate the fact that no one was above the law. Royal officials, the council decreed, were to be treated with respect: 'This was made plain recently when the Lord King removed his first born and dearest son, Edward Prince of Wales from his household for well nigh half a year because he had uttered coarse and harsh words to a certain minister. Nor did he permit his son to come into his sight until he had made satisfaction to the said minister for the said transgression.'

The Prince had to dismiss a number of his yeomen, find jobs and homes for them and beg others to help out. Mary, his sister, a nun at Amesbury, invited her brother to stay with her. Another, Joan, sent him her seal to order goods, the fourteenth-century equivalent of a banker's card. She also informed her brother that he was more than welcome to stay with her. The young Prince, however, was determined not to let this situation continue for long. During June and July 1305, he followed his father through Sussex and Kent, though always at a healthy distance, in order to beg forgiveness and heal the rift.

By August matters had improved and by the late autumn the Prince had been returned to favour. Nevertheless, it was an incident he never forgot. He does not come across as weak or feckless but, in his own way, as stubborn as his father. Once Edward had become king, Bishop Langton was imprisoned whilst the treasurers public accounts were scrutinized.

During this great quarrel, two other incidents occurred which also provided an insight into Edward of Caernarvon's character. In the first instance, Edward became embroiled in a famous murder case. Mathilda, a widow of one of the powerful Mortimer family, who owned lands on the south-west along the Welsh March, was accused of poisoning her husband as well as encouraging her chamberlain to murder a certain Hugh of Kingsmead at Thameside in January 1305. Mathilda had been a lady-in-waiting to Queen Eleanor, Prince Edward's long-dead but beloved mother. Mathilda was indomitable and refused to plead so she was despatched to the Tower. Prince Edward intervened. He rebuked Kingsmead's brother and, despite the row with his father, persuaded the King to appoint two of the Prince's favourite judges to try the case. Once they were appointed, Prince Edward wrote to both judges asking for the matter to 'be well and speedily dealt with'. He also bluntly informed the local sheriff that he would hold him personally responsible for organizing 'suitable' jurors to be empanelled. Edward was intent on fixing the court and he was successful. Mathilda was not only released but given a pardon for all crimes of which she may have been accused.

The Prince also had a special affection for the Dominicans, choosing his confessors from this order of preaching friars. In 1305 the Dominicans of Northampton became involved in a bitter feud with the townspeople, who attacked their cloister. They asked for the Prince's help. He wrote immediately to the Mayor, who had played a principal role in the assault, warning him that, if he didn't make speedy amends, the Prince would 'make an example of him to all others'.[42]

The events of 1305 show a Prince in a different light from the heir ready to run obligingly after his father. He was prepared to confront the King, argue with royal ministers, interfere with the process of justice, and personally threaten those who hurt his friends. Edward of Caernarvon comes across as strong-willed, selfish and ruthless: a man not to be crossed, who gave loyalty and expected it to be returned in equal measure. This was to be the keystone of Edward II's character and reign: a very good friend or an inveterate enemy.

A great feast on 12 October 1305 at the Palace of

Westminster was the occasion of a formal reconciliation between father and son. The Prince presided as the royal guest of honour.[43] The King and his son had made their peace; they would act together to crush the Scots and, even more importantly, to escape from the hateful French marriage alliance. In May 1306 the Prince, together with 300 other candidates, was summoned to the Palace of Westminster to be formally knighted. The problem of catering for and providing lodgings for such a vast crowd was so great that the buildings of the Knights Templar near Ludgate were requisitioned, and tents and pavilions erected in the gardens. On the night of 21/22 May, the young Prince presided, not in prayerful vigil and meditation, but over revelry and feasting. On the morning of the 22nd the Prince was knighted in the chapel in the Palace of Westminster. This was followed by a great banquet where eighty minstrels played and royal dishes of swans were served. The wine must have flowed, soothed tempers and loosened tongues. The old King swore how, once he had brought the Scottish rebel Robert Bruce to heel, he would go on crusade. The young Prince also took a solemn oath that he would never sleep in the same place twice until he had reached Scotland.[44]

Father and son then swept north across the Scottish border and launched a reign of terror in which the young Prince demonstrated that he could be as brutal as his father.[45] The ravaging of Bruce's new kingdom lasted until the autumn. When the English retreated to Lanercost Priory near Carlisle, they found the papal envoy, Cardinal Peter, waiting to insist on the young Prince's marriage to Isabella. The English court spoke fair words in response but neither father nor son showed themselves eager to fulfil the promises made years earlier.

On 3 July 1307, Edward I once again marched towards the Scottish border. He arrived on Burgh-on-Sands three days later, just near the ford across the Solway Firth. The following day, determined to bring further devastation to Scotland, Edward arose, shouting at his attendants to arm him, only to fall back dead in their arms.[46]

Suddenly, the old King was gone, but the last weeks of his life had once again been marred by a very serious quarrel with his heir. This time it was not over hunting dogs or lavish expenses but his suspicions about the influence of the Prince's constant companion, the Gascon, Gaveston. The quarrel was violent, the King had seized his own son, tearing his hair out and kicking him to the ground. The Prince had rashly demanded that Gaveston be elevated, probably to the Earldom of Cornwall. The King's response was bitter in the extreme. 'You base-born whoreson!' Edward screamed at his son. 'Do you want to give away lands now? You, who never gained any! As the Lord lives, if it were not for fear of breaking up the kingdom, you shall never enjoy your inheritance!'[47]

As a result Gaveston was banished. The Prince himself even accompanied him to Dover to see him off to Northern France.[48] But the old King's words were prophetic. His heir had found the love of his life, not his father or some princess, but Piers Gaveston.

T W O

Isabella and the King's Favourite

'The King of France's messengers let it be known
that, unless Piers Gaveston leave the kingdom,
their master will pursue as his mortal enemy, all
who support the aforesaid Piers.'

Anonymous newsletter, April/May 1308

By July 1307 Edward of Caernarvon was twenty-three years of age, with considerable experience in administering his own estates and large household. 'Fair of body and great of strength,' reports one chronicle, 'Of a well proportioned and handsome person, a good horseman, a skilled hunter.'[1] The beautiful statue carved on top of the sarcophagus in Gloucester Cathedral bears out these descriptions, showing a well-proportioned face; the hair and well-clipped moustache and beard were probably blond. He had an excellent physique and stamina as his wife, Isabella, later found to her cost. Despite his relationship with Gaveston, Edward also had a reputation for being popular with the ladies: chroniclers accused him of 'consorting with harlots'.[2] He also had a bastard son, Adam,[3] and his wife Isabella bore him four children: Edward, John, Eleanor and Joanna.

35

There were high hopes at his accession. His anonymous biographer declared: 'Oh, while he was Prince of Wales, what high hopes. All such hopes vanished when he became King.'[4] Indeed, the real problem was that Edward didn't really want to be king. After his father's death, he clung to the friends of his youth, acted on their advice and ignored the leading barons. In any case, this group of well-armed, well-born ruffians were really no better than their new King. Thomas, Earl of Lancaster, his cousin, was dismissed as rapacious and lecherous. The Earl of Warwick proved himself to be an assassin and the Earls of Surrey and Hereford had few redeeming features. The only exception was Aymer de Valence, Earl of Pembroke, a moderate, faithful servant of the Crown who did good work as a diplomat abroad. In the main, these earls were young men who viewed themselves, with a certain degree of legitimacy, as the King's natural advisers. Edward delighted in upsetting the status quo: his reluctance to rule and determination to ignore the great barons was clearly expressed in his deep infatuation, even obsession, with Piers Gaveston.

Gaveston was the younger son of Arnaud, lord of a manor near Bearn on the borders of English-held Gascony. He was probably born around the same time as Prince Edward.[5] Like the new King, Gaveston had lost his mother at an early age, whilst his father spent most of his life fighting on behalf of Edward I in both France and Wales. In 1296–7 his father had been held hostage in France but escaped and fled to England, probably bringing his young son with him. The young Piers is described as a 'squire'. Edward I, as a reward for the Gavestons' loyalty, appointed Piers to his son's household.

The relationship with Prince Edward blossomed. Whether

it was homosexual or not is still a matter for speculation. Piers, like Edward, married and produced a child,
Joan. Nevertheless, the chroniclers were unanimous in
condemning the King's infatuation with the Gascon,
whom he loved 'beyond measure' and 'uniquely'. The
Westminster chronicler refers to Edward II's love for
Gaveston as an 'illicit and sinful union which led to the
rejection of the sweet embraces of his wife'. Another
chronicler describes the rumour 'that the King loved an
evil, male sorcerer more than he did his wife, a most
handsome lady and very beautiful woman'. The Meaux
chronicler is more blunt: Edward was a sodomite and
sinned excessively.[6] A more charitable explanation is given
by the anonymous author of the *Vita Edwardi Secundi*. He
compares the bond between Gaveston and Edward to that
of Jonathan for David in the Old Testament, 'whose love
David valued above the love of all women'.[7]

The sexual nature of their relationship cannot be proved.
A more satisfying interpretation lies in comparing the
psychological make-up of these two young men. Both
lost their mothers in childhood and were left to their
own devices. Both had a psychological and emotional
void which needed to be filled. Children who are lonely
often invent a mythical brother or sister, a close friend
whom others cannot see. Prince Edward went one step
further: Gaveston had been put into his household as a
squire and Edward transformed him into a blood brother.
There are many references to this. Edward often called
him 'Gaveston his brother'. He told the barons to stop
persecuting 'his brother Piers'. The Annals of St Paul
claim that, because of his excessive love for Gaveston, he
called him 'brother'. Another chronicler states that Edward

had been doing this for years, even when he was Prince of Wales.[8]

No physical description of Gaveston exists but he comes across as an arrogant, ostentatious man – and a foreigner, which made matters worse. Yet he was no court fop. He was courageous and proved his skill as a warrior during the savage war in Scotland. When he was exiled to Ireland, Gaveston brought the wild tribes into submission and executed rebel chieftains. The Irish regarded him as a very noble knight and were overawed by his martial skill and lavish vice-regal status.[9] He was also a skilled jouster. At the Wallingford tournament of December 1307, Gaveston rubbed salt into open wounds when he and a collection of nonentities successfully toppled some of the great earls of England in the tourney lists.[10]

Prince Edward was deeply attracted by this reckless, headstrong young man, who loved to snub his nose at authority. Gaveston also had a tart tongue and caricatured the nobles by bestowing offensive nicknames on them. Thomas, Earl of Lancaster, was dismissed as 'the Fiddler'; the Earl of Pembroke was 'a Jew'; Gloucester was 'a cuckold bird'; and Warwick, 'the black dog of Arden'. Gaveston considered such objects of ridicule as unworthy of his attention and never let slip an opportunity to put the barons in their place.[11] Edward championed him in this. Indeed, he regarded Gaveston as a second king, his joint ruler, being only too willing to share the burdens of the Crown with 'his brother'.

Both young men lacked the political foresight to realize this situation would never be accepted. However, Gaveston's recall from exile was one of the new King's first acts. Edward I died at three o'clock in the afternoon of 7 July 1307. Four days later, the news reached the Prince in London. Not only was Gaveston recalled immediately but, even before he arrived in England, around 13 August, the new King, having issued orders for officials to take care of his father's corpse, drew up his first royal charter at Dumfries (on 6 August), in which he granted the Earldom of Cornwall to Gaveston, his 'beloved brother'. A mercer, Geoffrey of Nottingham, was also ordered to supply green and indigo silk to make heraldic arms for the use of the Earl of Cornwall.[12] The Charter is a brilliant piece of calligraphy, its borders decorated with the Gaveston eagles. Smaller drawings mingle the heraldic arms of England, Gaveston, Cornwall and, more importantly, de Clare, an eloquent indication of further honours to be bestowed on Gaveston.

Edward was determined to bring Gaveston into the royal family by giving him in marriage his niece, Margaret de Clare, daughter of his favourite sister Joan and her first husband, Gilbert, Earl of Gloucester. The wedding took place at Berkhamsted on 1 November 1307. Edward attended, adding a personal touch by providing the rather generous amount of £7.10s.6d. in pennies to be thrown over the heads of bride and groom when they met at the church door to exchange vows.[13]

The barons had no say in Gaveston's meteoric promotion to the Earldom of Cornwall, a title last held by a royal half-brother, or in Gaveston's marriage to one of the richest heiresses in England. The barons, the papacy and Philip IV had no choice but to accept this rapid sequence of events, which transformed a minor Gascon exile into one of the most powerful men in England.

Other friends and supporters were benefited, though to

a lesser degree. Anthony Bec, Bishop of Durham, who had quarrelled with Edward I but shown great favour to his son, was restored to his bishopric. He was also given the task of escorting Edward I's funeral cortège back to Westminster. There the late King was buried, with due ceremony, under a slab of black Purbeck marble.[14] Walter Reynolds, whose acting ability Edward had always admired, was made Treasurer. Because of his friendship with the young King, Reynolds would later be promoted to Bishop of Worcester, then Archbishop of Canterbury. Edward did not forget his friends – or his enemies. Walter Langton, Bishop of Coventry and Lichfield, was immediately stripped of all office and possessions and sent for a short sojourn in the Tower.

In the main, such changes were greeted with relief in the happy expectancy of a new reign. The old King had been resented and feared: his constant warring and military expeditions had become a heavy drain on the Treasury and resources. Great things were expected of the young King: 'God has bestowed every gift on him', wrote one chronicler. 'And made him equal to, or indeed, more excellent than other Kings.' Other commentators were not so sure: they likened Edward I to Solomon and the new King to Rehaboam, Solomon's feckless heir.[15] Robert the Bruce was more perceptive, saying he feared the dead King's bones more than his living heir. The Scottish rebel was soon proved correct. The great campaign organized by Edward I was called off. Military matters north of the border were left to the competent Earl of Pembroke whilst Edward II, having received the homage of leading barons from both sides of the border, journeyed south.

Philip of France now saw his opportunity. The wily King

was fostering two plans. The first, to bring the marriage of his daughter Isabella to a happy conclusion: the second, an all-out attack on the Templar Order. Philip's treasury was bankrupt. For years he'd lusted after the wealth and treasure of this religious order of fighting monks, who owned estates, manor houses, and acted as international bankers throughout Europe and the Middle East. Late in 1307, Philip launched his attack, ordering the sudden arrest of all Templars in France. The papacy, now in exile at Avignon, was forced to agree with this. Philip depicted the Templars as corrupt, obscene, indulging in secret rites and satanic practices. Their leader, Jacques de Molay, put up heroic resistance but could not withstand the furious assaults of the French King which were now sanctioned by Pope Clement V.[16] It might be argued that Philip, who laid such emphasis on the alleged sodomititic practices of the Templars, should not have been enthusiastic about marrying his twelve-year-old daughter to a King whose relationship with a favourite was, to put it mildly, highly questionable. But Philip, ever pragmatic, would not have cared about this. Kings had their favourites, their public virtues and private vices, and he himself was surrounded by lawyers, clerks and advisers of relatively humble birth. Such notions had to be subordinate to Philip's grand designs for his dynasty.

But Philip was to encounter an unexpected obstacle. The new King of England refused to believe, and rejected as lies, the allegations against the Templars. On 4 December and again on 10 December 1307, Edward II proclaimed his views to the rest of Europe.[17] Philip was furious. If the Templars had found a champion in the English King then his campaign might be halted and brought under greater public scrutiny. More importantly, Philip, who had vouched for the allegations personally, was being branded as a liar throughout the courts of Europe by a young and inexperienced ruler.

Greater shocks were in store for Philip when he reminded Edward about his obligations to marry the twelve-year-old Isabella. Edward, revelling in the company of his favourite, was in no hurry to honour treaty obligations or enter into connubial bliss. Indeed, he began to question the whole treaty. What profit, he argued, could be had from his marriage to Isabella? Edward II even ignored members of his own council, who strongly advised that such an attitude could lead to all-out war and the loss of Gascony. Philip was nonplussed.

Through his spies and informers Philip discovered that not all of the English royal council were opposed to the marriage. Some were very fearful at the consequences of its repudiation. Philip began to plot and his envoys specifically targeted those of Edward's council who were advising Edward to reject Isabella's hand in marriage. 'Gascony,' Philip warned, 'had only been restored to the English Crown because of Isabella: "Et les enfants Qui en naistront", and the children she would bear.' He branded as fools and liars those who claimed that the English King would gain nothing by his marriage to the daughter of the King of France.[18] No doubt he was referring to Gaveston – the new Earl of Cornwall was a Gascon, whose family had always been opposed to the French Crown.[19] Gaveston would have played on the naturally rebellious attitude of Edward, encouraging him to attack and upset his future father-in-law as he had Edward I of England.

Gaveston and Edward II were thoroughly enjoying the

game they were playing, and it soon proved to be merely a game. In truth, secret preparations were in hand to comply fully with French demands. By mid-December 1307 Edward realized the game had gone on long enough. Five days after he'd condemned the allegations against the Templars as a lie, Edward ordered their secret arrest and the confiscation of their property throughout his kingdom.[20] Preparations were made for the reception of Edward's young queen. Royal apartments at Westminster were refurbished. The gardens were newly turfed and replanted, fish ponds cleared and restocked. The Queen's Bridge, a special pier jutting out from the Thames near Westminster Palace, was mended and put in order. Ships and barges were repaired and gathered at the mouth of the Thames to receive the young Queen.[21]

Edward agreed to meet Philip on Sunday, 21 January 1308. Whether by accident or design, he failed to leave England until the 23rd, still engrossed with Gaveston. To add insult to injury, he proclaimed his favourite Regent of the kingdom during his absence. He arrived at Boulogne on 24 January, three days late to meet his new father-in-law.[22] On Thursday, 25 January, Edward and Isabella met at the door of the cathedral church of Notre Dame Boulogne where they exchanged vows and were married. The young Princess's preparations for her wedding and consequent journey to England were magnificent. A lavish trousseau had been ordered: gold crowns ornamented with gems, precious drinking vessels, dishes, porringers and spoons, wardrobes and chests full of garments made of gold and silver stuff, velvet and taffeta. Six dresses of green cloth, six of green-gold and six of scarlet were included. Besides many furs and costumes, Isabella also brought seventy-two coifs or head-dresses, 420 yards of linen, and tapestries embroidered with lozenges of gold, displaying the arms of France, England and Bourbon.[23]

Edward was seemingly captivated when he eventually met his young bride. One chronicler even claims he neglected the war in Scotland because of his desire to marry the beautiful Princess as soon as possible.[24] The wedding was a major event for European royalty. The guest list included Mary, the Queen Dowager of France, Isabella's brothers, Louis, Philip and Charles, the Arch-Duke of Austria, the Duke of Brabant and other European nobility.[25] On Sunday, 28 January, there was a general wedding feast. On the 30th, Edward acted as host at a great banquet arranged for the French court. The King and his new Queen took lodgings near the cathedral, the rest of his retinue sheltering in canvas tents which had been set up around the harbour town of Boulogne.[26]

Naturally, Philip IV mixed business with pleasure. He presented a list of grievances to Edward, who retaliated by dismissing them and sending the French King's wedding gifts, including jewels, rings and other precious articles, back home to Gaveston.[27] This led to a bitter row. The French and English lords were tired of Edward's games: the wedding celebrations were marred by a general manifesto issued by the English nobility, and certainly backed by the French, complaining of 'certain oppressions', the opening shot of their later campaign against Gaveston.[28]

On 2 February 1308, Edward and his new bride left France and landed at Dover on the 6th. Isabella was greeted by the wife of the Earl of Norfolk, the Countess of Hereford, and other noble ladies. Gaveston must have

taken great pleasure in issuing the summons himself, deliberately bringing them to Dover at least four days before the
new bride arrived, an uncomfortable sojourn in a bleak
channel port in the dead of winter.[29] As soon as the
King disembarked, he ran to Gaveston, embraced him and
called him 'Brother'.[30] In an atmosphere of heightening
tension, the royal party made its slow progress to London
via royal palaces at Rochester, Eltham and London. On
19 February 1308, Isabella was formally lodged in the
royal apartments at the Tower from where she would
be taken to be solemnly crowned with her husband. By
now Isabella's French relatives were also seething. Her two
uncles, Louis of Evreux and Charles of Valois, joined the
English barons in threatening to postpone the coronation
until Gaveston was exiled. Edward prevaricated and then
promised reforms.[31]

The coronation took place on 25 February 1308 but it
was a fiasco. Gaveston, not Isabella, appeared to be the guest
of honour. Two London upholsterers received advances of
five pounds sterling, 'for making tapestries with the arms
of the King of England and of Piers Gaveston, Earl of
Cornwall against the King's coronation'.[32] It was a public
insult to the French, who demanded that Isabella's arms,
not some Gascon upstart's, be arrayed alongside those of
her new husband. Further surprises were in store. The
coronation of a king and the first wearing of his crown
was a very solemn event. Ceremonies such as the carrying
of the crown, the bearing of the royal sword, Curtana,
and the fastening of the King's spurs, possessed a symbolic
significance: these were always undertaken by leading
nobles. However, on this occasion, these ceremonial tasks
were given to Gaveston. He carried the coronation crown

of the Confessor. He held Curtana and also fastened the spurs onto the King's left foot. In appointing Gaveston to discharge these solemn and sacred duties, Edward was proclaiming that his favourite was, in fact, superior to the high nobility, whether of England or France, such as Thomas, Earl of Lancaster, and Charles of Valois.[33] Passions ran high; so much so that swords were drawn and a fight nearly broke out during the coronation. According to the chroniclers, only the presence of the Queen and the sacredness of the occasion, prevented bloodshed in Westminster Abbey.

Gaveston, as Regent, had also been responsible for the preparations for the coronation – and his organization left a great deal to be desired. The crowd was not properly marshalled and one man was trodden to death. It was three in the afternoon before the solemn consecration was over and long after dark before the formal banquets got underway. The food was badly cooked and ill-served, yet Edward II didn't seem to mind. He chose the occasion to publicly insult both his bride and his guests by sitting with the Gascon rather than his Queen.[34]

It is difficult to understand why, at least from July 1307 to the end of February 1308, Edward II went out of his way to publicly insult everybody he could. The only logical explanation could be that he was at last voicing his resentment, and that of his favourite, at their former treatment at the hands of his father, Edward I. Secondly, Edward was determined that everyone should accept Gaveston as his co-ruler, England's second king, his blood brother: public ceremonies provided the best stage for this. Edward II may not have deliberately wished to insult a twelve-year-old French Princess. Isabella was, as usual, regarded as a pawn to be used in her husband's confrontation with both her father and his barons.

Nevertheless, Edward II had sown the seeds for his later betrayal. Stubborn as ever, he attacked those who opposed his favourite and the easiest targets were the weakest. The Manor of Hailes, as well as Berkhamsted Castle, which belonged to Isabella's aunt, the Dowager Queen Margaret, were taken from her and given to Gaveston. Isabella herself was treated even more harshly. No dower lands were given to her, and there is no record of Isabella receiving even petty sums to set up and run her own independent household. Until July 1308, Isabella had to accompany Edward to royal palaces and manors at Westminster, Reading, Wallingford and Windsor. Nor was she given any patronage, such as the right to promote clerks or priests; nothing is recorded, except for three criminals receiving pardon 'at the Queen's insistence'.[35] Philip IV grew concerned. Why had lands not been granted to his daughter? Edward replied evasively he would love to do so but his Council was preventing it.[36]

Finally, Philip decided to intervene. An autocrat himself, he was reluctant to support rebels against any king, but the treatment of his daughter and sister were the final straw. Two anonymous newsletters of May 1308 mentioned how Philip had sent envoys to England to proclaim his hostility to Gaveston and that anyone who supported the royal favourite was now France's mortal enemy. Philip also despatched monies to encourage the English opposition.[37] Young Isabella was drawn into this too. Two months earlier Philip had sent a secret agent, a trained clerk, Ralph de Rosseleti, to England to carry Isabella's privy seal.[38] This trusted French clerk now took over the despatch of Isabella's letters and any sent to her. She was now her father's principal point of contact with the rebel barons in England.

Edward then conceded defeat, at least to create a breathing space. If he continued to support Gaveston, he would not only face war in the north against Robert the Bruce but uprisings throughout England led by his leading earls and supported by French troops. So Edward changed tack. Gaveston was honourably exiled to be Edward's Regent in Ireland, while the English King worked furiously to detach the French court from his baronial opponents. This opposition was now making itself felt in every walk of life. For example, in the late spring of 1308 the monks of Westminster were bitterly divided over the appointment of their new abbot, Kedyngton, a protégé of Gaveston. His opponents, led by Roger de Aldenhan, urged his colleagues to petition Queen Isabella, who would do anything to hinder Gaveston's nominee because of her hatred for him.[39]

Once Gaveston had left, Edward desperately tried to bring such partisan policies to an end. Isabella was immediately given certain estates in the French counties of Ponthieu and Montreuil as a sweetener. She did not attend Gaveston's departure from Bristol on 25 June 1308; instead, she waited for her husband at Kings Langley before travelling on to Windsor to console him on the loss of his favourite. The new Queen now began to be treated with increasing honour. She attended a Parliament at Northampton in August and afterwards entertained the nobility with a great banquet at Westminster.[40] Edward now hoped, through his wife and dowager aunt, to win Philip's approval. Bishop Langton, whom Margaret had defended, was released,[41] whilst property given to Gaveston was restored to her. Even greater generosity was shown to Isabella: huge grants of money were issued from the Exchequer and she received the ownership of manors in England and Wales and the right to appoint priests and clerks to benefices. Moreover, Isabella was now constantly in Edward's company. Hardly surprisingly, Philip withdrew his opposition to Gaveston who, in 1309, rejoined the King.[42]

Over the next two years, 1309–11, Isabella was the King's constant companion and supporter, so much so that the baronial opposition led by Thomas of Lancaster regarded her as Gaveston's ally. She even sheltered the favourite's supporters in her household. The barons demanded their removal, especially Henry Beaumont and his sister Isabella de Vescy, who'd become the Queen's regular companion. The barons had their way but Isabella refused to give up the friendship, writing constantly to de Vescy and sending her delicacies of wild boar meat and cheese.[43]

By the end of 1311 Isabella was still only fifteen years of age but nevertheless a Queen in her own right, a powerful landowner and a lavish patron. She had a household of over 200. Her tailor, John Falaise, employed sixty seamstresses to maintain and repair the Queen's robes. Falaise also supervised the Queen's treasury in the Tower of London – huge iron-bound coffers containing Isabella's jewels, plates and precious cloths, which were supplemented by gifts from the King. She was given rich wardships and the control of lands, whose owners had yet to come of age. The manors of Bourne and Deeping, as well as the royal manor of Eltham, with additional lands in Kent, were added to her estates. She attended her husband, graced state occasions and made royal tours, such as her pilgrimage to Becket's shrine at Canterbury, being awarded £140 to defray the costs.[44]

At the beginning of 1312 Isabella received extra money to accompany the King and his favourite north but this was no mere court outing. Edward II now faced a sea of troubles. Since 1307 Robert the Bruce and his commanders had transformed their guerrilla campaign in Scotland into a full-scale war against the English occupier. South of the border, the baronial opposition led by Thomas of Lancaster, with his extensive estates in Lancashire, Yorkshire and across the Midlands, was on the brink of civil war over Gaveston's continued preferment. Any opposition by Isabella to the Gascon favourite had now evaporated. She travelled with him and the King, she sheltered his friends and, on her husband's behalf, intervened to seek the support of her father and the French court.[45]

This strange triangular relationship can only remain a matter of speculation. Edward and Isabella certainly lived as man and wife, as did Gaveston and Joan of Gloucester. The latter gave birth to a daughter and by March 1312 Isabella herself was pregnant with her first child and sharing the good news with everyone.[46] The spring of 1312 was a happy one for the court. The King and his Queen were sheltering at York, well away from the intrigues at Westminster, but close enough to keep an eye on developments along the Scottish border. At the end of February Gaveston's daughter was christened and the court was entertained by 'King Robert' and other minstrels. There is even evidence of horseplay between the King's and Queen's households. On Easter Monday, 27 March 1312, the ladies of Isabella's chamber indulged

Edward's well-known love of practical jokes. Payments were made to a group of them for catching the King asleep in bed and dragging him from it.

This was a well-established custom connected with the story of Christ's resurrection: any man found in bed on Easter Monday morning could be dragged away as a prisoner and forced to make payment for his release. Edward apparently loved this, paying the ladies concerned a most generous sum.[47]

Once the Easter season was over, however, the King and his Queen had to face the grim reality of war. Bruce was now threatening the border whilst Lancaster and the other barons were calling up troops. Edward journeyed further north to Newcastle, while Isabella retired to Tynemouth Priory for sanctuary. Edward's stay in the north demonstrated his fecklessness: he, his favourite and his pregnant Queen were caught between the Scots and the baronial army moving north. The royal forces were few in number and eventually any organized command amongst Edward's forces collapsed. The King became a hapless fugitive in his own kingdom, desperately fleeing his enemies. Lancaster and the others followed in pursuit, forcing Edward and Gaveston to join the Queen at Tynemouth. The barons continued their harassment, threatening to besiege the Priory. Isabella was forced to flee with her husband and his favourite, leaving most of her baggage train behind. Lancaster wrote to her, assuring the Queen of his good will. Isabella ignored this and adhered to her husband.[48] The royal party fled south, to Scarborough, and Gaveston was left in its castle, perched high on the cliffs above town and sea for his own safety, whilst Edward and Isabella continued on to York.

An entry in Isabella's household book for the period 1311–17 shows that she was not simply a spoilt, young woman, who collected lands, possessions and money, more intent on her status than anything else. The Scottish war had devastated the north, towns and villages were burnt, farms ransacked. It was a cruel guerrilla war, of ferocious cross-border raids: Bruce's commanders used the terrain of lonely valleys, dense woods and empty moorland to terrifying effect. They burnt and plundered, swelling the stream of refugees south. Isabella found one of these refugees, a young boy whom she called Tomolinus. The Queen, 'being moved to charity by his miseries gave him food and raiment and sent him to live in London with Agnes the wife of Jean, one of the Queen's musicians, providing money for both doctors and teachers.'[49]

Even so, Isabella and Edward were themselves refugees in a hostile country, devoid of any baggage train and unable to call up sufficient troops. The King could do little to save his favourite. The barons followed them in hot pursuit and besieged Scarborough Castle. Aymer de Valence, Earl of Pembroke, gave every assurance that if Gaveston surrendered, he would be well looked after. Edward was unable to send help and the besieged favourite was now running short of food and supplies. On 19 May 1312, Gaveston surrendered. The King was beside himself, offering a thousand pounds for his favourite's safety whilst despatching the most begging letters to the Pope and Philip IV, asking for their help.

Gaveston was supposed to be taken to the King. On 9 June Pembroke reached Deddington in Oxfordshire and left Gaveston in a rector's house whilst he went to visit his wife and family. Historians have debated whether

Pembroke was simply naive or treacherous. The fact remained that Gaveston was now unprotected, and the Earl of Warwick arrived at Deddington only too pleased to seize the man who'd called him 'The Black Dog of Arden'. Pembroke acted the role of the injured innocent. 'The Black Dog', however, summoned the other great earls to his castle at Warwick and decisions were made. Gaveston, stripped of his finery, was put on trial before hastily assembled royal justices and condemned to death as a traitor. On 19 June he was taken from Warwick and moved into Thomas of Lancaster's territory. Gaveston, knowing he was to die, jokingly asked that, 'because of his good looks his head not be cut off'. The barons handed their prisoner to a group of Welshmen, who took him some distance away to Blacklow Hill in Warwickshire. One ran him through the heart with his dagger, the other cut off his head, which was despatched to Lancaster to confirm that his mortal enemy was dead.

Edward's grief was immeasurable, though all the chroniclers claim he dissimulated well. Nevertheless, the die was cast. From that day on, whatever peace treaties were made, whatever pardons were issued, the King and his earls were mortal enemies. The country teetered on the brink of civil war. Edward wrote more begging letters, demanding papal and French help. Philip IV truly believed the time had come to intervene. His daughter Isabella was now expecting a possible heir, whilst her husband was pleading for his help. French lawyers were despatched to England to mediate. A peace treaty was arranged but these were mere words, as one chronicler reported: 'Because of Gaveston's death, there rose a mortal and long lasting hatred of the King for his earls.' Isabella herself might have been secretly relieved: she was pregnant, being shown every favour by her husband, while the royal favourite had been removed with no blame to herself. The bond between King and Queen seemed strong.[50]

In the summer of 1312 Isabella moved from York to Westminster and on to Windsor for the royal lying-in. Her delivery was overdue and Edward and his court moved backwards and forwards to Windsor Castle in the weeks preceding the royal birth.[51] On Monday, 13 November 1312, Edward's patience was finally rewarded when two members of the Queen's household, Jean Launge and his wife, informed him that Isabella had given birth to a healthy son. This was proclaimed to the waiting capital,[52] and on 16 November 1312 the baby was christened in the royal chapel at Windsor. Present at the occasion was Cardinal Arnold, the papal legate and Isabella's uncle, Louis of Evreux, who had arrived in England to help Edward in his difficulties, and Hugh de Spencer the Elder, representing the family who would soon take the place of the dead Gaveston in the King's affections.[53]

However, the birth of the royal child caused more friction. The French wanted the boy named Louis after Philip IV's grandfather, but the English earls objected. Edward conceded to his barons and England was deprived of ever having a king called Louis I.[54] The barons protested stridently at the influence of France and their objections demonstrate how vulnerable Edward had made himself. During the Gaveston crisis, the King had attracted little military support but Philip of France was a different matter: the French had intervened in earlier English civil wars and could do so again.

During the Christmas festivities of 1312 the French

envoys clashed with leaders of the baronial opposition: harsh words were exchanged, but peace was maintained.[55] London had been waiting to celebrate the royal birth and, at the end of January 1313, when she was strong enough, Isabella solemnly processed through the city. The London guilds staged a magnificent celebration in her honour, the climax being a glorious pageant by the powerful Fishmongers' Guild, who accompanied the Queen from Westminster to the royal palace at Eltham.[56]

Edward II had gained an heir, but his problems still remained and he needed all the help he could get, if not at home then from abroad. He now began to act as if the French King was his overlord and master. In spite of the objections of his barons, Edward agreed to take his wife and heir to Paris. They left England on 23 May 1313 and reached the capital at the beginning of June. There were many things to discuss: Gascony, French interference in Scotland and Philip's assistance against Edward's opponents in England. There were also the Templars. This once-powerful fighting Order, under its Grand Master Jacques de Molay, was now ruined, its possessions and treasures seized. Many of its leading officers had either been barbarously executed or disappeared into the dungeons of Philip's castles up and down the country. Pope Clement V, sheltering in Avignon, had been bullied into accepting Philip's series of despicable allegations against the Templar Order and ordered their dissolution in a Bull, *Vox in Excelso*. Edward, to his eternal shame, had also seized Templar lands in England, and those knights who did not escape were committed to prison. Nothing was said about his earlier defence of this distinguished order.[57]

Philip relished his new-found power, and prepared a

series of ostentatious banquets and pageants for Edward's benefit. Both Kings, conscious that the suppression of the Templars would leave a gap in the great crusading movement, took solemn oaths that they would pursue a joint crusade against the Turks.[58] Isabella, too, was involved in this: she also took the cross, vowing to accompany her husband if he left for Palestine.[59] Once the flowery declarations and empty promises had been made, Philip and Edward moved to Pontoise where the French King could continue his display of glory. A set of six gorgeous miniatures, still kept in the Bibliothèque Nationale in Paris, commemorate Edward's visit. In these paintings the French King is the constant centre of attraction, always flanked by members of his own family. One miniature in particular has him seated in glory, attended by the English King, bound to him by kinship as well as gratitude for favours received.[60]

One incident marred this glorious pageant. The English court had followed Philip to Poissy, residing not in palaces but in specially erected silken pavilions set up for their comfort. Here an accident occurred when the English royal tent caught fire and was burnt down. Edward escaped unscathed but Isabella, probably trying to rescue some possessions, had her hand badly burnt. For months afterwards physicians were tending to it with rose water, olive oil and lead plasters.[61]

By July 1313 the King and Queen were back in England, armed with French support and lawyers to combat the demands of the barons. However, Edward was personally more concerned with the corpse of his dead favourite, which the barons had at last released for burial. The King had it carefully embalmed at his favourite manor of Kings Langley in Hertfordshire and then moved to the Dominican House in Oxford. It lay above ground for two more years until Edward, due to pressure from the Church, reluctantly agreed to have the corpse of Gaveston interred.[62]

The injury to the Queen's hand still affected her and she remained at Westminster until after Christmas before travelling to Canterbury in January 1314 to give thanks for the safe birth of her son and recovery from her injuries. She also attended the consecration of her husband's friend and acting companion, Walter Reynolds, as Archbishop of Canterbury.

Afterwards the Queen prepared to return to France to continue negotiations. The Italian financier, Pessagno, hired a splendid ship from Sandwich for the Queen's crossing together with twenty-six cogs (a merchant ship which could be converted to a war ship) and thirteen barges for the rest of her household and escort. The Treasury was equally generous, releasing almost £5000 to cover the Queen's expenses abroad.[63] Isabella was now being used by her husband to reach a final *rapprochement* with Philip IV. She achieved considerable success in Paris but her visit led to the uncovering of a great scandal. During the festivities around the Île de France, Isabella noticed that three silken purses she had given to her sisters-in-law after the knighting of her brothers on her previous visit, were now being worn by three knights of the French court.

The rest of Paris, meanwhile, was distracted by other occurrences. During the spring of 1314, the same time Isabella arrived in the capital, Jacques de Molay, the Grand Master of the disgraced Templar Order, had been displayed on a public scaffold to recant his wrongs and seek the absolution of Philip IV. As matters turned out, de Molay used the occasion to loudly proclaim and protest his innocence and that of his Order. De Molay stridently condemned the Pope, Philip IV and other western princes for their greed and rapacity. He made this statement on 14 March together with Geoffrey de Charnay, both men proclaiming their defiance for all of Europe to witness. The following day, 15 March 1314, de Molay and de Charnay were burnt to death over a slow-burning charcoal fire on an island in the river Seine. According to one report, de Molay continued screaming from the flames. He summoned Philip and Clement to appear with him before God's tribunal within the year and cursed Philip's family to the thirteenth generation.[64] Historians have been quick to point out that de Molay's curse did, indeed, become reality: Louis XVI, Marie Antoinette and their young son spent their last days during the French Revolution in the ancient fortress once owned by the Templars. But, de Molay's curse took effect more speedily: within the year both Philip IV and Pope Clement V were dead and, in the very month de Molay died, Isabella reduced her father's carefully constructed diplomatic triumphs to ashes.

The scandal began with the purses. Isabella was intrigued and informed her father. Her household expenses mention ten torch-bearers who took her by night to Philip's quarters in the royal palace to consult with the King.[65] Philip ordered the matter to be carefully investigated and the three knights were watched and followed. In fact, they were regularly meeting all three of Philip's daughters-in-law at a palace, the Tour de Nesle, on the outskirts of Paris. There they would feast and dine, turning these nights into one long orgy. Philip was aghast. A secret court was convened. The three women confessed to their adultery and were sentenced to life imprisonment, being virtually walled up in different establishments throughout France. The three knights faced a more barbaric fate. One of them fled to England but was swiftly extradited and joined his two friends at Montfaucon, the bloody execution yard in Paris, where they were strapped to huge wheels which were spun while their limbs were shattered with iron bars.[66]

The Templars had their vengeance. A year earlier Philip had portrayed himself as master of Europe. Now his three sons were publicly proclaimed as cuckolds and their lives ruined. There is considerable evidence that the scandal soured relations between England and France, while Isabella was viewed as a *persona non grata* by the French court.

On her return to England, however, Isabella had to face a greater crisis. Edward II had left for the north, intent once more on crushing the Scots. An uneasy peace had been negotiated between Edward and his barons, with the exception of Thomas of Lancaster, and plans drawn up for an all-out invasion of Scotland. Many English lords, who owned estates there, buried their differences to face the common enemy. Writs were issued, troops raised and the English army crossed the border, threatening bloody retribution. The campaign ended in the greatest military disaster England ever suffered in Scotland. On 24 June 1314, Bruce and his army met the English invaders at Bannockburn and inflicted a devastating defeat. The Earl of Gloucester was killed, thousands perished in the battle and many were taken prisoner. Edward himself, although he fought bravely, had to be dragged from the battlefield, losing his own seals as well as his honour. Isabella was waiting for him at Berwick where she did what she could for both her husband and other casualties. She attended to her husband's wounds, even cleaning his armour; she also loaned him the use of her own seals to authorize documents, then accompanied him south to attend Parliaments held at York and Westminster.[67]

Isabella continued to do her best to support her husband during the traumatic period following Bannockburn. Thomas, Earl of Lancaster, who had sulked in his tent like Achilles during the Scottish campaign, now emerged as an alternative ruler in England and seized the reins of power. Isabella, like Edward, was subjected to Lancaster's strictures and dislike and grants to her dried up. The Earl again attacked the Beaumont family, who were driven from her household. Isabella did not retaliate but over the next two years, 1314–16, stayed with her husband until her lying-in for the birth of her second son John, who was born at Eltham on 15 August 1316 and baptized some five days later.[68] Edward was ecstatic, and his delight was expressed in generous grants of land to Isabella, including the county of Cornwall and treasure from his Lombard bankers, the Bardi.[69]

Apart from this, 1316 was to be the 'Annus Horribilis' of Edward's reign. Not only was he fighting a losing battle against the Scots but was now forced to begin humiliating negotiations with the hated Lancaster. It was also the year of the Pretender. A young Oxford clerk came forward to claim that he, not Edward II, was the real King of England. The Pretender, with his cat, was taken before the Justices in Oxford and told the most fantastic story. He pointed out that he was missing an ear, the principal proof for his claim to kingship. He then informed the astounded Justices how, many years earlier, he had been playing in the courtyard of the royal castle when he had been attacked by a sow. The animal had bitten off his ear and the nurse, terrified of the old King's rage, had exchanged the royal child for the son of a peasant. That, the Pretender triumphantly concluded, was why he was making his claim and why the present King was more interested in rural pursuits and hobbies than good governance. The case caused great scandal and not a little merriment. Isabella was very upset by the story and eventually the comedy began to wear thin. The Pretender was closely interrogated, broke down and confessed that he had been walking in Christchurch Meadows in Oxford when the devil had appeared to him in the form of a cat, which he produced in court as evidence. The devil had instructed him to go in front of the royal Justices, tell his story and all would be well. The judges listened attentively then, tired of the situation, had the Pretender hanged on the town gallows with the cat suffering the same fate alongside him.[70]

The story illustrates Edward's lack of popular support and a growing realization of his failure to act like a king. Isabella decided the continuous decline of her husband's fortunes had to be stopped. Robert the Bruce was an opponent they could do little about. During 1316–17 England was ravaged by a great famine and Edward lacked the men, resources and will to defend the Scottish March. Lancaster was a different matter and Isabella gleefully opposed him at every opportunity. When the powerful bishopric of Durham became vacant in 1316, on the death of Anthony Bec, Isabella successfully backed the candidature of Lancaster's enemy, Louis de Beaumont, brother of Henry and Isabella's close friend, Isabella de Vescy. Isabella promised her husband that Louis would 'be a stone wall' against the Scots and a powerful ally in the north. She had her way and Lancaster was frustrated.[71] Isabella had now acquired the same privileges that Gaveston had enjoyed: she attended council meetings, patronized court knights and, when Dowager Queen Margaret died in 1318, was rewarded with a generous portion of her landed inheritance.[72] On 18 June 1318 Isabella gave birth to their third child, a girl, Eleanor, and Edward was present with her at Woodstock for the lying-in and birth.[73]

By 1319 Isabella's pre-eminence had also attracted the attention of Robert the Bruce. Scottish forces had driven the English out of Scotland and were busy ravaging the northern shires. Edward and Lancaster decided to bury their differences and concentrate on trying to recapture the powerful northern fortress of Berwick, which dominated vital routes into Scotland. During the summer campaign of 1319, Isabella remained at a manor near York. She thought she was safe, but in fact she was now the real object of Scottish military strategy. James Douglas, Bruce's war leader and a skillful guerrilla chief, had decided to capture her. This would not only humiliate Edward throughout Europe but be a powerful negotiating counter in forcing both England and France to recognize Scottish sovereignty. Douglas gathered a highly mobile force, outflanked the English army gathering around Berwick and, at the beginning of August 1319, penetrated deep into Yorkshire. He was nearly successful but the Queen was alerted and fled to the security of Nottingham Castle. Douglas had to content himself with harrying the countryside and defeating a hastily assembled English force at Mytton on 12 September 1319. Douglas would have continued his audacious foray south but England's northern levies now rallied. They threatened to block his route back to Scotland so Douglas had no alternative but to retreat.

Douglas's campaign to seize Isabella illustrates how the Scots, like Lancaster, had realized the Queen's standing with Edward II: she was the mother of his three healthy children, a Queen who loyally supported him and had done good work for the Crown in its tangled negotiations with France. Her capture would have been a national disaster and a personal humiliation for Edward. More importantly, and rather ironically, Isabella would have, once again, been used as a powerful counter in diplomacy. Kings and princes of the fourteenth century were accustomed to using royal captives to negotiate favourable terms – Philip IV of France himself had seized the Count of Flanders's daughter. Later in the century, Isabella's war-like heir would use the imprisoned kings of both France and Scotland to gain favourable terms, especially rich ransoms and concessions of territory. If successful, Bruce would have done the same: demanding heavy compensation for the ravages by English forces and Edward's approval of territorial concessions, even Scottish sovereignty itself.

Accordingly, Douglas's raid to seize the Queen must have been carefully planned. The Scottish war leader must have gained vital information about the movement of English forces along the north-east coast and, more importantly, that the English Queen was not protected behind the fortifications of York but residing in a 'parva villa iuxta' – 'a small manor house nearby'.[74] Treachery was suspected and Lancaster was accused. The real villain of the piece was most probably a Yorkshire knight, Edmund Darel. Darel was a member of the King's household and closely involved in royal decisions: as a northerner he was also known to the Scots. Moreover, although he had been pardoned with the rest, Darel was under suspicion of being a turn-coat, of having a hand in Gaveston's capture and death in 1312. Darel was an argumentative, war-like man, involved in brawls with his neighbours, quick to pick up the sword and often tried to achieve his ends by force. Like many northern knights, he had been impoverished by the Scottish raids and susceptible to the large bribes the Scots offered to facilitate Douglas's raid to capture the Queen.[75]

Darel was arrested for betraying the Queen but the prosecution had little evidence. Nevertheless, he lost his place in the King's household and was summarily deprived of the royal manor of Westcliff in Yorkshire. Due to the courage of the Archbishop of York and the fighting qualities of the northern levies, Isabella escaped this attack on her freedom and honour but it was an incident remembered by others. Edward was both horrified and embarrassed by his Queen's plight and gave Isabella jewels and other presents as some consolation for the indignities she had suffered.[76]

Isabella returned to London with Edward in January 1320 and stayed with him for most of that year. She then accompanied him to France to meet her brother Charles IV. The meeting with the new French King had two agendas. Ostensibly, they went to discuss the usual problem of English possessions in France. Secretly, Edward was now determined to crush the baronial opposition and, once again, was looking for French assistance.

In the eight years since Gaveston had died Edward had had the support of old colleagues like Walter Reynolds, Arcbhishop of Canterbury, a number of earls and, of course, royal officials and clerks, and had worked hard to build up a court party loyal to him. However, he not only wanted revenge for Gaveston but needed to fill the emotional void created by the death of his favourite. Before long a new star emerged from the court party: a more sinister figure than Gaveston, the astute and rapacious Hugh de Spencer. De Spencer's father, also called Hugh, had been an administrator, a King's man in every sense of the word. He was the King's constant companion and won Edward's undying loyalty by being one of the few courtiers who had supported Gaveston. In doing so, however, he had incurred the implacable wrath of Lancaster and his clique. Naturally, the King rewarded him but it was de Spencer's son, Hugh the Younger, who emerged as Edward's personal favourite.

Hugh de Spencer the Younger was of similar age to Edward, and had been knighted on the same day. Although he had opposed Gaveston, Hugh eventually followed his father's line, deserting the barons and becoming chamberlain to the royal household. He was quick to criticize Lancaster and, in the period 1318 to 1321, drew closer to the King. Edward, delighted by this, supported the de Spencers' ambitions in South Wales where they were busy carving out a small empire for themselves. The Earl of Gloucester had died at Bannockburn in 1314 without a male heir, and his vast territories in South Wales and along the Welsh March fuelled a power struggle amongst the other great landowners in that region: de Spencer was one and his implacable opponents Roger Mortimer of Chirk and his war-like nephew, Mortimer of Wigmore. De Spencer's territorial ambitions, not to mention his undoubted talents, also brought him into conflict with many of Lancaster's party who owned lands in Wales. He won royal support in the principality whilst his power was also felt at court, where he emerged as Edward's closest councillor and confidant. While de Spencer used the King to further his own ambitions, Edward saw de Spencer as the means to destroy his enemies and avenge himself for the death of Gaveston.

De Spencer the Younger, however, was not a second Gaveston. Hugh was a war lord, a politician and administrator. He understood the machinations of Edward's baronial opponents and was not frightened of championing the King's cause against all comers. Isabella may have liked the father – the old de Spencer had been present at the baptism of her first child – but his son was quickly viewed as a rival. In 1321 Isabella was twenty-three years old, the King's favourite and the mother of his three children. She did not take kindly to her husband's attentions being distracted elsewhere. De Spencer's rise was piecemeal but Isabella was at loggerheads with him from the start.

In 1320 the first signs of a rift between the Queen and the new favourite became apparent. De Spencer the Elder was supposed to pay her £100 per year from the profits of his manor at Lechlade, but failed to do so. The following year his son followed suit over £200 due from the profits of Bristol. They refused to pay the debts or to enter into any negotiations over these debts.[77] Isabella retaliated and the court became involved in a petty feud between the Abbot of St Albans and William Somerton, Prior of the Abbey Cell at Binham in Norfolk. The Abbot appealed to de Spencer for help. He despatched some of his henchmen to arrest Somerton and hand him over to the Abbot who threw him into gaol. De Spencer's enemies worked hard to get Somerton released and enlisted the patronage of the Queen. The issue was petty but it masked deeper antagonisms, which were about to surface.[78]

By August 1321, the barons were alarmed at the de Spencers' growing influence, both at court and in South Wales. Lancaster and his supporters retaliated by adopting the same tactics used against Gaveston and demanded their exile. Edward refused. The barons gathered their armed men and entered London. Edward was forced to concede, particularly when his Queen went down on her knees to beg for the expulsion of the favourites in order to avoid civil war, an empty political gesture by Isabella which allowed Edward to gracefully concede defeat.[79] The eldest de Spencer went into hiding: the younger de Spencer travelled to the southern ports, hired men and ships, and assumed the life of a pirate in the English Channel: he was successful enough to capture a Genoese galley worth some £1000.

Edward, meanwhile, now finally emerged from the depression caused by Gaveston's death. He had lost one favourite, he was determined not to lose another. Isabella had opposed de Spencer over the Somerton case and pleaded for their exile, but she was still the King's favourite, the recipient of his generosity: moreover, she was pregnant with their fourth child, a daughter Johanna, who was born at the Tower in July 1321.[80] Isabella disliked de Spencer but she also had no love for Lancaster and his coterie, and so co-operated with her husband's secret schemes to bring the favourites back to court.

De Spencer had been exiled in August 1321. By October Edward had decided to fight back and the hand of the astute, scheming Hugh de Spencer can be seen in

Edward's changed approach. This time Edward did not go wandering the lonely northern shires but stayed near London, plotting not only de Spencer's return but the destruction of his enemies. In the previous summer both the Tower of London and the custody of the Great Seal, the King's official signature to all charters and letters, had been entrusted to Isabella,[81] who was now also drawn deeply into Edward's plot to remove baronial opposition around London. The King selected his chosen victim prudently. One of Lancaster's more reluctant lieutenants was Bartholomew Badlesmere, a great Kentish landowner. The county of Kent was of strategic importance: whoever controlled it would also control the entire south bank of the Thames, the coastline of south-east England, including its valuable ports stretching from the Medway to Romney, the perfect sanctuary for de Spencer playing pirate out in the narrow seas.

In September 1321, Edward despatched a number of knights to seize Dover Castle, thus gaining control over the most important southern port in England. If Hugh de Spencer the Younger was to return, Dover would provide a natural door into the kingdom. Badlesmere retaliated by placing all his castles in Kent on a war footing and moving through the county, banners displayed, in a show of strength, to Canterbury.[82] Edward watched and waited. He and Isabella travelled to Thanet Island secretly to meet de Spencer, who had brought in his pirate fleet. The finer details of their plan were finalized. Edward was determined to seize Leeds Castle, Badlesmere's principal stronghold, where he had placed both his treasure and his wife.[83] The court gathered at Whitley in Surrey with the kingdom on the brink of civil war.

THREE

The New Favourite and Isabella's Disgrace

'To the Queen. The King has frequently ordered her, both before and after the homage, to come to him with all speed, laying aside all excuses . . .'

Edward II to Isabella, *Calendar of Close Rolls, 1323–1327*

'I have not forgotten the great wrong that was done to my brother Piers.' Edward's words, reported by his anonymous biographer,[1] lie at the root of the blood bath and terror that occurred after the seizure of Leeds Castle in 1321. It is easy to play the psychologist and read into people's actions particular theories or explanations. Nevertheless, the chroniclers are unanimous and Edward's actions confirm their statements: the King had never forgotten, not even for a day, the murder of Gaveston by his baronial opponents. The chroniclers dismiss Edward as a light-weight ruler, more interested in his pleasures and his games than policy, but the events of 1321–6 prove them wrong. Edward had been obsessed, infatuated with Gaveston. He had made mistakes since the favourite's murder, but he had managed to dissimulate and to hide both his anger and raging desire for revenge. He waited for an opportunity and de Spencer the Younger provided it.

Hugh de Spencer comes across as a buccaneer, a pirate, a noble, who feared neither God nor man. He became Edward's foil, his dagger to strike at the heart of the likes of Thomas of Lancaster and others. Edward wanted revenge and de Spencer would serve up the dish. For the first and only time in his life, Edward proved he was his father's son: a shrewd plotter and a cunning general, who managed to divide his enemies before ruthlessly destroying them.

Edward's and Isabella's strategy was simple enough. The baronial opposition was divided into three centres of resistance: Kent, which, because of its proximity to turbulent London, always posed a threat; Mid-Wales under the two Mortimers, Roger Mortimer of Chirk and his redoubtable nephew Roger Mortimer of Wigmore; and finally the Midlands, under the power of Lancaster. Edward, through his friend and ally Walter Reynolds, was able to control the Church and he also had the support of the so-called royalist earls, Pembroke and Richmond. All the King needed was a *casus belli* – and Badlesmere could be provoked to provide it.

The Kentish landowner was already watchful and fearful. The whole county was prepared for war when Isabella, under the guise of visiting her favourite shrine at Canterbury, went on pilgrimage through Kent. The traditional pilgrim route bypassed Leeds Castle but this time Isabella headed straight for the castle, arriving there late on 2 October 1321, with a considerable armed force, using the excuse of nightfall to demand entrance and shelter. The defenders refused to open the gates. Isabella declared this was treason and her soldiers attempted to force an entry, only to be driven off with the loss of six of their company.[2] The following day, 3 October 1321, Isabella communicated the news to her husband, who had travelled south to Portchester to meet the younger de Spencer. On 7 and 8 October Edward responded. Royal levies were raised and Leeds Castle was placed under siege. The King moved his headquarters to Rochester. Isabella joined him and was given custody of the Great Seal, a gesture of great trust for this now gave her control of the Chancery, the civil service of the time.[3]

Leeds was a powerful fortress but it was cut off by a royal army led by six earls: Pembroke, Surrey, Arundel and Richmond, together with the King's own half-brothers, Thomas of Brotherton, Earl of Norfolk and Edmund, Earl of Kent, accompanied by a powerful detachment of Londoners. The castle surrendered immediately. Badlesmere had already fled but his wife, together with his kinsmen, were imprisoned in the Tower of Dover Castle. Thirteen of the garrison were summarily hanged for their affront to Isabella, who also shared in some of the plunder looted from the castle.[4] The execution of Badlesmere's knight, Walter Culpepper, along with other leading members of the garrison, was the first indication of the martial law which Edward intended to impose on his kingdom. Edward was also serving notice that those caught in arms against the King would no longer merely endure a period of imprisonment, a possible fine and, at the appropriate time, a pardon, but rather summary execution, the imprisonment of their kinsfolk and the confiscation of all their property.

Civil war had commenced. Isabella moved back to

London and in December 1321 was safely lodged behind the defences of the Tower.[5] Edward moved to Cirencester on 8 December and, despite the winter, began his campaign against the Mortimers. Advancing up the Severn Valley, the King moved with a speed which surprised his opponents. He was joined by the de Spencers. The Mortimers hoped that the Severn river would provide a natural defence but Edward crossed at Shrewsbury and the Mortimers had no choice but to surrender in January 1322. They negotiated their submission which is probably why they weren't executed on the spot. Some of their contingent fled to Lancaster but the two Mortimers were sent as prisoners to the Tower and their chief henchman, Maurice Berkeley, to Wallingford Castle.[6]

The King now controlled London, the southern Shires, South Wales and the Welsh March as he advanced north against Lancaster. Isabella, still in London, played her part in Edward's military preparations by despatching letters to Andrew Harclay, Warden of Carlisle, to advance south to oppose Lancaster. She also issued similar instructions to Simon Ward, Sheriff of Yorkshire.[7]

Edward's strategy in the early spring of 1322 was simple. He hoped to catch Lancaster in a pincer and destroy him. The Earl lost his nerve and retreated further north to Pontefract, with Edward following in hot pursuit. Lancaster continued his withdrawal, possibly hoping to seek help from Robert the Bruce, only to be trapped by Harclay and his Cumberland and Westmoreland levies on the river Ure near Boroughbridge, north-west of York. Lancaster and his captains foolishly divided their forces and attempted to ford the Ure, only to be driven back. The Earl of Hereford and a party of knights led other Lancastrians to the bridge held by

Harclay. Their attack was also a complete failure. Hereford died a grisly death, being speared in the anus by a soldier who had managed to get beneath the bridge.

Lancaster was forced to withdraw and his troops began to desert. On 17 March 1322, Simon Ward, Sheriff of York, arrived and the trap was closed. Lancaster, together with other leading adherents, was taken prisoner. Edward was delighted: vengeance was to be swift, public and brutal. Lancaster was tried in the Great Hall of his own castle at Pontefract. The court was really a military tribunal, chaired by the King and a number of royalist earls. Lancaster was accused of a litany of offences and not permitted to speak in his own defence. On 22 March 1322, Thomas, the great Earl of Lancaster, dressed as a penitent and mounted on a sorry-looking nag, was led out of the castle to a small hill, a grisly reminder of Gaveston's death. Spring was late that year, there had been flurries of sleet and, on his way to execution, the hapless Lancaster was pelted with snowballs. Perhaps the same freezing weather numbed the executioner. He was clumsy and took some time to hack off Lancaster's head, which was shown to the King before the Earl's mangled remains were handed over for burial in Pontefract Priory. The reign of terror, 'of horror piled upon horror', had begun.[8]

The chroniclers are unanimous in their condemnation of what took place after 1322. 'Oh calamity,' the anonymous biographer of Edward II wrote, 'To see men, so recently clothed in purple and fine linen, now tied in rags bound and imprisoned in chains.' The same author, a contemporary observer of the dreadful events, commented how, after Boroughbridge, 'the harshness of the King has today increased so much that no one, however great or wise, dares to cross his will . . . The nobles of the realm are terrified by threats and penalties. The King's will has free play.' He then concludes: 'Thus today Might conquers Reason for, whatever pleases the King, although lacking in reason, has the force of law.'[9]

Four years later, at the time of his own trial, the young de Spencer was specifically accused of extortion and a veritable catalogue of brutal crimes against the widows and children of executed Lancastrians.[10] Even the Pope intervened and begged the King to show some restraint. However, after his great victory at Boroughbridge, Edward sated his desire for revenge with this blood-letting, which may have unbalanced his mind to some extent. Subsequently he became a pliable tool in the hands of the De Spencers. Hugh the Younger in particular, comes across as nothing better than a gangland boss, determined to acquire treasures and lands, showing little mercy to anyone.

The list of wholesale executions continued. Many of Lancaster's knights were put to death on the same day as their leader died at Pontefract. All of them faced the same military tribunal as Lancaster, who had protested in vain: 'This is a powerful court, and must be great in authority, where no answer is heard or any excuse admitted.'[11] Lancastrians were executed at Bristol, Windsor and Cambridge. The hapless Bartholomew Badlesmere was despatched in a particularly hideous manner, by being fastened to a hurdle and dragged at the tail of a horse through the city of Canterbury, before being hanged at the crossroads. His head was struck off and put above the gates of the city, a grim reminder of the penalties for treason.[12]

Besides the executions, between seventy and a hundred other knights and lords were imprisoned in castles throughout the kingdom, often in straitened circumstances, being allowed only three pence a day for their maintenance. Children were separated from their mothers; Mortimer's three daughters, Joan, Margaret and Isabelle, were incarcerated in priories in Lincolnshire, Norfolk and Bedfordshire.[13] Lancaster's widow, Alice, together with her mother, the Countess of Lincoln, were also imprisoned and Alice was personally harassed by the two de Spencers. They claimed she was the real cause of her husband's execution and should suffer the fate specially reserved for the murderers of husbands – being burnt alive. Terrified, Alice agreed to do whatever they wished. Another, Lady Baret, the widow of Stephen Baret of Swansea, was tortured at the orders of the de Spencers; her limbs broken, her injuries were so terrible that she went out of her mind.[14]

Isabella could only be a helpless bystander as these horrors unfolded. She joined the King at York in May 1322 where Edward's power, and that of de Spencer, was enshrined in statute law. However, the younger de Spencer's harsh treatment of high-born ladies and arrogant assumption of power must have alienated the Queen. This time Edward did not reward his wife with the plunder after Boroughbridge, a sinister sign that de Spencer was perhaps poisoning his mind against Isabella. Indeed, he was determined, by whatever means, to remove her influence over the King. In 1319 Isabella had almost been captured by the Scots. The de Spencers decided once again to place the Queen in danger.

After the Parliament of York in May 1322, Edward and his favourite, in their first flush of triumph, resolved to defeat Bruce once and for all. Later that summer an English army crossed the Scottish border, taking the war deep into the enemy camp. On 6 September Edward wrote briefly to the Bishop of Winchester: 'We have found no resistance', and on 18 September, to Archbishop Reynolds, Edward spoke of his high hopes for the success of the expedition. But a month later the campaign had turned into an unmitigated failure. Bruce counter-attacked, driving deep into England, harrying Yorkshire and defeating the English forces at Byland Abbey on 14 October, capturing many of Edward's followers, including the Earl of Richmond.

The defeat was a major military setback. Andrew Harclay, the hero of Boroughbridge, who had been created an earl by his grateful king, was so affected by the disaster that he attempted to negotiate an independent peace treaty with the Scots. For this he was arraigned on a charge of treason and executed.[15] The news of the Byland disaster travelled south. The city fathers in London demanded an immediate audience with Roger Swynnerton, Constable of the Tower, asking if Bruce intended to launch an attack on London itself.[16]

Meanwhile, in the north, Isabella had once again been caught up in the chaos. In his wild retreat back into England, Edward had left Isabella at Tynemouth Priory on the north-east coast while he hurried further south to raise fresh troops. This was a foolish move because the Queen was now effectively imprisoned there with the surrounding countryside under the control of a marauding Scottish army. From the start, Isabella was anxious about Edward's plans and a row broke out between them over who should be responsible for her safety. Edward had asked Thomas de Grey, constable of a nearby castle, to keep an eye on Isabella but Grey already had his hands full.[17] In the Public Record Office there are a number of almost illegible drafts of letters apparently dictated at great speed by the King as he retreated from Scotland in the autumn of 1322. The first is addressed to two of his commanders: he orders them to gather men from the troops of the younger de Spencer to fortify Tynemouth and protect the Queen. However, Isabella did not want de Spencer, or any of his men, anywhere near her. In a second letter to his Queen, Edward carefully removed any reference to de Spencer.

The Queen's panic is understandable. The Scots were pouring over the border and flight by sea was equally dangerous. A Flemish fleet was patrolling the north-eastern waters, giving aid and sustenance to the Scots. Isabella was caught between the hammer and the anvil: capture by either Scots or Flemish pirates. Once again she sent urgent pleas for help, though still insisting that de Spencer come nowhere near her. Edward wrote back that he would send a French knight, Henry de Sully, with troops 'more agreeable than the others'.[18] But De Sully never reached Tynemouth; he was caught up in the general rout and fell back with Edward's army to Byland, where he was captured. The heroes of the hour proved to be a group of young squires from Isabella's own household.[19] On the landward side they fortified the priory, drove off the Scots and then arranged flight by sea. The Scots renewed their assault during embarkation and did grave injury to Isabella's party. One of her ladies-in-waiting was killed and another died later of her injuries. Nevertheless, the squires were successful and Isabella and her household managed to escape along the coast to a secure place and travelled inland to join her husband at York.[20]

Isabella was incensed by this harrowing experience at Tynemouth. According to the chroniclers, she held de Spencer personally responsible and four years later, when de Spencer was arraigned for trial, the deliberate desertion of the Queen at Tynemouth was one of the principal allegations levelled against him. It would be easy to dismiss such accusations as groundless, that Isabella's experiences at Tynemouth were merely the fortunes of war. Moreover, Edward's letters showed that Isabella, even when in considerable physical danger, refused to have Hugh de Spencer the Younger anywhere near her. She hated him, found his presence offensive and certainly would not have entrusted her safety and security to his hands. Subsequently, the rancour between them grew. This animosity was not just due to de Spencer's rapacity, his cruelty to high-born ladies or even the execution of knights who had once served in her household. More than anything Isabella feared de Spencer's influence and control over her husband: she suspected that he would be only too pleased to see the back of her, whether in some lonely Scottish castle or a Flemish port. In Isabella's eyes, the débâcle at Tynemouth was a deliberate attempt to get rid of her.

Relations between Isabella and her husband now became very strained. Edward protested that he had done his best in the north and turned on Isabella's friends, the Beaumonts. In February 1323 Edward took Louis de Beaumont, Bishop of Durham, to task. He reminded Louis that he had been appointed to that powerful bishopric at the request of his friends, including the Queen, because they said he'd be 'a stone wall against the Scots'. Three months later Louis's brother Henry also quarrelled bitterly with the King at a council meeting on 30 May 1323 at Bishopsthorpe. Angry words were exchanged and Henry was asked to leave the meeting. He replied he could think of nothing better, for which contumacy he was placed under arrest.[21]

Isabella was not present at the meeting at Bishopsthorpe. She and her husband were now living separate lives. On 23 December 1322 Edward had informed his sheriffs that his Queen was about to embark on several long pilgrimages to various places in the kingdom. Isabella's absence from the court was to last almost a year until 13 October 1323. She did rejoin her husband for a short while but their deteriorating relationship became only too apparent. Isabella no longer exercised patronage, received gifts or any of the plunder taken by the de Spencers from their defeated opponents. De Spencer, meanwhile, was strengthening his control over the King. Nobles like Henry de Beaumont were being forced to take great oaths on the gospels, 'To live and die with the de Spencers'. Isabella was offered such an oath but refused to take it.[22] The King's new favourite was determined to reduce Isabella to a mere cipher.

In 1324 de Spencer seized on a new opportunity to denigrate the Queen. The new French King, Isabella's brother, Charles IV, resurrected the Gascon question. Once again England and France edged towards war. De Spencer had no love for France. Charles IV was sheltering exiles from Boroughbridge and further, in 1321, the French had refused de Spencer sanctuary or permission to dock in French ports.[23] Edward reminded Charles IV that peace between England and France was the reason he had married Isabella in the first place. Charles ignored this. Edward and de Spencer retaliated. On 18 September 1324, under the pretext of a possible French attack, all of Isabella's lands were taken back by the King, and on 18 November, Edward instructed the Exchequer to take over the running of Isabella's household.[24] In addition he ordered the arrest and imprisonment of all Frenchmen in England as well as the confiscation of their property. This was clearly intended to hurt Isabella directly. Twenty-seven French members of her retinue, including her chaplains, her doctor Theobald and the Launge family, were imprisoned under reduced circumstances in monasteries and convents throughout the kingdom.[25] And even greater cruelty was to come: the Queen's young children were removed from her and entrusted to Eleanor de Spencer, Hugh the Younger's wife, and another court favourite, Isabella Hastings.[26]

Both England and France now drifted into war over the duchy of Gascony. Edmund, Earl of Kent, the King's half-brother and Commander-in-Chief of English forces there, made a complete mess of the military defence of the duchy. Charles IV pressed his assault while demanding that his sister be treated more fairly. At length the French grew more insolent, insisting that Edward come to France and negotiate over their mutual difficulties. De Spencer was terrified of the King leaving the kingdom. All of his opponents were sheltering at the French court and the favourite had good reason to believe that Edward might be seized, even assassinated, while abroad.

In fact, by 1324, de Spencer was living in a nightmare. Secret agents were stealing into England, despatched by exiled Lancastrians to kill the King and his favourites, although the plot was discovered and the agents caught.[27] At the same time a magician, John of Nottingham, appeared before King's Bench, accused of making wax effigies of the King and his favourites in an attempt to slay them by necromancy.[28] De Spencer, fearful of being killed by black magic, wrote to the Pope asking for his special protection. John XXII replied: 'In answer to his complaint that he is threatened by magical and secret dealings, the Holy Father recommends him [i.e. de Spencer] to turn to God with his whole heart and make a good confession and such satisfaction as shall be enjoined. No other remedies are necessary beyond this general indulgence which the Pope grants him.' The Pope also wrote to de Spencer complaining at the harsh treatment of Edward's Queen and sharply upbraided him for his lack of good government.[29]

More practical reasons existed for Edward and de Spencer's reluctance to leave England. Despite their great victory at Boroughbridge, the country was seething with unrest. Criminal gangs, such as the Folvills of Leicestershire, were terrorizing their neighbours and waging a private war. Prisoners at Wallingford Castle, led by Maurice Berkeley, nearly broke out but were recaptured.[30] Edward II, faced with crises, both at home and abroad, reluctantly agreed in February 1325 that Isabella was the best person to represent his interests in France. He failed to realize that the Queen's departure to France was the result of a carefully laid plot.

By 9 March 1325 Isabella was in France with strict instructions to be back by midsummer. The Queen arrived in Paris where she successfully arranged a new truce over Gascony and despatched a loving letter to her husband, explaining how she could not return immediately because of outstanding problems over the duchy.[31] She kept Edward informed of proceedings and spent her leisure time visiting churches and entertaining dignitaries.[32] Edward was supposed to join her in Paris but was still reluctant to leave England: the de Spencers were fearful of accompanying him yet did not wish to be left in England by themselves. Eventually it was decided that, instead of the King going to France, his thirteen-year-old son and heir would do homage for him. On 12 September 1325, the Prince of Wales left for Dover and performed homage for Gascony.[33] Edward II believed a satisfactory conclusion had been reached, only to discover that the real crisis of his reign was about to emerge.

On 18 October 1325 Edward sent a letter to the Pope, complaining about the French but, more importantly, expressing deep concern at his wife's failure to return home.[34] Two weeks later, Walter Stapleton, Bishop of Exeter and the King's Treasurer, one of Edward II's most faithful ministers, abruptly arrived back in England. He informed the King and the de Spencers that he had become concerned about his own personal safety in Paris. English exiles, refugees from the de Spencer regime, were now making public appearances at the French court. A plot had been hatched to kill him, forcing Stapleton to flee Paris by dead of night.[35]

A month later, John Stratford, the wily Bishop of Winchester, also returned to England, bringing letters from the Queen.[36] She had now taken the young Prince of Wales into her custody. More dramatically, Isabella was now publicly dressing as a widow, claiming that she had lost her husband and openly announcing: 'I feel that marriage is a joining together of man and woman, maintaining the undivided habit of life. Someone has come between my husband and myself, trying to break this bond. I protest that I will not return until this intruder has been removed but, discarding my marriage garment, I shall assume the robes of widowhood and mourning until I am avenged of this Pharisee.' Edward immediately cut off all financial payments to his wife and the crisis had begun.[37]

No doubt de Spencer, the intruder to whom Isabella refers, played a major role in this marital crisis. He was undoubtedly a thug, a gangster, a man with few redeeming qualities apart from courage, yet he was no worse than many of his contemporaries. Isabella may have been repelled by his treatment of widows and orphans but, during her four years of glory 1326–30, she proved herself to be no faint heart when it came to taking life or other people's property. At this time what is striking is Isabella's clever deception of her husband and his favourite. They apparently regarded her as a political nonenity. Isabella, however, brilliantly deceived both her husband and de Spencer, becoming so submissive and obedient they thought she posed no danger. They undoubtedly placed spies in her household whilst she travelled France and kept strict control of the purse strings. For seven months, between March and October 1325, Isabella sustained the pretence. Edward and de Spencer became so confident they then compounded their fatal mistake by allowing her eldest son, the thirteen-year-old Prince of Wales, to join her. Once she had custody of her son, the heir to the English throne, Isabella set up an alternative government in Paris, attracting all the refugees from Boroughbridge as well as two royal earls, who found it impossible to return to England because of the débâcle in Gascony – Edmund of Kent, half-brother to Edward, and the Earl of Richmond.

In one of his letters to Isabella and to her brother Charles IV, Edward expressed deep concern at the appearance of

English rebels who lay in wait for Stapleton, Bishop of Exeter. He also alluded to someone advising the Queen, the shadowy and sinister Roger Mortimer of Wigmore, who had made his first public appearance beside Isabella. In a further letter to Isabella's uncle, Charles of Valois, dated 18 March 1326, Edward showed he now realized the full implications of Isabella's deceit: she has forsaken him and the kingdom; she had refused to return home or acknowledge his writ, and she had set up an alternative government and was personally involved with an escaped traitor, who appeared to be both her lover and her adviser.

'Now at last,' Edward wrote,

When the King sent to seek her, she then showed the feigned matter for the first time, which was never heard or suspected by anyone, unless by her: wherefore, the matters being considered, one ought not to give faith to such feigned invention against the truth. But, indeed, the King fully perceives, as the King of France and everybody may, that she does not love the King as she ought to love her lord, and that the matter that she speaks of the King's said nephew [i.e. de Spencer] for which she withdraws herself from the King, is feigned and is not certain, but the King thinks it must be of inordinate will when she, so openly and notoriously, knowingly, against her duty and the estate of the King's crown, which she is bound to love, has drawn to her and retains in her company of her council the King's traitor and mortal enemy the Mortimer, and others of his conspiracy, and keeps his company in and out of house, which evil-doer the King of France banished from his power at another time as the King's enemy, by virtue of the alliance between his and the King's ancestors.[38]

This letter publicly names the person Edward holds responsible for advising the Queen – Roger Mortimer of Wigmore. The King not only accuses his Queen of treason but of sexual misconduct. The phrase 'in and out of house' is a diplomatic way of saying 'in bed and out of bed' with Mortimer. The appearance of this English rebel and his involvement with Isabella must have sent shock waves through Edward's council. At no time, before the Queen's departure to France, had there been even a whisper of scandal about her conduct. Now she was openly consorting with a rebel and a traitor.

Roger Mortimer of Wigmore was a contemporary of Edward and de Spencer. Born in the mid-1280s he had been knighted with the Prince and de Spencer at the great ceremony of 1306. He had then proved himself to be an ambitious Welsh magnate, intent on building up his estates both in Wales and in Ireland. Mortimer of Wigmore was also one of Edward II's more successful generals. When Robert the Bruce had sent his brother Edward to invade Ireland in May 1315 and raise rebellion against the English Crown, Mortimer had made a successful landing on the Irish coast and brought the Gaelic tribes back under English rule. Mortimer kept to himself, on the fringes of baronial intrigue, more intent on pursuing his own ambitions along the Welsh March. Only when he and de Spencer clashed over territorial claims in South Wales did Mortimer and his uncle, Roger Mortimer of Chirk, rise in rebellion.

Both Mortimers had been defeated in the winter campaign of 1321–2. They were sent to the Tower and kept under tight security. Incarcerated for life, Mortimer of Chirk, probably injured in the skirmishes around Shrewsbury, fell seriously ill and eventually died, either of his injuries or his treatment in the Tower. His nephew was made of sterner stuff. Late in 1322 the Mortimers were challenged about further disruption in Wales and sentenced to death. The younger Mortimer decided that if he stayed any longer in the Tower, he would either starve to death, suffer an 'accident' or be taken out and formally executed. A plot was hatched to free him, supported by Mortimer's close friend and adherent, Adam Orleton, the ruffianly Bishop of Hereford. Orleton was to figure prominently in Isabella's circle for a while. He regarded Mortimer as his patron and his stance exemplifies how de Spencer had alienated the Lords Spiritual. Very few bishops would, in the last resort, support Edward and de Spencer: they were either, like Orleton, opponents of the favourite, or, as in many cases, simple spectators. The only exception was the able and scholarly Stapleton of Exeter, founder of Exeter College in Oxford.

On 1 August 1323, the garrison of the Tower celebrated the feast of Peter Ad Vincula – St Peter-in-Chains – after whom the Tower chapel was named. At the banquet the guards were drugged and Mortimer, with further help from two wealthy London merchants, John de Gisors and Richard de Betton, escaped from the Tower by a rope ladder. He lowered himself down, swam the Thames and reached the pre-arranged meeting place, where a group of horsemen took him to Portchester from where he crossed to France.[39]

Historians have always wondered if Queen Isabella, in the light of her later liaison with Mortimer, had anything to do with Mortimer's escape. The Marcher Lord was undoubtedly resolute and highly versatile. No physical description of Mortimer exists but he comes across as a tough, wily, resolute fighting man: a warrior, used to danger and physical hardship. His escape from the Tower, crossing the Thames and flight from England, is one of the most successful in the history of that bleak fortress. Mortimer, moreover, had not been a leading member of the baronial opposition; he had been much more involved in Ireland and along the Welsh March and he loyally supported the King until he clashed with the de Spencers over lands in South Wales. In 1311, Isabella had assisted Roger Mortimer in the release of a Chamberlain of North Wales imprisoned on the suspicion that he had deliberately lost his accounts.[40] She also corresponded with him,[41] supporting him and the others in the Somerton case, whilst her bailiff at Macclesfield, John Hinkley, had been in the Mortimers' retinue when they fought against the de Spencers,[42]

On 17 February 1323, Isabella wrote a letter to the treasurer begging for relief for Roger's wife Joan who had also been imprisoned.[43] Isabella was in, or around the Tower during August 1323 when Mortimer escaped. Her friendship, and implicit understanding of Mortimer's grievances, may have blossomed into a deeper relationship, and she may have persuaded the French court to give Mortimer a sympathetic reception. Edward specifically accused Charles de Valois, Isabella's uncle, not only of supporting Mortimer but of being involved in his escape.[44]

Isabella's liaison with Mortimer might have begun before her departure to France: because of de Spencer, she may have already regarded her marriage as null and void. During those first few months at Paris, Isabella and Mortimer must have kept their relationship very secret. However de Spencer's spies in her household may have alerted the King and his favourite while the visit of Walter Stapleton, Bishop of Exeter, would have brought matters to a head, resulting in the good bishop's abrupt flight from Paris. He took back firm evidence of the liaison and thereafter Isabella dropped all pretence.

Edward's anger is clearly apparent in his letters. His wife and heir were now in rebellion and he was being proclaimed a cuckold throughout the courts of Europe. He threatened to disinherit his son and heir too and use him as an example so that all sons would learn to obey their fathers.[45] De Spencer, and Edward also, realized the matter would have to be settled by the sword. Watches were set up along the south-east coast to prevent secret agents landing with arms or messages. Suspects were rounded up, including Mortimer's mother Margaret, who was imprisoned in Elstow Abbey.[46] The King issued firm instructions that, if his Queen and Prince returned in the ships he'd sent for them, they were to be treated honourably. However, if they landed with banners displayed and armed men, Isabella, Prince Edward and the Earl of Kent were to be taken as prisoners, and the rest were to be executed under martial law.[47]

Edward and de Spencer also initiated a widespread campaign of bribery both at Avignon and the French court in an attempt to buy themselves out of trouble. Papal legates travelled between Paris and London. The King even despatched Thomas Dunheved, his Dominican confessor, to the Pope to seek a divorce from Isabella. Charles of France was receptive to the bribes; the resolute John XXII was not. He believed Isabella's grievances and made his feelings felt. When Edward sent a gift of 5000 florins, Pope John graciously thanked Edward but bluntly added that he would take the gift as part payment of an outstanding debt and he looked forward to receiving the rest as soon as possible.[48]

Charles IV began to grow tired of his sister. De Spencer's gold and, perhaps, memories of the Tour de Nesle scandal led to a cooling of their relationship.[49] Once Isabella realized which way the wind was blowing, she and Mortimer left the French court in the summer of 1326 and entered the territory of William, Count of Hainault. Isabella promised a settlement of all maritime disputes between Hainault and England and the marriage of her eldest son Edward to William's daughter Philippa. In return William offered troops, a fleet of eight men-of-war as well as 132 fishing smacks, or herring ships, for transport to assist with any invasion.[50]

Edward and de Spencer became almost hysterical in organizing watches along the coast, issuing letters to sheriffs, strengthening castles, seeking out traitors and spies.[51] But their efforts were fruitless. Many of de Spencer's secret enemies now emerged from the shadows and the King and his favourite did not know whom to trust. Prominent members of their administration, such as Robert Bellers and Robert Sapy, were horribly murdered. The latter's eyes were torn out and all his limbs were broken before he died.[52] The de Vescy family attacked royal officials in Yorkshire while other de Spencer opponents appeared at fairs and markets, openly flouting their resistance and subjecting royal manors to a series of bloody attacks.[53] By March 1326 Edward was bemoaning how the secret agents of his enemies were able to move in and out of the country at their ease: he was soon to discover the reason why.[54]

On 21 September 1326 Isabella and Mortimer set sail from Dordrecht in Hainault,[55] crossed the North Sea and made a safe landing on the Suffolk coast, to take up position off a small Suffolk port with their mercenaries and all the malcontents from England. Edward had put his fleet on a war footing and a special squadron was supposed to take up position off the small port of Orwell, the very route Isabella's ships would have to follow.[56]

On 24 September 1326, the rebels landed on the Colvasse peninsula near Walton-on-Naze, on the tip of the approach to the port of Orwell.[57] Isabella led about 1500–2000 men and, more importantly, she met with no opposition. The King's fleet did not materialize – it apparently sailed in the opposite direction – while the levies of Essex, who were supposed to block her from landing, went over to her side. It would be wrong to suggest such treachery was due solely to devotion to Isabella. In truth, it was a clear expression of the hatred felt for Edward II and the de Spencer regime: very few were prepared to support them.

Edward and de Spencer, who had set up their head-quarters in London, were aghast at the reports which now flooded in. Thomas, Earl of Norfolk, the King's half-brother, immediately joined the Queen. Henry of Lancaster, the dead Earl Thomas's brother, collected levies at Leicester and marched south to link up with the inva-ders.[58] Worse, the London merchants were quietly distrib-uting bribes to their mob leaders. Edward and de Spencer, fearful of being trapped in the city, made preparations to flee into Wales to raise troops. The royal Chancery issued letter after letter telling this sheriff or that official to raise troops to muster at certain points to oppose the Queen.

Mortimer was branded an outlaw: a reward of a thousand pounds sterling was put on his head, dead or alive. But no one was interested.[59] The King, his favourites and a select group of clerks, with a mobile treasure of about £29,000, fled London on 2 October for the safety and security of de Spencer's strongholds in Wales.[60]

The Queen's march inland became a triumphant progress. She reached Oxford where the University greeted her as a saviour. For the time being Queen Isabella observed the niceties. She lodged with the Carmelites whilst Mortimer was given a chamber at Osney Abbey.[61] A special convocation of the University took place. Adam Orleton, Bishop of Hereford, emerged from hiding to deliver a violent sermon against de Spencer. Preaching on a text from Genesis: 'I will put enmity between thee and the woman and between thy seed and her seed, she will bruise thy head.' Orleton applied the text to de Spencer the Younger, describing him 'as a seed of the first tyrant Satan who would be crushed by the Lady Isabella and her son the Prince'. Orleton's speech was a clear warning of the violence to come.[62] The Leicestershire chronicler, Knighton, reports how the Queen and her party had decided on the eradication of the entire de Spencer family, root and branch, so that never again would a de Spencer rise to power and threaten the throne.[63]

Edward's star was plunging fast. On 11 October he reached Gloucester, offering free pardons to any outlaw who joined him and was reduced to making twelve archers of his household swear they would never leave him. He asked the bishops to intervene but he was calling into the darkness.[64] A few bishops met at Lambeth on 13 October to draw up plans for a peace conference at St Paul's.

Walter Reynolds, Archbishop of Canterbury, now revealed that he had been sending secret funds to the Queen, and the King's cause was pronounced lost. The meeting broke up.[65] The only bishop loyal to Edward, Stapleton, Bishop of Exeter, unwisely decided to return to London, now a very dangerous place for any adherent of Edward or de Spencer. Isabella had issued a proclamation saying that the Londoners would be punished if they did not destroy de Spencer. The royal favourite had placed a thousand pounds on Mortimer's head dead or alive: Isabella responded by doubling that for de Spencer. The mob rose in revolt. The Tower was stormed and de Spencer's men were killed. Poor Stapleton chose that very moment to enter London. He was seen by one of the robber gangs, nicknamed 'Rifflers', who pursued the bishop and his two squires to St Paul's. They were captured in a nearby stableyard, stripped naked and hacked to death. Stapleton's head was sent to the Queen.[66]

Isabella was fully intent on capturing her husband. However, although England had deserted the King, the Mortimers were not liked in Wales and Edward hoped that a fresh royal army might be gathered there. The elder de Spencer, exhausted, took shelter in Bristol. On 18 October Isabella arrived before the city. For eight days the favourite's father held out, trying to negotiate terms to guarantee security of life and limb. It was futile: his garrison refused to fight, the gates were opened and, on 22 October, the elder de Spencer was arraigned before a military tribunal manned by adherents of the dead Earl of Lancaster. Isabella pleaded for his life – after all, the elder de Spencer had shown friendship to her in the early years of her marriage. The Lancastrians, now a powerful part of her army, reminded her of her promise that all de Spencers were to die. The elder de Spencer was charged, not allowed to answer and found guilty 'by clamour of the people'. He was sentenced to be hanged in a surcoat quartered with his own arms, which was to be burnt and destroyed for ever. The old man suffered the full rigours of a traitor's death, hanging, drawing and quartering, on the common gallows outside Bristol. His severed head was sent to Winchester and his decapitated corpse displayed on the gallows before being hacked up and fed to dogs.[67]

The pursuit of the King was then resumed, although the constitutional niceties were observed. A council meeting was held and it was decreed that, as the King had fled from his kingdom, his eldest son would take over as 'Custos' or Keeper.[68] Edward, meanwhile, had taken a ship across the Bristol Channel in an attempt to flee abroad. He offered money to de Spencer's confessor, Richard Bliton, to pray to St Anne for a favourable wind. The saint proved to be of no assistance and they were forced to return to Wales. They had a brief respite at Caerphilly Castle but, frightened of being besieged, de Spencer and Edward fled once more. They left the castle in control of the royalist John Felton who held out for weeks before negotiating his own surrender.[69] The King continued to issue writs and raise troops, but it was all over. His household accounts end abruptly on 31 October, a sign that the royal clerks were deserting him. Edward moved to Neath Abbey and, on 10 November, made one last-ditch attempt to negotiate with his wife.[70] It failed. Edward tried to hide in the countryside but troops, led by Henry of Lancaster, were not far behind. Certain Welshmen, for a sum, offered to lead Lancaster to the King. Edward and his party were captured. Most of them were released but de Spencer and Simon de Reading were sent under chains to the Queen at Hereford.[71]

Edward surrendered to Henry of Lancaster and was taken first to Monmouth then on to Kenilworth Castle. The King was finished and the 'She-Wolf' had come into her own.

Edward II's downfall was inextricably linked to the collapse of his marriage to Isabella. Even in a modern marriage, which disintegrates in the full glare of the public media, it is difficult to ascertain what is the cause and who is at fault, and the difficulty is compounded by speculating on such events which occurred 700 years ago. Nevertheless, some evidence does exist for the tragedy which swept away Edward II and the de Spencers in 1326. What is most surprising about the whole affair is the speed with which Edward and Isabella's relationship disintegrated and transformed into conspiracy, treason and bloody death.

Edward II was in his early twenties when he married Isabella; she was probably approaching her thirteenth year. They both had to face considerable personal and political difficulties. They had not met before, nor was there any indication of a desire by either party to marry: they were simply political pawns, managed and manoeuvred by their respective fathers. Matters were certainly not helped by Edward II's conduct after his marriage. He went out of his way to insult his in-laws and openly favoured his 'sweet brother' Gaveston. Nevertheless, Gaveston proved to be no real threat to Isabella. Whatever the exact relationship between the Gascon favourite and the King, Isabella did not harbour the same intense hatred for him as she did for de Spencer.

Gaveston and Isabella apparently travelled together and

their households mingled. Isabella may have been secretly relieved at the favourite's execution but there is no evidence of mutual antipathy, nor a shred of proof that Edward II regarded Isabella as playing any part in Gaveston's downfall. Indeed, until 1322, the relationship between the King and his young Queen appears to have been harmonious, with no hint of acrimony or confrontation, either privately or in public. Isabella was treated with every respect. Like other queens before her, she had a sumptuous household and a host of retainers; she was a powerful landowner with estates throughout the length and breadth of the kingdom. She received gifts and was honoured in every way. In turn, Isabella produced four healthy children for her husband; she participated in the King's negotiations with his barons, and helped to maintain fairly harmonious relationships with France. True, there was a clash between Isabella and the de Spencers over certain rents due to her: she opposed the favourite's nominees in the Somerton case and played a public role in begging for the de Spencers' exile in 1321. Even so, this may well have been an empty diplomatic gesture, which allowed the King to save face and concede to his baronial opponents.

Of course, there may have been personal reasons why the relationship between Edward and Isabella weakened and frayed. Yet the violence of its final collapse is truly breathtaking, especially in view of the major role Isabella played in the King's military preparations against the barons during the winter of 1321–2. Documentary evidence does exist, which hints at certain causes for such a disastrous marital collapse, in the form of letters between Edward and Isabella during the Queen's self-imposed exile in France as well as the formal charges levelled against de Spencer after his downfall. Three principal accusations emerged from these: de Spencer's seizure of Isabella's estates, the Tynemouth incident and de Spencer's 'intrusion' into her marriage. The first two must be regarded as symptoms rather than causes: the 'intrusion' may lie at the root of the matter. Isabella's public statement, once she had decided to break with her husband and set up an alternative government in exile, is very clear. She took the young Prince of Wales into custody, publicly dressed in widow's weeds and loudly proclaimed the reason for her actions: 'I feel that marriage is a joining together of man and woman, maintaining the undivided habit of life. Someone has come between my husband and myself, trying to break this bond. I protest that I will not return until this intruder has been removed but, discarding my marriage garment, I shall assume the robes of widowhood and mourning until I am avenged of this Pharisee.'[72]

The important sentence here is 'Someone has come between my husband and myself trying to break this bond.' Of course, that someone was de Spencer, and the 'intrusion' could refer to a relationship between de Spencer and the King which Isabella found repulsive and unacceptable. Nevertheless, would this account for the intense rancour between the Queen and the royal favourite? It could be argued that Isabella's liaison with Mortimer was the real cause and that the Queen was simply making 'bricks out of straw', using Edward's relationship with de Spencer as an excuse and pretext for treason, conspiracy and adultery.

Certain letters sent by Edward to his estranged wife and the French court shed more light on the matter. The first is dated 1 September 1325.

To the Queen. The King has frequently offered her, both before and after the homage, to come to him with all speed, laying aside all excuses: but, before the homage, she was excused by reason of the advancement of the affairs, and she has now informed the King, by the Bishop of Winchester, with her letters of credence, that she will not return now for danger and doubt of Hugh de Spencer. The King marvels at this to the extent of his power, especially as she always behaved amiably to him, and he to her, in the King's presence, and particularly at her departure by her behaviour, and after her departure, by the very special letters sent to him, which he has shown to the King. The King knows for truth, and she knows, that Hugh has always procured her all the honour with the King that he could: and no evil or villainy was done to her after her marriage by any abetment and procurement.[73]

The second letter, to the King of France on the same date, develops this theme a little further.

To the King of France. The King has received and understood his letters, delivered by the Bishop of Winchester, and has also understood what the Bishop has told him by word of mouth concerning the matters . . . for peril of her [Isabella's] life and for the doubt that she has of Hugh de Spencer. It is not fitting that she should doubt Hugh or any other man living in the King's realm, since, if either Hugh or any other man in the realm wished her evil, and the King knew of it, he would chastise them in such a manner that others should take example; and such is, and has been, and always will be the King's will, and he has sufficient power to do this. He wishes the King of France to know that he could never perceive that Hugh, privately or openly, in word or deed, or in countenance, did not behave himself in all points towards the Queen as he ought to have done to his lady: but when the King remembers the amiable countenance and words between the Queen and Hugh that he has seen, and the great friendships that she held to him upon her going beyond sea, and the loving letters that she sent him not long ago, which Hugh has shown to the King, he cannot in any manner believe that the Queen, by herself, can understand such things concerning Hugh. Whoever has, out of hatred, made her so understand, and the King cannot believe it of Hugh in any manner, but he believes that, after himself, Hugh is the man of his realm who wishes her most honour, and this Hugh has always shown, and the King testifies to this in good truth. He prays the King of France not to give credence to those who would make him understand otherwise, but that he will believe the King's testimony, because the King has, and by reason ought to have, much greater knowledge of this matter than others . . .[74]

Now, a possible hypothesis for this violent estrangement could be that Edward II was bisexual, that his relationship with Gaveston was intimately physical but that Gaveston proved to be no threat to the Queen at the time, as she was then in her early adolescence. Moreover, by the time she was sixteen, this rival for her husband's affections had been brutally removed. It might then be argued that, after Gaveston's death, Edward's and Isabella's relationship became more amicable. The Queen matured: she supported Edward through all his difficulties but objected to his relationship with de Spencer. This new favourite, however, not only enjoyed an intimate relationship with her husband but openly ridiculed and humiliated her and drove her from the King's presence. However, this does not explain why de Spencer allowed Isabella to travel to France or why Isabella immediately began a very scandalous relationship with the exiled Mortimer.

A review of the evidence indicates a much more complex situation. There is no doubt of the mutual hatred between Isabella and de Spencer. Isabella's treatment of the fallen favourite is powerful testimony to her feelings whilst, during her exile, de Spencer's detestation of Isabella was also well publicized. On 15 June 1326, during the height of the crisis, the King and de Spencer travelled to Rochester to meet its venerable, but very astute bishop, Hamo de Hethe. The bishop entertained the King and his favourite, during which de Spencer launched into a savage diatribe against Isabella. The King turned to de Hethe (the conversation was recorded almost word for word) and asked: 'Isn't it true that a Queen who once disobeyed her husband was deprived of her Queenship?' De Hethe retorted: 'Who ever has told you that has given you very bad advice.' The bishop then baited de Spencer with allusions from the Old Testament on the fate of evil councillors, but de Spencer would neither relent or concede. The incident illustrates both de Spencer's deep opposition to the Queen and gives the lie to any hope of compromise or reconciliation.[75]

By 1325 Isabella was a young woman of twenty-nine. There is no hint of infidelity on her part before this crisis: she was a loyal wife, a good partner and had provided Edward with four healthy children. She began her liaison with Mortimer whilst in France, but this was a result rather than the cause of her alienation from her husband. Something had driven Isabella away from her husband, and I suspect it was more than just a homosexual relationship between the King and his favourite. After their victory in 1322, de Spencer may have reminded Edward how his marriage to Isabella had been forced upon him by Edward I and Philip IV of France. On the other hand, Isabella had fulfilled all expectations: she had produced healthy heirs; she had tolerated her husband's foibles and done good work for him both in England and abroad; she had played a crucial role in Anglo-French relations and supported Edward against his hated opponent Lancaster. Edward II's sexuality may have been suspect, but Isabella had accepted the relationship with Gaveston, once Edward accorded her the honour due to her as his wife and Queen. De Spencer, however, was a different matter. Even before the battle of Boroughbridge Isabella's hostility and resentment towards him were apparent, and the Tynemouth incident only crystallized this. Isabella talks of 'intrusion' and Edward's letters, both to her and the King of France develop this theme further. Edward's assertion to Isabella is most telling: he does not defend any relationship between himself and de Spencer but refers to that between de Spencer and Isabella: 'The King knows for truth, and she knows, that Hugh has always procured her all the honour with the King that he could: and no evil or villainy was done to her . . .'

What was this villainy, this evil? Edward's letter to the

King of France returns to this elusive matter, rebutting the allegation that Isabella is in fear of her life from de Spencer, a probable reference to the Tynemouth incident, but then mentions something else. 'He, [i.e. Edward] wishes the King of France to know that he could never perceive that Hugh, privately or openly, in word or deed, or in countenance, did not behave himself on all points towards the Queen as he ought to have done to his lady.'

It seems that Isabella had levelled serious allegations of a very sensitive nature against de Spencer. If it was simply the seizure of her estates and household, or a clash over political and administrative issues, this would be apparent. Instead the King himself does not wish to spell out what de Spencer allegedly said or did to Isabella which she, in turn, had reported to the French court. In my view, Edward is referring to some sexual misconduct, which Isabella found offensive and disgusting. More importantly, it was something which upset Charles IV of France and his council and accounts for Isabella's determination not to return, as well as her assuming the dramatic role of a widow. It could also explain her elder son's adherence to her as well as the sustained support she received from both the papacy and the English hierarchy. I suspect that Edward may have tried to pressure Isabella into accepting an open marriage in which de Spencer wished to play a part. Admittedly, few details exist of this. One Hainault chronicle (Isabella stayed there before she launched her invasion of 1326) claims that Edward II was having an affair with his own niece, de Spencer's wife Eleanor.[76] Did Edward II reciprocate? Wife-swapping is not a phenomenon solely reserved for the twentieth or twenty-first centuries. Did de Spencer who, after Boroughbridge, was given virtually everything else, demand Isabella as well?

De Spencer was by all accounts a rapacious villain: his harsh treatment of Lancastrian widows is well documented. Did he employ similar tactics towards Isabella and, when she refused, humiliate and disgrace her? It could well explain Isabella's conduct. She may have pretended to submit to de Spencer's demands, which would account for him believing she was no longer a threat but a pliant tool who would do whatever he demanded. Isabella dissimulated, pretended to comply and then escaped to France. Once she was safe with her son, she dropped the mask. De Spencer's sexual harassment of her would also explain Isabella's conduct with Mortimer. Because of de Spencer's 'intrusion', she may have regarded her marriage as null and void. If her husband insisted on playing the pander and allowing his favourite into her bed, why shouldn't Isabella choose for herself and, who better than de Spencer's sworn rival and enemy in Wales, a seasoned soldier, a warrior who now led the exiles plotting against the King and his despised favourite?

This argument would certainly explain Isabella's hatred for de Spencer, her dissimulation and desire to flee abroad, not to mention her ruthless pursuit and total destruction of her husband and his favourite. It also provides a powerful insight into Isabella's character. Early in Edward's reign, Isabella had proved to be an effective negotiator with the French court. During her exile she displayed similar abilities in building up resistance abroad, moving to Hainault and persuading its Count to give her financial and military support for an invasion of England. Isabella comes across as a hard-headed, resolute, very able woman who could practise deception with the best. Once abroad, she gave full vent to her fury, though hiding it well before she left for France. However, the wise Henry Eastry, Prior of Christchurch, Canterbury, and a close friend of the Queen, sensed the dangers. Isabella visited him shortly before leaving for France and asked him to look after her greyhounds. They had a long conversation and Eastry may have even acted in the role of her confessor. He became very concerned by what he learnt and shortly afterwards, wrote to Walter Reynolds, Archbishop of Canterbury, advising that Isabella should not be allowed to leave the kingdom until her estates and household were restored and full reparation made to her.[77] It was Edward's tragedy that his old acting friend, the vacillating Archbishop, failed to persuade the King to act on this sage advice.

FOUR

The She-Wolf Triumphant

'Quo audiens, Populus universus, unanimo, manus
extendetes, clamabat, Fiat! Fiat!' – 'On hearing
which all the people, unanimously, hands extended,
cried "Let it be! Let it be!"'

The reaction of Parliament, January 1327, to
Archbishop Reynold's declaration that
Edward be deposed

Isabella's and Mortimer's loathing for Hugh de Spencer
the Younger was given full vent in his gruesome death.
The fallen royal favourite had no illusions about what was
in store and tried to starve himself to death.[1] Exhausted
by his sudden collapse from power, flight across England
and wandering through Wales, de Spencer was already in
poor shape. The Queen would have liked to have taken
him back to London and displayed him before the mob,
but did not want to risk him dying on the way, either from
sheer weakness or by committing suicide. De Spencer's
son-in-law, the Earl of Arundel, had already faced summary
execution at Hereford and the same city was therefore
chosen for the public humiliation and execution of Hugh.

First, he faced a military tribunal composed of Lancaster, Mortimer and other lords: a list of charges were read out, encompassing all his crimes since 1321. His treatment of Isabella figured high in these. He was blamed for the collapse of the Queen's marriage, coming between man and wife, of humiliating Isabella, seizing her estates and wealth and bribing the French court against her.[2]

De Spencer, like his father, was not given a chance to reply and he was too feeble to protest. He was found guilty and taken to the gates of Hereford. There he was dragged from his horse, his clothing stripped off him and the surcoat bearing his arms reversed. A crown of nettles was fashioned and forced on his head. His enemies drew knives and scratched into his bare skin verses from the scriptures denouncing his evil arrogance. He was then forced back on his horse and led into the city to the bray of trumpets and the mocking tunes of a bagpipe. The mob were allowed to have their way. Everything at hand was hurled at both him and his marshal, Simon of Reading, who was forced to walk in front carrying de Spencer's disgraced, polluted standard. The fallen favourite was suffering so much that, according to one chronicle, such a horrid sound came from him as had never been heard before. Judgement was again pronounced. De Spencer was dragged off his horse, tied to a sled pulled by four horses, and taken into the town square to be hanged on a specially erected gallows fifty feet high. Still conscious, he was cut down, his body sliced open, his intestines plucked out and burnt before his eyes before decapitation put an end to his pain. Simon of Reading, his marshal and principal henchman, was despatched on a smaller gallows next to him. The entire proceedings were watched by the Queen, Mortimer and others, who feasted and celebrated. De Spencer's head was sent for display in

London, the quarters of his corpse to different cities of the realm.[3]

For the rest of de Spencer's supporters Isabella and Mortimer acted with restraint. There was no witch-hunt, no general purge. Many were pardoned and the clerks, the civil service, who had been so close to Edward, de Spencer and leading ministers like Stapleton, were allowed to continue in office. But Edward and de Spencer's households at Westminster and the Tower of London were ransacked and £8000, an incredible sum at that time, was seized, with Isabella and Mortimer acquiring the lion's share.[4]

Supporters were rewarded, lands restored, prisons opened and some form of compensation was paid to the victims of the de Spencer reign of terror. Isabella and Mortimer now faced one serious problem. Nobody would mourn de Spencer but the imprisoned King was a different matter. He was the Lord's anointed, their tenant-in-chief. Medieval lawyers could draw a distinction between the Crown and its wearer but how could the two be separated? Edward of Caernarvon was King by primogeniture and God's grace; he was the 'Christus', the Anointed One. In the eyes of medieval man, the coronation ceremony was very similar to a marriage and 'what God has joined together no man should put asunder'. And, of course, there was the more sensitive problem of Isabella's adultery. She may have been much suspected but nothing was ever proved. Now that de Spencer had been removed, surely the King could reign once again and the Queen rejoin her husband?

Meanwhile Edward II was being held in honourable custody by his cousin Henry of Lancaster. He had reigned for almost twenty years, he'd shown himself to be feckless, but he had also shown that he never forgot. If released, he would eat humble pie, bow and beg, accept any conditions. Never-theless, time would pass and Edward, once again, would plot revenge. He was only forty-five years of age; his father had lived to be sixty-eight. New favourites might emerge?

Isabella had murder in her heart. De Spencer had been killed. Why couldn't Edward die as well? Like de Spencer, he, too, had committed hideous crimes and brought the kingdom to its knees. She had to move quickly. Already the flush of victory was fading, secret sympathizers of Edward were emerging while Isabella was having to face the hard grind of government. Robert the Bruce had been held back by a secret agreement between himself and Isabella,[5] but there were other, equally urgent problems. London had risen in rebellion. De Spencer's agents were being taken and beheaded in the streets. Bands of rifflers, robber gangs, roamed the city pillaging churches, attacking the Italian bankers, mobbing any official of Edward II who dared to show his face. The unrest had spread to the countryside. Lambeth was attacked. Rochester lurched under mob rule. Merchants fled and commercial life collapsed as farmers refused to bring produce into the markets.[6]

Edward II had first been taken to Monmouth where he handed over the Great Seal to his cousin Henry of Lancaster. By 23 November the Seal was with Isabella,[7] and she began to issue writs, sometimes in her husband's name, sometimes 'by the King on the information of the Queen', 'by the Council', 'by the Queen and the King's first born son'.[8] Isabella was intent on keeping government in her hands. She personally supervised the Great Seal, kept the Hainault mercenaries in her household and did not allow her fifteen-year-old son out of her sight. She tried to bring London back to the King's peace. But the

Londoners, now holding her second son, John of Eltham, refused to co-operate. When she tried to assist a German merchant, Hildebrand, they rudely retorted that no enemy of London could be a friend of the Queen and she was to mind her own business.[9]

Isabella resolved to act. A small force of Hainaulters secretly entered the capital and seized the Tower.[10] Castles around London were given to trusted servants of the Queen and, by supporting her own nominee as Mayor, Isabella was able to take control of the situation.[11] Next she travelled to Wallingford via Gloucester, Lichfield and Witney. A great council was held there during Christmas 1326 to discuss what steps to take next. Isabella and Mortimer showed their hand: there were calls for the King's execution, prompted by Isabella, but these were not taken up. Henry of Lancaster, the King's cousin, would never have accepted this; his treatment of Edward had always been honourable. The bishops, too, would have balked at such an outcome. Nevertheless, for a while the argument was maintained: Edward should stand trial and face the full penalty for his crimes. The council became divided on the issue, but the decisive voice was that of the mercenary leader, John of Hainault. He argued that Edward was an anointed king: he could not be harmed and they had no right to try him. The council eventually came down on his side. Edward would be constitutionally deposed and confined to a castle for the rest of his natural life. Isabella had, at least, won half a victory.[12]

Parliament was summoned at Westminister for January 1327 to depose Edward II and make way for his elder son.[13] The entire proceedings were pure pantomime. A deputation was sent to Edward at Kenilworth, inviting him to attend the Parliament and face the charges against him. According to chronicle sources, the delegation, led by two bishops, received a savage rebuff from Edward. He called them traitors and said he would have nothing to do with the proceedings. It is doubtful whether Edward said anything of the sort. The two bishops who led the delegation – Orleton of Hereford and Stratford of Winchester – were firmly in the Queen's camp. Edward may have personally reviled them but he would have loved an opportunity to speak in public at Westminster, attack his Queen and take her to task for her failings. Of course, his enemies never intended the imprisoned King to be given a public forum at Westminster. Once again, Edward was depicted as being recalcitrant and unwilling to co-operate, so at this point Mortimer emerged from the shadows. He declared that the King should be deposed in his absence.

The play-acting continued, with the parliamentary pro-ceedings, punctuated by speeches from Isabella's bishops, Orleton of Hereford and Stratford of Winchester. The chronicler Swynbroke dismissed these two worthies as 'Alumpni Jezebele' and 'Baal Sacerdotes', 'the assistants of Jezebel', 'the Priests of Baal'. Isabella herself is described as a '*virago ferrea*', 'an iron virago'. Orleton certainly protected the Queen's interests, loudly proclaiming how Edward of Caernarvon was too dangerous for the Queen to live with. According to Orleton, the imprisoned King carried a knife in his hose to kill the Queen and, if he was disarmed, he would slay her with his teeth. Orleton's comment that Isabella could not rejoin her husband, was a pointed reminder to those bishops who were beginning to murmur about the sanctity of marriage vows, as well as those amongst the victorious magnates who argued that the Queen had done her duty and should now withdraw. Of course, once she was gone, Mortimer's power would be weakened.[14]

Orleton finally asked Parliament to consider whether Edward should be deposed or not. The hapless Archbishop Reynolds, who had made his peace with the Queen, put forward the Articles of Deposition against Edward II: incompetence, relying on bad counsel, destroying the Church and many noble families, defeat abroad, breaking his Coronation Oath, dissipating the realm's treasure and being totally unwilling to change his ways.

Prince Edward, now almost fifteen years of age, was then led into Westminster Hall. The people were asked to choose between father and son: with one voice, the people cried they would choose the son. Isabella played her part to perfection: dressed in black, a sorrowful countenance, 'La Grande Dame du Douleur', torn between grief at her husband's deposition but bravely smiling through the tears at her son's accession.[15] Archbishop Reynolds then delivered another sermon, '*Vox Populi, Vox Dei*', and Stratford followed with a discourse on what happens to a kingdom 'When its head was sick'. Orleton concluded this marvellous piece of theatre by choosing the theme, 'Woe to the kingdom whose king is a child'. A nice touch. No one was sure whether he was speaking about Edward the father or Edward the son but it was a timely reminder that the young king would need the protection and guidance of a royal council, in which Mother, as well as 'Uncle Roger', would play a prominent part. The young prince was then proclaimed to cries of '*Ave Rex!*' followed by the hymn, 'Gloria, Honor, Laus . . .'

A second delegation was then sent to Edward at

Kenilworth. Again, the King supposedly refused to have anything to do with it, cursing them as traitors. Isabella was in a quandary. She didn't want the King coming to Parliament but, at the same time, she needed his co-operation. Secret messages were sent to Kenilworth, this time with a different slant. The deposition would go ahead but, if Edward didn't co-operate, there was a possibility Parliament would choose a king from another family. This may have been an empty threat or even an allusion to Parliament choosing Mortimer. If that had happened the kingdom would have slipped into civil war. Henry, Earl of Lancaster, not to mention Edward II's half-brothers, had legitimate claims to the throne. Nevertheless, Mortimer placed great emphasis on his supposed descent from the legendary British King Brutus. He was steeped in the Arthurian legends and possibly saw himself as founding a new dynasty.

Edward II's resistance was broken and he decided, or was forced, to concede. A formal delegation, with the Lancastrian knight William Trussel as their spokesman, was despatched to Kenilworth. Edward met them in the audience chamber clothed from head to toe in black. He was weak, almost swooning with grief, but reluctantly abdicated in favour of his son. On 21 January, Trussel, on behalf of the whole kingdom, read out the renunciation of homage. Sir Thomas Blunt, Edward II's steward, broke his staff of office to show the royal household was dissolved and Edward was then led away. The abdication was proclaimed on 29 January and the young King was crowned at the beginning of February 1327.

At the coronation Isabella was still playing the role of a stricken queen. The historian Walsingham talks of her face and posture being that of 'A woman of sorrow', but adds that it was a great pretence.[16] Indeed, Isabella must have been delighted. De Spencer was gone, Edward II was deposed, her young son was King, while she controlled both him and the council. She was with Mortimer and had a cast-iron excuse not to go back to Edward.

Isabella busied herself acquiring lands and treasure. The allegation of one chronicler that she eventually owned almost two-thirds of England is exaggerated, but she became a byword for rapacity, especially amongst the de Spencer family. They later informed the garrulous chronicler, Froissart, that 'Isabella had been an evil queen and took everything from them'.[17] Between 1 December 1326 and 13 January 1327, Isabella received cash grants of almost £32,000. The great alliance she and Mortimer had formed with the other barons began to fall apart in the face of such greed. Moreover, sympathy was growing for her deposed husband, as became apparent at a council meeting at Stamford on 16 April 1327. According to rumours, Edward regretted his former reluctance and pitifully demanded to see his wife and children again.[18] The deposed King was now spending his time making heart-rending pleas and engaged in writing doleful poetry:

> In winter woe befell me,
> By cruel fortune threatened.
> My life now lies a ruin.
> Once was I feared and dreaded,
> But now all men despise me
> And call me a crownless King,
> A laughing stock to all.[19]

Throughout English history members of the royal family who fell into disgrace managed to elicit a great deal of sympathy, be it Richard III, Charles I or Edward VIII. The same was true of Edward II. His loyal supporters had been caught off guard by the rapid events of autumn 1326. Now they were beginning to gather both in secret and at court. The moderates amongst them argued as follows: Edward II was deposed, shouldn't he now be allowed to live as a country gentleman, and wasn't it time his wife Isabella rejoined him? The Queen and Mortimer grew alarmed. They thought they had settled the matter at Wallingford and, later, at the Westminster Parliament. At the Stamford meeting of April 1327, however, the questions were posed again and this time with some force. Some of the bishops, particularly Melton, Archbishop of York, and Hethe of Rochester, had not taken too kindly to the revolution and felt genuinely sorry for Edward. They were also alarmed by the Queen's liaison with Mortimer. Others were more mischievous, beating the drum in the hope that they could detach Isabella from Mortimer and thus block the Welsh Lord's ascendancy. Once again Orleton came to Isabella's aid. He reminded the council that the Queen had been forbidden to rejoin her husband because of his great cruelty and no one could answer this.[20]

Isabella eventually won the debate but the dispute at Stamford hid a deeper cause – a radical change in Edward II's status. At the time of his deposition, he had been under house arrest. By the time the Stamford council met, he had been taken from Kenilworth and imprisoned under tighter security at Berkeley Castle in Gloucestershire. From the moment Edward had first been imprisoned, Isabella's and Mortimer's agents were warning that Kenilworth was not the securest place in the kingdom for a deposed king. First, it was in the public eye. Secondly, it was controlled by Henry of Lancaster, Edward's cousin, and a man whose sympathy for his deposed cousin was understandable. Even more urgently, a powerful gang had formed in the Midlands with a view to freeing the deposed King. The moving spirits behind this plot were two brothers: Thomas and Stephen Dunheved. The former, Edward II's Dominican confessor, had been despatched to Rome to seek a divorce for his master from Isabella. The mission had proved fruitless. Dunheved returned and was forced to go into hiding when Isabella landed in 1326. His brother Stephen was Lord of Dunchurch on Dunsmore Heath in Warwickshire, so the brothers were well situated to free their lord from nearby Kenilworth.[21] The conspiracy came to a head in March 1327 when members of the Dunheved gang were named. They included the Dunheveds, William Aylmer, the parson of Donnington Church, William Russell, Thomas Haye, Edmund Gascelyn, William Hull and John Morton.[22] During March, April and May 1327, the Dunheveds and their followers faced a barrage of writs and orders for their arrest, with the added proviso that if they were caught they were to be immediately taken to the Queen.[23] However, the gang were quick on their feet and, hiding out on Dunsmore Heath, were able to evade capture.

Isabella and Mortimer grew alarmed. Lancaster himself protested that he could not guarantee his royal prisoner's safety and security.[24] Thus the decision was taken to move Edward, and on 21 March two new keepers were appointed, Thomas Berkeley and John Maltravers.[25] Isabella and Mortimer chose their men well. Lord Thomas Berkeley was Roger Mortimer's son-in-law. He had risen in rebellion against the de Spencers, only to see his lands, manors and castles pillaged and ransacked. He and his father Maurice had been placed under strict confinement at Wallingford. Maurice had died there, and although the resourceful Thomas had attempted to break out, he was kept in captivity until liberated by Isabella's invasion. Sir John Maltravers was Berkeley's brother-in-law and a fervent Lancastrian. He had managed to flee the kingdom, one step ahead of de Spencer's agents, and spent four years in exile, while at home his father had waged a savage guerrilla war against de Spencer. He, too, would have little love for the King.[26]

At first sight Berkeley Castle seemed a poor choice to confine the deposed King, a short distance from the Welsh border, where Edward still had considerable sympathy as well as some political and military support. On the other hand, Berkeley, even today, is a fairly lonely spot: a secure castle, surrounded by woods, it was also near Mortimer's power base on the Welsh March and well away from public view. A northern fortress would be vulnerable to attack by Bruce or Edward's Scottish supporters like Donald of Mar. The London mob were too fickle to be trusted and the Tower would be far from ideal. Berkeley Castle was, in fact, perfect and both Maltravers and Lord Berkeley were given extensive powers in the area, being made Commissioners of the Peace for almost all of south-west England. This made them military supremos in the area and were to summon up military help, raise levies and pursue malefactors.[27]

The transfer of responsibility for Edward from Lancaster to Berkeley and Maltravers was done properly. When the prisoner was collected from Kenilworth an indenture, a solemn agreement, was drawn up, Lancaster, like Pilate, washed his hands of Edward, and Berkeley and Maltravers travelled south with their prisoner.[28] He was escorted by a powerfully armed troop and careful measures were taken to create diversions so that people would be uncertain as to the King's real whereabouts.

Berkeley and Maltravers were commissioned to take over the custody of Edward on 21 March. On 3 April 1327, it was agreed they be given £5 a day for the prisoner's needs.[29] Historians have concluded that the transfer actually took place on the 3 April and Edward completed the fifty-mile journey from Kenilworth to Berkeley and was in his new prison cell by 6 April at the latest. Berkeley and Maltravers, together with another knight, Thomas Gurney (who was to play a prominent part in the deposed King's treatment), secured the deposed King in the last week of March and then took him, by a very circuitous route, to Berkeley. They visited Corfe Castle, then Bristol. On the night of 5 April, Palm Sunday, the royal prisoner reached Gloucester and spent the night at Llantony Abbey near Hay-on-Wye, the guest of the Augustinian Canons. The following day, hoping they had fooled the Dunheved gang, Berkeley and Maltravers deposited their prisoner at Berkeley Castle.[30]

However, there are reasons to question this evidence. Adam of Murimouth, a Canon of St Paul's, who wrote his history some time around 1335, says that Edward was taken to Berkeley but then removed to other places because of conspiracies to free him.

And because they were afraid of certain persons coming to him to effect his release, Edward was secretly removed from Berkeley by night and taken to Corfe and other secret places but, at last, they took him back to Berkeley but after such a fashion that it could hardly be ascertained where he was.[31]

Accordingly, there are three versions of events. First, that Edward was moved swiftly from Kenilworth to Berkeley. Secondly, Edward was moved from Kenilworth to Berkeley but removed secretly by night so as to distract his supporters; he was then taken to places such as Corfe Castle in Dorset (a stronghold of Maltravers) before being moved back to Berkeley. Thirdly, Edward was taken from Kenilworth by a circuitous route, including places like Corfe, to throw off pursuers, before being confined for life in Berkeley Castle. The third explanation seems most likely. Berkeley and Maltravers would hardly travel directly from Kenilworth to Berkeley Castle; they would do their level best to lay false trails and provoke suspicions about where the royal captive really was. Once they had Edward in the fastness of Berkeley Castle, they would surely be reluctant to take him out again around the southern shires where they would certainly be vulnerable to attack. This issue is an important one in that Edward II's link with Corfe Castle was to play a vital part in the legends which later grew up around his imprisonment.

The forced journey of the King from Kenilworth to Berkeley marked a rapid decline in his fortunes. The chronicler Swynbroke claims that Edward was subjected to appalling abuse: his new captors crowned him with a crown of hay and shaved his head and beard by the roadside with ditch water; they clothed him in rags, forced him to ride through the night, forced him to eat food that was barely edible, and, mocked and reviled him. Historians have been quick to reject such allegations, and accuse the chronicler

Swynbroke of sensationalizing events. However, Edward II was no longer a king but a deposed prince, fast becoming a public nuisance, and his execution had even been debated at a formal council meeting. Moreover, the hatred heaped upon de Spencer the Younger, the cruelties inflicted as he was led out to execution, illustrate the deep resentment of many against Edward's former rule.[32] In the history of deposed princes, it is remarkable how, once the fall from power has been completed, the minions of those who brought about the collapse, are only too quick to join in the fun of cruel mockery against one who once lorded it over them. The indignities, the rough shaving, the poor clothes, would also have been necessary to disguise the King. It is hardly likely that Edward would be allowed to ride openly through the countryside, even with a powerful escort, in a state in which former subjects might recognize him.

Edward was in his new prison by 6 April 1327 and the Berkeley records show that capons, eggs, meat and other foodstuffs were supplied to the King. Isabella also sent her husband certain delicacies.[33] Such evidence appears to clash with Swynbroke's story that Isabella was really intent on killing Edward by contagion. However, five pounds for his upkeep, the Berkeley estates producing fresh food for the King and Isabella sending delicacies to him, are perhaps not evidence enough to reject the allegations of ill-treatment. Swynbroke maintains that the carcasses of rotting animals were placed in the deep pit near the King's cell in Berkeley keep in the hope that he would catch some infection and die. The stories could well be true. After all, at Wallingford, Isabella and Mortimer seriously considered executing Edward; their treatment of his favourite had been cruel in the extreme, and Isabella and Mortimer had proved they could be as ruthless as de Spencer if they encountered opposition. Moreover, Edward not only suffered physical indignities, but the psychological torture must also have been great. Here was a man who, a year previously, had been lord of his kingdom, to whom everyone bowed at the knee and to whom everyone deferred. Within a matter of weeks, he had lost everything – his crown, his kingdom, his wife, his family and now his freedom.

Edward may well have cursed his wife and threatened to kill her – even with his teeth – but he was also the father of their four children: Edward of fifteen years, John of Eltham, eleven, Eleanor, eight and Johanna only six years old. There is no record of the King being allowed to see any of his children during his incarceration. In fact, no real evidence exists that Edward was *not* ill-treated. The sums of money, the supplies, the delicacies may well have gone to others. In the final analysis, it was in Isabella's and Mortimer's interests that Edward should not survive long. He was a danger to them politically and, as the council at Stamford proved, there was a growing concern, especially amongst the bishops, that Isabella should honour her marriage vows and return to her husband.

The Queen had every confidence that Berkeley Castle would take care of her problem husband. The fortress stood in the wilds of Gloucestershire countryside, close to the Severn Estuary, on a natural shelf of red sandstone, surrounded by fresh and salt water marshes of about 200 acres in extent, and standing at an altitude of sixty-three feet. The castle had a good view of the surrounding countryside and was strategically placed to guard the main Bristol to Gloucester road. The castle itself would be difficult to attack. Assailants would have to cross the treacherous marshes, ford the moat and scale the curtain walls. Even if they were successful in seizing the gatehouse and the outer rim of defences, defenders could fall back to the Keep and continue their fight. Isabella and Mortimer would have also ensured that Berkeley Castle was well manned, not just by local levies but household troops, veterans who would be able to guard the prisoner and put up a stout resistance against any attack.

Isabella and Mortimer confidently regarded the deposed King as a minor problem and, like Edward II and De Spencer before them, began to marshal their troops for yet another military expedition across the Scottish border. English defeats in Scotland had characterized Edward II's reign: his débâcles there had been a contributing factor to his fall from power. Isabella and Mortimer knew that to gain public approbation they would have to settle the Scottish problem – and the auguries were good. In the main the kingdom was now united: the great lords were willing to participate and Mortimer was an experienced general, who had won considerable success against Bruce's brother in Ireland. If the Scots could be checked once and for all, then Mortimer's ascendancy would be confirmed. Military preparations began, assembly points were chosen and writs despatched. However, on 3 July 1327, Thomas Berkeley was excused from the general muster 'being charged with the special business of the King'. This 'special business' entailed dealing with the irrepressible Dunheved gang. They had discovered where Edward was incarcerated and were mustering their forces for another attempt to free the deposed King.[34]

The Dunheved gang included a monk from Hailes

Abbey, a canon from the Augustinian order, as well as the usual rifflers, eager for easy plunder. They had stirred up a riot in Cirencester, disappeared and then turned up in Chester. The gang was highly mobile, organized and well resourced. The government continued to issue writs against them but were careful not to reveal their real purpose, saying simply that the members of the gang were to be arrested for evading military duty in Scotland.[35]

But the Dunheveds laid their plans well. Berkeley Castle was heavily fortified but King's Wood, Michael Wood, Berkeley Heath, and the wild heathland of Berkeley Vale, provided natural cover for this roaming band of outlaws. At first Isabella and Mortimer dismissed them as mere gadflies. They would have been armed with long bows, arrows, swords and shields, but they would need siege equipment to penetrate such a closely guarded castle. Security at Berkeley would have been very tight; entrance only being allowed by a special pass. However, the Dunheveds were successful. A letter, published by the historian Tanquerery, dated some time in July 1327, informed Isabella and Mortimer that the Dunheveds had not only attacked and plundered Berkeley Castle but had even managed to get the King out of his cell. The writer of the letter was a high-ranking clerk, John Walwayn, who had been despatched to Berkeley to investigate the raid. Walwayn doesn't just say the castle was attacked, but actually plundered, and the royal prisoner 'taken from our care' – a remarkable feat for a gang of ruffians and a few rebel priests.[36]

In the Middle Ages a castle could either be taken by storm or by means of treachery. A possible explanation in this case is that Lord Thomas Berkeley, although concerned about his prisoner, was also anxious to carry through major repairs after the castle had been ransacked only a year earlier by the de Spencers and their forces. The Berkeley records prove this building work was going on. One chronicle relates how carpenters actually saw the King and heard his cries and groans of desperation.[37] This also would confirm the view that the King was not being well treated. Rumours of possible torture would have spurred the Dunheveds to act quickly. They would have most likely used craftsmen involved in this building work, or one of the priests in their gang to secure their surreptitious entrance to the castle. Once this had been obtained, it would be easy to open a postern gate and let in the main body of attackers. The assault was probably launched at night. Guards and sentries were quickly despatched of, the place ransacked and Edward II freed. The letter from Berkeley specifically says, '*D'avoir ravi*', namely, they 'actually seized' the King from his prison, and escaped from the castle. The hunt then began to bring these malefactors to justice. But what of the deposed King? The accepted story is that he was quickly recaptured and taken back to Berkeley.

On 1 August 1327, special powers were given to Thomas Berkeley to hunt down the gang and bring them to trial – but this commission makes no reference to Edward being on the run.[38] By 20 August, one of the gang, William Aylmer, had been arrested at Oxford. We can assume the king had been recaptured because Isabella told the sheriff there that Aylmer was 'to be indicted for trying to free Edward of Caernarvon'. She then added a surprising postscript: 'That Aylmer was to be released on bail, pending a personal appearance before the King on the

7th October.'[39] Instead of fleeing, Aylmer actually turned up in court, only to have all evidence against him quashed and his innocence established.[40] The other outlaws were not as fortunate. They were all tracked down, apart from Stephen Dunheved, who managed for a while to evade his would-be captors, but his brother, Thomas disappeared into Newgate where he died from gaol fever.[41]

Aylmer's arrest and the fate of Thomas Dunheved is quite remarkable. The evidence suggests Aylmer was deeply involved in the plot to free Edward. Seven months earlier, during the first week of March 1327, William Aylmer, parson of the church of Doddington, had been specifically named as a leading member of the Dunheved gang. He had tried to free the King from Kenilworth in the early spring and he definitely took part in the attack on Berkeley Castle. It is remarkable that clemency was shown to such a dangerous man: in 1326–7 he had been publicly named as one of de Spencer's leading clerks and, two years earlier, he had been on a commission sent into Wales to try adherents of Mortimer. Isabella and Mortimer should therefore have been delighted to have such a rebel promptly hanged. [42]

As for other members of the gang, Thomas Dunheved, so rumour had it, was brought immediately before the Queen, then thrown into Newgate prison. Thomas was a Dominican friar and should have been given the benefit due to clergy; and the same courtesy extended to other members of his gang, who were also tonsured clerics. Isabella totally ignored the law and, apart from Aylmer and Stephen Dunheved, the rest of the gang appear to have disappeared off the face of the earth. A possible solution is that Aylmer turned King's evidence and, in return for his freedom, betrayed the rest of the gang to government agents. On a later occasion, in 1329–30 a certain Gregory Foriz was prosecuted for murder before King's Bench. The case was run of the mill, except for two significant features. First, Henry of Lancaster intervened as a guarantor of Foriz and, secondly, William Aylmer was also named as an associate of Foriz,[43] establishing a connection between a magnate, fast emerging as the leading opponent to Mortimer and Isabella, and the band of outlaws. This connection between Lancaster, Foriz and Aylmer suggests that the Dunheved attack had not been some mad escapade by a group of wild adherents sheltering in the forests of Michael Wood or the waste lands of Berkeley Heath. It also accounts for their success both during the attack and afterwards, when making their escape. Such a gang would need arming: bows, arrows, swords, hauberks, supplies, money and, above all, fast horses; they would need guarantees that they could be hidden in certain places and a blind eye turned to their passing. Nor was Dunheved's attack simply a one-off. In his letter from Berkeley, the royal clerk Walwayn spoke about other crises, begging the government for greater powers and saying: 'I understand, from a number of sources, that a great number of gentlemen in the county of Buckingham and in adjoining counties, have assembled for the same cause', namely, the freeing of the deposed King. So it would appear that the conspiracy to free Edward stretched right across the Cotswolds, with more than one group feverishly plotting to attack Berkeley and free the King.[44]

Walwayn's letter tantalizes in its vagueness about what actually happened to the royal prisoner. This, in turn, begs other questions. If Berkeley had proved to be unsafe, why not transfer the King elsewhere? Yet this did not occur and Edward of Caernarvon was returned to his old prison. His gaolers were not reproved and apparently continued as his keepers. Some historians maintain Edward was moved between several castles but there is agreement that, by the beginning of September, he was definitely back at Berkeley.

Isabella, meanwhile, had not only to answer to other members of the royal council for her husband's fate but also to her Welsh lover. In September 1327, according to the accepted story, matters were brought to a head. Another plot was hatched to free Edward, but this time it wasn't a roaming band of outlaws but a number of Welsh gentry, loyal to the old King, and very eager to weaken Mortimer's power in Wales.

On 4 September, Roger Mortimer was commissioned to resume his duties as Justice of Wales and, on the 8th, empowered to arrest all those breaking the peace in Wales.[45] He kept a close eye on government. In the fourteenth century, one of the ways the monarch indicated who was in favour was by asking them to witness charters issued under the Great Seal. Mortimer had been with the court at Doncaster where he witnessed a charter on 26 August. After that date, this Welsh lord, whose name is rarely absent from the list of charter witnesses, did not act in this capacity again until 4 October 1327 at Nottingham.[46] Apparently, the situation along the Welsh March had become so serious that Mortimer was obliged to tear himself away from the Queen and return to Wales to deal with the problems there, to ensure that Edward remained captive.

This crisis did not become apparent until several years later when in April 1331, William Shalford, Mortimer's lieutenant in Wales during 1327, was accused by Howel Ap Griffith of being party to Edward II's death.[47] The case was referred to King's Bench where it was quashed due to Griffith's non-appearance. Griffith's testimony is still extant, published by T. F. Tout in his article, 'The Captivity and Death of Edward II'. It reads as follows:

Howel Ap Griffith appeals William Shalford and others of his Council, of encompassing the death of Edward, father of our Lord the King whom God protects, who was feloniously and traitorously slain by murder. Namely, that on the Monday after the feast of the birth of Our Lady, September 14th 1327, at Rhosfair in Anglesey, that same William sent a letter to Lord Roger Mortimer at Abergavenny. In this letter he maintains that Rhys Ap Griffith and others of his coven had assembled their power in South Wales and in North Wales, with the agreement of certain great lords of England, in order to forcibly deliver the said Lord Edward, father of our Lord the King, who was then detained in a castle at Berkeley. And he also made clear in that letter that, if the Lord Edward was freed, that the said Lord Roger Mortimer and all his people would die a terrible death and would be utterly destroyed. On account of which the said William Shalford, like the traitor he is, in that same letter counselled the said Roger that he ordain such a remedy in such a way that no one in England or Wales would ever think of effecting such deliverance. The said Lord Roger Mortimer showed that letter to William Ockle [In the manuscripts he is called William Docleye]. And commanded him to take the said letter of William Shalford to Berkeley and to show it to those who were guarding the said Edward. And Mortimer charged him to tell them to take counsel on the points contained in the letter and to quickly remedy the situation in order to avoid great peril. The said William Ockle took charge and carried out the orders of the said Roger. On account of which the said William Ockle and others, who were guarding the Lord Edward, traitorously killed and murdered him . . .

Shalford was furious. He challenged Griffith to mortal combat and, when the case appeared before King's Bench in April 1331, Shalford brought a host of witnesses to testify to his innocence. Griffith, however, fell mysteriously ill on his journey to London and was unable to press the appeal, so the case was dropped. The incident may have had more to do with the rancorous clan hatred in Wales than any love for the deposed King or even resentment against Roger Mortimer. However, Griffith's appeal does seem to fit in with the accepted chain of events. Shalford was Mortimer's lieutenant in Wales and Mortimer had left the English court and was based at Abergavenny. According to Griffith, Mortimer decided to take matters into his own hands and find a way of getting rid of Edward for good. Shalford wrote his letter on 14 September and, within a week of that letter, Mortimer had sent agents into Berkeley and Edward II was reputedly killed on or about the feast of St Matthew, 21 September.

Other evidence proves this story. The *Annals of St Paul*, a fairly contemporary account, simply says, the King died at Berkeley. The *Bridlington Chronicle* alleged: 'With regard to the King's decease, various opinions were commonly expressed. I myself prefer to say no more about the matter, for sometimes, as the poet says, lies are for the advantage of many and to tell the whole truth does harm.' Adam Murimouth reported: 'It was commonly said that he was slain, as a precaution, by the orders of Sir John Maltravers and Sir Thomas Gurney.' Historians place a great deal of trust in Murimouth, but even he is not totally accurate. The Somerset knight Sir Thomas Gurney, together with William Ockle, were specifically named as the King's assassins, and Maltravers had to face other charges.

Higden's *Polychronicon* which was translated into English by John Trevisa, vicar of Berkeley, when Thomas, Lord of Berkeley, was still alive, agreed that Edward II was killed in the gory way as described in Swynbroke's chronicle, 'by a red hot poker being thrust up into his bowels'. The Leicestershire chronicler, John of Reading, claims that this horrible death was not just a matter of rumour but based on the confession of the guilty parties. Swynbroke, that garrulous and very hostile witness to the rule of Isabella and Mortimer, provides the detail with great relish. He first tried to exculpate Thomas, Lord Berkeley, who was responsible for both the castle and the prisoner, saying that, until the actual death, Berkeley had treated the fallen King with kindness but he was not really the gaoler. Ockle's arrival put an end to all this. Lord Thomas Berkeley, angry that he was no longer master in his own house, said farewell to the imprisoned King and took himself elsewhere – he was to make this same excuse three years later when he had to appear before Parliament to answer for his actions. He claimed to have been very ill and had retired to his manor at Bradley near Wootton-Under-Edge.[48]

Swynbroke actually put someone else's name in the frame for the murder of Edward II – that confidant of Mortimer and deliverer of powerful sermons, Adam Orleton, Bishop of Hereford. According to Swynbroke, Orleton, acting on behalf of Mortimer, was the one who issued the specific order for Edward's death. Orleton was asked by the former King's gaolers what they were to do with their prisoner. Orleton sent the following message back: '*Edwardum occidere nolite timere, bonum est.*' This can be translated two ways, depending where the comma is placed. Either: 'Do not fear to kill Edward, it is a good thing.' If, however, the comma is moved back to follow '*nolite*', it can be translated: 'Do not kill Edward, it is good to be afraid.'[49]

It's a fanciful story but Swynbroke seems to have fabricated it. First, it is taken from the tale about the death of a Hungarian queen, as recounted by the chronicler Matthew Paris almost ninety years before.[50] Secondly, by September 1327, Orleton was no longer in favour with Isabella and Mortimer because he had secured a transfer to the prosperous bishopric of Worcester against their orders. Thirdly, Orleton was not even in the country when Edward was killed, but at the papal court of Avignon on business of his own. Finally, after Mortimer and Isabella fell from power in 1330, Orleton was challenged about his involvement in the regime of Isabella. The good bishop issued an 'Apologia' in which he clearly demonstrated that his hands were not stained with innocent blood, as he was not party to, and had not consented to, the late King's death.[51]

It is understandable that historians take Swynbroke's lurid description of Edward's death with more than a pinch of salt: Swynbroke describes him as being pressed down, suffocated with great pillows and then killed with a plumber's iron, burning hot, applied through a horn up into the bowels to burn the organs and intestines. Nevertheless, the same manner of death is described in Higden's *Polychronicon* and in the Meaux Chronicle.[52] Such a grisly death would leave no visible mark on the royal corpse. Murimouth, writing at a time when Lord Thomas Berkeley was still alive, does admit that the deposed King was 'craftily killed'.[53] On the published date of the death there seems little doubt. Fifteen days later, on 6 October 1327, the nearby Abbot of Crokesden Abbey agreed to hold an anniversary Mass every year for the late King on the feast of St Matthew, 21 September.[54] The deed was done but how was it to be proclaimed and the after-effects managed?

FIVE

The Burial of a King

'Edmund Earl of Kent acknowledges that the Pope charged him, on his benison, that he should use his pains and diligence to deliver Edward, his brother, sometime King of England.'

Edmund, Earl of Kent's confession, March 1330,
Chronicle of Adam of Murimouth

Isabella may have sent her husband delicacies during his imprisonment at Kenilworth and Berkeley but, in reality, it was a case of 'out of sight, out of mind'. In her eyes Edward became a non-person. There is no evidence that Isabella allowed any members of her family – sisters, brothers, children, or other kinsmen – access to her imprisoned husband. The attempts to free Edward II were a threat to her position: they brought him firmly back onto the political scene. The news of his death, therefore, had to be carefully managed and his funeral staged to excite as little interest as possible.

According to the Berkeley accounts, on 28 September 1327, Thomas Gurney was sent to the Parliament at Nottingham[1] where Edward's demise was simply reported, according to an independent source, as a *'fatalis casus'*, a fatal accident.[2] This elliptical quote from the Northern Registers epitomizes Isabella's and Mortimer's initial public reaction. There was no reference to disease or illness and the impression given was that the former King had 'slipped and fell' and that was the end of the matter. The truth, of course, was very different. A manuscript source proves that Isabella knew about her husband's death as early as 23 September, at least a week before the news was proclaimed at Nottingham, where the court arrived on 30 September. Gurney had taken two days to travel from Berkeley to Nottingham, the same amount of time it took for the mysterious messenger, who must have left Berkeley immediately the King died, to notify the Queen at Lincoln on 23 September.[3]

Isabella was clearly no passive participant in these events: she apparently learnt the news of her husband's death and planned the announcement a week before Parliament met. Moreover, the alleged assassins were also members of her clique and she would have direct control over them. At her request Thomas Gurney was made Constable of Bristol Castle. Ockle became a 'scutifer' or squire in her son's household. Isabella also favoured him, writing letters demanding that certain debts should not be exacted from him.[4]

According to the established story, though, Edward II died on 21 September but it was another three months before he was solemnly interred in Gloucester Abbey. At no time did Isabella, or any of her family, go to view the corpse or take up residence in or around Berkeley or the Gloucester area. Indeed, as far as Isabella was concerned, it was business as normal. No evidence exists that she even went into mourning. She had been publicly acting the 'widow' since 1325 and simply continued with the same role which, initially at least, had won her such sympathy. She stayed at Nottingham until 10 November before moving to Coventry where, on 10 December 1327, she summoned another Parliament to meet at York the following February.[5] Far from grieving over her husband, Isabella was much more concerned with pressing political problems.

Of course, her husband's corpse had to be buried somewhere and there was considerable debate about the former King's last resting place. According to the history of St Peter's of Gloucester, its abbey was chosen because no other place dared accept the royal corpse for fear of offending Isabella and Mortimer. However, the muniment room of Westminster Abbey holds a list of expenses incurred by a delegation of monks, sent to Isabella to request that Edward II's body be buried in the royal mausoleum, alongside that of his father, mother and grandfather, Henry III. The request was refused.[6] Isabella was fearful of carting the royal corpse across the country: it might have provoked a violent demonstration against her and Mortimer, while the London mob was as fickle as ever.

Moreover, Thoky, Abbot of St Peter's, was a kinsman of Mortimer. His abbey was near Berkeley and within striking distance of Mortimer's territories along the Welsh March. The *Lanercost Chronicle* says the choice of Gloucester was at Isabella's insistence. Edward II may have been a king but he died a deposed prince.[7] Further, he was not the first king to be buried away from Westminster Abbey. His great-grandfather John, who also lost his kingdom and died in disgrace, had been interred at Worcester. Isabella was simply supporting a family tradition: disgraced kings were not buried at Westminster.

By the end of October 1327, Edward's sudden death at Berkeley would have been common knowledge. It seems to have taken his adherents and supporters completely by surprise. There is no evidence of agitation or protests, the conspiracies and supporters melted away, not a voice was raised in protest. People may well have been shocked: princes died in battle or, like Edward I, in harness, still fighting his enemies. Even the death of John, who fell ill at Newark and died of something he ate, took place publicly and was witnessed by courtiers, clerks and soldiers. Only Rufus, slain by an arrow whilst hunting in the New Forest, died in what were considered fairly mysterious circumstances. In the end, though, Edward II's death may have been greeted with relief in many quarters. In life he had not been popular and in captivity he had been an embarrassment, not only to his opponents but also to his friends, who felt bound by oaths of fealty.

Isabella and Mortimer deliberately dragged their feet over arranging the obsequies and the state funeral which Edward, whatever his failings, certainly deserved. They wished to avoid any allegations of hurrying the deposed King to his grave as well as trying to cover up what had really happened. The order for Edward's corpse to be interred at Gloucester wasn't issued until 10 November 1327. Isabella and Mortimer showed some cunning in arranging the funeral in the depths of winter in the West Country. In the balmy days of autumn 1327, the height of the campaign season, it was easy for messengers to gallop from Berkeley to Lincoln or Nottingham. In December, with the proximity of the Christmas festivities, notables would find it difficult to travel the muddy, makeshift trackways to Gloucester. In the meantime, the custody of the royal corpse was left to others, although Isabella took very careful precautions. She may not have been in mourning but she worked hard to avoid any suggestions that her husband's corpse was not honourably treated.

The corpse remained at Berkeley until 21 October.[8] Lord Thomas Berkeley's rather surprising declaration that he was ill at Bradley didn't stop him submitting his accounts to the Exchequer for looking after the imprisoned King. This showed him in the prime of health, supervising the corpse until 21 October and, according to Murimouth, inviting local citizens and churchmen up to Berkeley Castle so they could view it. Murimouth, however, added that this public viewing was 'very superficial and from afar off'. Apart from this very controlled lying-in-state, where local visitors were allowed a quick glimpse, only two other people were allowed near the dead King. The first was a sergeant-at-arms, William Beaukaire, who stayed '*juxta corpus regis*', 'near the body of the King', from 21 September until 20 December. This solitary sergeant-at-arms was, apparently, the only guard of honour. The other person was a 'certain woman' responsible for the corpse's embalmment.

Glanville, the clerk in charge of the royal funeral arrangements, put in a bill for his own wages, but only from 23 October, when the body was in Gloucester, until the funeral on 20 December 1327. He then made a further claim for extra days, after the burial of the King, when he was obliged to journey from Gloucester to meet the Queen at Worcester. His entry reads: 'Escorting a certain woman who disembowelled the King to the Queen . . . for two days staying there one day and then returning to York, for four days.' Glanville also took the dead King's heart, placed in a silver casket, to the Queen. His companion to Worcester, however, this mysterious old woman, was the only one who knew the real truth about Edward II's death. She, not a royal physician, embalmed the corpse: her involvement and Glanville's attempts to hide it, provide telling evidence that the story of death by a *'fatalis casus'* is highly suspect.

Accordingly, by 21 October 1327, Isabella and Mortimer could relax: Edward II was dead, the news had been published and the corpse embalmed. On that day the royal remains were placed in a cart and escorted by Thomas Berkeley and John Maltravers from Berkeley to the Abbey of St Peter's at Gloucester. It must be emphasized that the royal corpse was now hidden away in a heavy, sealed, lead casket, which was seen when the tomb was briefly opened in 1855. It would also account for the fact that the funeral cart had to stop for the horses or oxen to rest. According to a local tradition, people later planted an oak tree at each of these resting places.

Once they'd arrived in Gloucester, Maltravers and Berkeley had completed their task. They had been in charge of the deposed King, alive and dead, for 201 days. They claimed expenses amounting to over £1000, of which they received about £700. Berkeley, never at a loss to pursue what was his due, also put in for expenses for taking the body to Gloucester, for himself and his household, and even for the 'vase' of silver in which the dead King's heart was enclosed.

The dead King was taken into the abbey and laid before the high alter. Isabella issued elaborate arrangements for the custody of her husband's corpse as long as it remained above ground. John Eaglescliffe, the Dominican Bishop of Llandaff, was instructed to go to Gloucester and remain there, praying over the corpse. He was paid 13s 4d for his fifty-nine days stay. Eaglescliffe was chosen for two reasons: Llandaff's comparative proximity to Gloucester and because Eaglescliffe was a member of the dead King's favourite order and not one of the political bishops, like Hereford or Winchester, who served Isabella and Mortimer so closely. A military escort was also arranged. Two knights to watch the corpse were paid 6s 8d and 5s a day respectively. Two royal chaplains and two sergeants-at-arms were also in attendance, as well as the King's candle-maker, responsible for ensuring the candles which ringed the hearse were constantly replaced. The arrival of the royal corpse in the abbey excited public interest and brought sightseers flocking in; so great was the press that great oaken beams had to be erected to keep back the crowds.[9] They were disappointed to discover there was nothing really to see, so 40s was spent for 'carving a wooden image, in the likeness of the deceased King'; a copper gilt crown was also made for that image, costing 7s 3d, the first time such 'an image' was ever used at a royal funeral.

The corpse lay at Gloucester for almost two months. One reason for the delay in burying Edward was the long-drawn-out military expedition in Scotland; another was the deliberate ploy by Isabella and Mortimer not to complete the obsequies with unseemly haste. Mortimer had rejoined Isabella on 4 October at Nottingham, and they stayed there until 10 November before slowly moving across the Midlands. They only reached Gloucester on 19 December, the day before the funeral took place.[10] The service itself was lavish and conducted with solemn pomp. Quantities of gold leaf were bought for decorating the harness around the coffin. Four standards and twenty pennants were specially made for the funeral ceremony itself. More gold leaf was used to embroider the funeral robes laid over the casket. Four great lions, edged with the best gilt, carrying mantles displaying the arms of England, were specially fashioned by John Eastwick, the royal painter, and placed on each side of the hearse. On top of it, statues of the four Evangelists with eight angels were placed, carrying golden censers.[11]

On 20 December, after the funeral Mass and the 'Requiem', Edward's corpse was solemnly interred, amid gusts of incense, on the left side of the high altar. Isabella was garbed in widow's weeds, still publicly playing the role of the doleful Queen. Mortimer was also dressed in mourning, a piece of hypocrisy his enemies never forgot. The casket found its last resting place and the paving stones were replaced. Edward II was gone at last, his only memorial a splendid tomb in Gloucester.

The tomb has only been opened once, for a short while, in 1855. The description of it made by the sub-sacristan in 1855, can still be read in the archives of Gloucester Cathedral. It reads as follows:

On the 2nd October 1855, in the presence of Dr. Jeune, the Canon-in-Residence, Mr Waller, the cathedral architect, Allen, the sub-sacrist, and Henry Clifford, the master mason, the tomb of Edward II in the cathedral was opened, by removing the floor on the south side of the tomb: only just below the flooring, immediately under the tomb. We came first to a wood coffin, quite sound, and after removing a portion of this, we came to a leaden one, containing the remains of the King: the wood, although light as cork, was still very perfect, and the lead one quite entire, and made with a very thick sheet of lead, its shape very peculiar, being square at the bottom, and rising on each side like an arch, and so turned over the body in an oval or arched form, and made to set nearly down upon the body. The tomb was never known to have been opened before this. It remained open but the space of two hours, and was then closed again, without the slightest injury being done to the tomb. The fact of his internment being now five hundred and twenty-eight years since, it was considered to be in a wonderful state of preservation.

Isabella must have been secretly delighted that the vexatious problem of her deposed husband had now been resolved. No courtier could object to her intimate relationship with Mortimer, no bishop demand that she return to her husband. Edward's corpse lay beneath the cold slabs of Gloucester Abbey and Isabella appears not to have given it a second thought. She and Mortimer had more important business in hand. A settlement was to be reached with the Scots whilst she had to honour her promise to the Count of Hainault that the young Edward III, now sixteen years of age, would marry his daughter, Philippa.

On 23 December, three days after the funeral, Philippa landed at Dover where she was met by household knights. She was rapturously received by the Londoners and travelled via Canterbury to York where, on 30 January 1328, the young couple were married in the city cathedral by Archbishop Melton of York and the Bishop of Ely.[12] No doubt the marriage was used to curry public favour, and distract attention from the ostentatious but empty ceremony in Gloucester a few weeks earlier, as well as from the distasteful policies Isabella and Mortimer were about to proclaim at the coming York Parliament. The historian John Froissart, who was lavishly patronized by Queen Philippa, visited Berkeley Castle in 1366 and made enquiries about the death of Edward of Caernarvon. 'An ancient squire told me,' he wrote, 'that he died within a year of coming to Berkeley. For someone cut his life short and thus died that King of England. Let us not speak long of him but turn to the Queen and her son.'

Once the wedding ceremony of her son was over, Isabella attended the York Parliament, which opened on 7 February 1328. Isabella and Mortimer were both determined on peace with Scotland. The council was divided about the issue but Isabella controlled the young King. On 1 March 1328, Edward III drew up formal letters containing a treaty agreeing to Scotland's sovereignty and bringing all hostilities between the two kingdoms to an end. At the end of April 1328, the Northampton Parliament ratified this peace treaty, in which Isabella also promised the hand of her youngest daughter, Joanna, to Bruce's heir, David. Scotland would pay some compensation but Bruce had won his war and his kingdom was recognized as both independent and sovereign, free of any English claims.[13] Isabella was exhausted and, for the first time since her invasion, completely withdrew from the court. Mortimer, too, was absent. The last time he had witnessed a charter was on 3 March 1328, and both the Queen and her adviser only reappeared towards the end of April at another council meeting at Stamford.[14]

Isabella and Mortimer were now living in a fool's paradise: their rapacity and monopoly of government tore holes in the great alliance which had toppled the de Spencers in 1326. Henry of Lancaster was not impressed. He and his followers had played a decisive part in the overthrow of the de Spencers. Now, within two years of their destruction, England had a new favourite and once again the party of Lancaster was marginalized. Earl Henry was supported by other dissidents, who resented Mortimer's ambitions in Wales as well as those who had lost estates as a result of the peace with Scotland.

Isabella had also created a breach with someone more important – her eldest son. King Edward III was now sixteen: married, old enough to bear arms, though still young enough to have to listen to the advice of his council. Edward was particularly angry with Isabella's management of Scottish affairs. He publicly proclaimed that the marriage of his younger sister Joanna to David Bruce did not have his blessing, so he would not be attending the wedding, scheduled to take place at Berwick on 16 July 1328.[15]

The young King kept to his word but his anger only increased when Isabella agreed to surrender the Stone of Scone. This was the holy relic of Scottish history on which former kings had been crowned until Edward I had seized it and brought it to London. Isabella insisted that her son order that the Stone of Scone be released and despatched to Berwick to be handed over to the Scottish Commissioners. Edward III obeyed the letter but not the spirit of her order. He issued a rather flippant instruction to the Abbot of Westminster to take the Stone of Scone to

Queen Isabella: 'in whatever part of the north of England she may be'.[16] The young King was being deliberately obstructive and the capital were infected by his mood. The Londoners staged a dramatic demonstration against the Stone's removal, so the Abbot wrote to Edward that he could not agree to surrendering it until the matter had been discussed further.[17] This was play-acting on the part of the monks of Westminster. They knew the King didn't want the Stone removed and so secretly co-operated with him. The incident demonstrated the young King's defiance and a growing restlessness against his mother's rule which others would support.

By February 1329, however, Isabella and Mortimer had managed to crush any opposition at home and, by brute force, obliged Earl Henry and the Lancastrian party to submit. Lancaster and his principal lieutenants were made to sign recognizances, or promises, guaranteeing their good behaviour and, if they reneged, he and his two lieutenants would face fines amounting to £55,000. They were also made to swear oaths on the gospels before the full King's council, that 'under pain of forfeiture of life, limb and property, they would do nothing against Our Lord the King, his mother the Queen, or any other great or small of their council'.[18] In effect Mortimer and his henchmen now controlled the young King's household.

At the Salisbury Parliament of the previous year, 1328, Mortimer had been created Earl of March,[19] and was beginning to emerge from the shadows and display the same unbounded ambition as his former enemy, de Spencer. The new Earl of March emphasized his descent from the mythical King Brutus of Albion and displayed his power in gorgeous extravangazas, in which he performed as Arthur with the Knights of the Round Table. Isabella, who had collected a number of books on the Arthurian romances, probably played Guinevere to Mortimer's Arthur. On 9 September 1329, the Queen's lover organized another demonstration of his glory and power at Hereford to mark the anniversary of de Spencer's downfall some three years previously. The occasion was the marriage of his two daughters: one to the eldest son of the Earl of Norfolk, the King's uncle; the second to the heir of the great landowner, John de Hastings. The latter provided Mortimer with more wealth. The marriage to Norfolk's heir, however, linked the Mortimers with the royal family and proclaimed their new position as one of the premier families of the realm. It was an ascendancy the Mortimer clan would develop and strengthen: by 1398, Roger Mortimer, the third Earl of March, was Richard II's acknowledged heir to the English throne.[20]

Isabella's paramour began to act more and more like a deputy king. Mortimer's self-glorification and pride became so well known that even one of his sons called him 'the King of Folly', not only a caricature of his father's ambitions, but a veiled warning against the reaction which his father's arrogance might provoke.[21] The astute and wily Pope John XXII was also receiving similar reports. He wrote to Mortimer and Isabella, quoting the Latin tag: 'That whatever they do, they do prudently and keep an eye on the end and to put up with minor irritations lest worse be thrust upon them.' The Pope may have been talking about their pride or subtly alluding to their adulterous relationship. In the winter of 1329–30, Isabella may even have become pregnant by Mortimer. During that period, and again in the summer of 1330, Isabella nominated Mortimer as heir to several properties in the event of her death.

After the celebration of the marriage at Hereford, Isabella and Mortimer travelled to Dunstable for another great extravaganza involving tournaments and pageants. After that, they removed themselves from the public eye once more, spending their time quietly at Northampton and Kenilworth before journeying into London for the coronation of the young Queen Philippa in January 1330. But their stay at Northampton and Kenilworth, however, was not simply a holiday from affairs of state. Their past deeds had returned to haunt them and the 'ghost' of Edward II refused to remain silent.

In January 1330 Isabella summoned a Parliament to meet at Winchester, ostensibly to discuss relations with France and the need to send men and supplies to Gascony.[22] The court left London and arrived at Winchester on 1 March, where the assembly were astounded by the sudden arrest of Edmund, Earl of Kent, Isabella's brother-in-law, the King's uncle, on a charge of high treason.[23] A court was swiftly assembled. Kent was brought before Robert Howell, coroner of the royal household, with Mortimer acting as prosecutor. The Earl of March, as he was now commonly known, produced certain letters and asked Kent if they belonged to him. Kent admitted that they did. Mortimer read them out and they revealed a most astonishing plot to free Edward II. Kent broke down and admitted everything: his published confession is still extant and makes lurid reading.

According to Kent, Edward II had not been murdered at Berkeley but in fact was still alive at Corfe Castle on the Dorset coast. Two friars, 'Edmund Savage and John', had confirmed the rumours and offered to act as intermediaries between Kent and his imprisoned royal half-brother. However, Kent had first been appraised of this matter via a Dominican whom he had met in Kensington: this friar, through the black arts, had raised a demon who had informed Kent that Edward II was still alive and well at Corfe. Edmund of Kent had shared this information with leading nobles and churchmen, including Melton, Archbishop of York and Gravesend, Bishop of London. He had been assured of financial and military support by these powerful men, as well as by exiles now living abroad, for freeing his brother and restoring him to his throne. The stamp of approval for the entire plot had been given by Pope John XXII, whom Kent had visited in Avignon and with whom he had conferred. Kent confessed he was so certain that Edward II was still alive, he had actually despatched letters to him through certain people and these documents had fallen into the hands of Mortimer.[24]

At first glance this must be one of the most bizarre plots in the history of the English royal family. Two and a half years after an ostentatious funeral, his half-brother, Edmund, firmly believed that Edward II was still alive and sheltering at Corfe Castle. Now there is no real evidence that the above confession faithfully reflected Kent's conspiracy. Edmund of Kent, son of Edward I and Margaret of France, was a young man whom very few people liked. Since the battle of Boroughbridge in 1322, he had demonstrated a predisposition for gullibility and inconsistency. In 1324 Edward II and the de Spencers had made him Commander-in-Chief of the English task force in Gascony, where Isabella's uncle, Charles of Valois, had tricked him into signing the disastrous Treaty of La

Reole. After that, Kent, frightened of facing the De Spencers, joined Isabella and the others in exile, becoming a prominent member of her council in Paris. Even then he compromised himself by secretly trying to assure Edward II that his intentions were not treasonable.

Once Isabella had staged her *coup*, Kent's allegiance swung back to his brother and he may have been one of the 'Great Ones of the Land', who supported the plots by the Dunheveds and Rhys Ap Griffith to free Edward II from Berkeley Castle. Kent opposed Lancaster but then changed his mind and joined Earl Henry. He proved to be more extreme than Lancaster, denouncing the young King personally for breaking his coronation oath and violating Magna Carta. However, when Kent realized that Lancaster could not possibly succeed, he deserted him and made his peace with Isabella. To all intents and purposes Kent was an unstable young man, with an obvious guilt complex about his betrayal of Edward II. Nonetheless, was he stupid or feckless enough to become embroiled in such an unlikely plot? In his confession Kent first implicates one of the most astute politicians of his day, Pope John XXII, reformer, theologian and poet, who probably wrote the '*Anima Christi*', the beautiful Catholic poem on the Eucharist. According to Kent, Pope John actually ordered him, with his blessing, to deliver his brother from prison and encouraged him to look for support among the English nobility. Kent, of course had already done this; indeed, he may have begun his machinations as early as the winter of 1328, when he first mentioned his secret to Lancaster. In a letter to the Londoners of 5 November 1328, Earl Henry refers to 'certain matters' told to him by the Earl of Kent but he was too frightened to put these into writing, although his messenger would report them by word of mouth.[25] This may refer to Kent's belief that his brother was still alive.

Kent attended Edward II's funeral, was at Gloucester when Edward was buried, and witnessed a charter there.[26] He did not see the corpse but he may have picked up rumours which he thought warranted further investigation. At the beginning of June 1329, Kent and Robert Taunton, another conspirator, were so convinced of the rightness of their cause, that they visited Pope John XXII at Avignon. Afterwards the Earl travelled to Paris, where he visited two refugees from Isabella's and Mortimer's government, Thomas Rosslyn, one of Henry of Lancaster's henchmen, and the loud-mouthed Henry Beaumont. The latter, together with the rest of his family, had broken all ties with Isabella over her treaty with Scotland, which had deprived them of estates and holdings north of the border.

On 24 March 1330, the young King, at Isabella's command, informed the Pope of the plot. They pointed out how Kent had been present at the funeral in Gloucester and that the source of his story was a demon-raising friar. Edward III added how his messenger, John Walwayn, would provide further details. On 15 September Pope John XXII wrote back to both Isabella and her son, expressing surprise that Edward II, whose funeral had been so public, could still be alive. The Pope added: 'That those who were present at the funeral could not possibly have been deceived and did not attempt to deceive. If the funeral had been in secret there would have been some grounds for suspicion but the funeral was public enough.' Moreover, the Pope added, if he'd really believed such a story he would have contacted the Queen and her son immediately and directly.[27]

The letter was a masterpiece of diplomatic evasion. Almost a year earlier, the Earl of Kent and the clerk Taunton had been in Avignon. However, the Pope was at pains not to deny that such a story was told to him, only that he didn't believe it, hence his silence for almost a year. He lays great emphasis on the public funeral. He protests his innocence but his doubts are tangible. His references to the obsequies at Gloucester are highly ironic. Had he seen through Isabella's strategies? Pope John XXII already had the measure of Isabella and Mortimer. He didn't tell them everything he knew, including the fact that the young King himself was now engaged in secret correspondence with the papacy, in direct opposition to his mother and Mortimer.

The story about the demon-raising friar in Kensington may have been a deliberate distortion by Mortimer and Isabella. The 'Dominican' in question was probably Thomas Dunheved's brother, Stephen, who, despite the best efforts of government agents, was still busy around the country on behalf of his former royal master. Kent may have been gullible but he would hardly commit high treason simply because a Dominican claimed he had been visited by the devil. In her letter to the Pope of 24 March 1330, Isabella repeats this story, knowing full well that it would put the focus on Kent as well as the source of his conspiracy.[28]

Nor would Kent have been able to convince others that his brother was still alive on the strength of a lurid story told to him by some devil-raising friar. The list of notable accomplices is quite extensive: the astute and saintly Melton, Archbishop of York, joined the conspiracy, pledging £5000. Melton, indeed, appears to have played a prominent part in actively encouraging Kent. The rest of his supporters were either fervent opponents of Mortimer or the heirs and adherents of de Spencer, who had managed to survive the crash of October 1326. The conspiracy, then, was widespread, even though the Earl of Kent was highly unpopular.

On 18 and 22 March the arrest of the principal plotters was ordered. On the 31st a list of more minor figures implicated was publicly distributed to the sheriffs. On the 21 March and 13 April 1330, commissioners, with wide, sweeping powers, were despatched into Norfolk, Suffolk and Northampton to search out and arrest possible adherents of the Earl of Kent. All were imprisoned and the more important, including the Archbishop of York, indicted for high treason before King's Bench. Proclamations were also issued on 13 April 1330, condemning people who persisted in spreading rumours that Edward II was still alive.[29]

On the one hand, Kent's conspiracy may appear lightweight and eccentric. A more critical examination demonstrates that it was well supported and far reaching, which explains how Isabella and Mortimer learnt about Kent's activities long before the Winchester Parliament of March 1330. Kent arrived back from France on 10 December 1329, when he rejoined the court at Kenilworth. According to his confession, two friar preachers, one called Edmund Savage, the other simply 'John', were 'the chief dealers in this matter'. The *Brut Chronicle* claims these friars approached Kent once he was back in England. They confirmed the rumour that Edward was still alive and claimed they had discovered that he was being kept at Corfe Castle. Isabella and Mortimer were responsible for infiltrating the Earl of Kent's clique with 'agents provocateurs'. The two Dominicans, Edmund Savage and 'Brother John' were never included in the lists of those to be arrested, nor has any documentary evidence of their existence ever been found. Possibly they were Isabella's own agents, luring Kent towards treason. Three months earlier, on 24 September 1329, John Maltravers, who had been associated with Berkeley in the custody of the deposed King, had been made custodian of Corfe Castle. Maltravers was later accused, together with Mortimer, of luring Kent to his death: it seems possible his appointment was part of the counter-plot and may prove that, as early as the autumn of 1329, Isabella and Mortimer's agents had informed them of Kent's conspiracy.[30]

Isabella and Mortimer had the Earl of Kent watched but, as Kent made clear in his own confession, the conspiracy was generally spread by word of mouth. Consequently, tangible proof of Kent's treason had to be found. Two further agents now emerged, Bogo Bayouse and John Deverel. They were later rewarded for their part in 'discovering the plot'. Bogo Bayouse was one of Mortimer's men; Deverel was described as a King's yeoman and a member of the garrison at Corfe Castle.[31] They encouraged Kent in his treason by showing him potential proof that Edward of Caernarvon was still alive, and persuaded the Earl of Kent and his wife to write letters to the deposed King. The Kents did this and Mortimer struck. The Earl was not immediately arrested; instead, a Parliament was called at Winchester, where Mortimer, who held the incriminating letters, challenged Kent before the King's coroner.

Kent might have expected a pardon: 'He wholly submitted himself to the King's will, to come in his shirt to

London or in this city barefoot, or where so ever the King shall appoint, with a rope round his neck, to do with him what it shall please.' Isabella and Mortimer, however, were in a hurry to get rid of him. The opening lines of Kent's confession give the impression that he was tried before the coroner and then repeated his confession before his peers in Parliament on 16 March. In fact, in early April rumours were circulating that Kent had been deprived of a fair trial and that once he had confessed he was hustled out to execution; his confession was later read out before Parliament. On 12 March, Kent's goods and chattels were taken into the King's hands. He was still alive on the 14th, detained under house arrest, when his wife and children were ordered to be confined in Salisbury Castle. By the 15th he must have been dead, as a reference in a proclamation is made 'To the late Earl of Kent'.[32]

According to the chronicles, Kent was condemned to death on 14 March and his pleas for mercy were totally ignored. Isabella herself played a decisive hand in his death. She swore 'By her father's soul that she would have justice'. Frightened that her son might exercise clemency, Isabella issued the order for the bailiffs of Winchester to have Kent summarily executed. The bailiffs, terrified at the responsibility thrust on them and aware that Kent's trial and condemnation had been irregular, led him out to the execution ground near the city gates, but they could find no one to carry out the sentence. The hapless Earl, dressed only in his shirt, waited there all day until shortly around Vespers. A dung-collector from the city prison was bribed with a pardon and carried out the sentence of decapitation.[33]

SIX

The Downfall of the She-Wolf

'*Edwardum occidere nolite timere, bonum est*: Do not fear to kill Edward, it is a good thing.'

'*Edwardum occidere nolite, timere bonum est:* Do not kill Edward, it is good to be afraid.'

Message sent by Adam Orleton, Bishop of Hereford, to Edward II's gaolers, September 1327, *Chronicle of Geoffrey Baker of Swynbroke*

The old adage 'those whom the Gods wish to destroy they first make mad', sums up the fall of Isabella and Mortimer in the autumn of 1330. Astute observers like Pope John XXII, who tried his best to advise them, realized their collapse was inevitable. Isabella had destroyed one tyranny and replaced it with another. Wales was seething with discontent: exiles abroad were plotting invasion. There was unrest in both London and the shires around the capital. Although there appeared to be no opposition from the barons – Kent was dead, Lancaster anxious not to suffer a similar fate – the real focus of discontent was in the royal household. The young King Edward III, married and now expecting an heir, watched the events of 1330 with growing anxiety. In less than three years Mortimer had achieved the destruction of two princes of royal blood: a King and his half-brother.

Later in the fifteenth century, during the Wars of the Roses, such violence became the norm but even then it was a case of generals and captains of defeated forces facing a military tribunal and summary execution on the edge of a battlefield or in the market square of some provincial town. Edmund of Kent's destruction had been illegal, violent and without precedent. A prince and half-brother to a King, uncle to another, was hustled from court, his pleas for mercy ignored, and made to stand before a city gate before a drunken dung-collector was bribed to kill him.

The Earl of March's arrogance was now notorious, with his tournaments, Round Tables and the constant emphasis on his mythical ancestry. Did Mortimer harbour secret notions of becoming King and wiping out the House of Plantaganet? Did he intend to marry Isabella and beget a new dynasty? There is some proof that Isabella was pregnant by him though we have no firm evidence. Mortimer certainly saw himself as Master of the Kingdom, as did the Queen. According to Swynbroke, by 1330 Mortimer even refused to give way to the young King, relating to him as if he was his equal.[1]

Edward III looked around him for support. He may have received passive assistance from Lancaster but, when he struck, the young King showed a shrewdness beyond his years. He gave a glimpse of his diplomatic skills after 1330, which would enable him to unite the baronage around him and bring to an end the bitter court-faction politics and the threat of civil war which had plagued the kingdom since his father's accession in 1307. Edward III put his trust in no one except the clerks and knights from his own household, in particular, the young William Montague and Edward's personal secretary, the scholar Richard Bury, Keeper of his Privy Seal.

Edward III also needed the Church, the blessing of the papacy and, at least, the tacit support of the bishops. In September 1329, William Montague visited the Pope at Avignon. Montague explained to John XXII the restrictions under which the young King was having to work. The Pope replied that Edward III should use some secret sign in his letters so he could distinguish between letters sent by the King from those merely sent in his name. It is remarkable how the Pope was so eager to offer Edward his counsel and support. One wonders if the Pope had offered the same support to the Earl of Kent. It also demonstrates the Pope's growing dislike of Mortimer and Isabella: their open adultery and acquisitiveness had lost them support amongst the episcopacy, except for one perennial time-server, Henry Burghesh, Bishop of Lincoln. Prelates like Adam Orleton, now Bishop of Worcester, must have briefed the Pope on the precious pair ruling England. The papacy realized that it was only a matter of time before Mortimer and Isabella made a mistake and followed the de Spencers into the dark.

On his return to England, William Montague reported back to the King and Richard Bury. Edward III immediately wrote to Pope John XXII informing him that, only letters beginning with the words '*Pater Sancte*' (Oh Holy Father) would come direct from him, anything else was the work of Isabella and Mortimer. Edward's letter also stipulated that he would use the secret sign to promote people of his own household, particularly to bishoprics.[2] The Queen Mother was intent on controlling the Church and recommended men such as her secretary Robert Wyville to the powerful bishopric of Salisbury, a cleric whom the chronicler Murimouth dismisses 'As of little learning and even less personality'.[3]

Slowly Edward built up his own party. Montague and Bury were joined by court knights such as William Clinton and Robert Ufford. Montague was made Commander of the King's guard. He signed a contract to stay by the King with twenty men-at-arms for life.[4] Such a force was essential. Mortimer was no fool and wherever he went a huge retinue of 'Wild Welshmen' went with him. The young King had to be careful. His own household was riddled with spies whilst a guard of 200 armed men under Mortimer's henchman, Simon de Beresford, watched his every move.[5] Nevertheless, this loyal party of adherents grew, drawing in John Neville of Hornby and the Bohun brothers, William and Humphrey. Such preparations did not go unnoticed and Mortimer and Isabella were warned of the young King's growing opposition to them. Both parties kept up a pretence of civility and court protocol. Even as late as June 1330, Isabella was calling Richard Bury her 'dear clerk',[6] though she must have known what mischief Bury was plotting. Her son was not helpless: if Mortimer could spy on him and buy information, then Edward could do likewise. A considerable number of Mortimer's adherents, Oliver Ingham and Thomas Berkeley, as well as the high-ranking clerk John Wisham, were all rather suspiciously well treated by Edward after Mortimer's fall.[7] The real problem was how 'to bell the cat', or 'eat the dog'. Mortimer and Isabella were always accompanied by a well-armed retinue and it would be difficult to seize them.

In the autumn of 1330 a Parliament was called at Nottingham. It opened with council meetings on Monday, 15 October, where the deep animosities of the court surfaced. Mortimer and Isabella were informed by spies that the young King was looking for an opportunity to overthrow them. Isabella and Mortimer panicked. They moved into Nottingham Castle, put guards on every exit, ordered the castle to be barred at night, while Isabella herself kept the keys to the gates.[8] Mortimer, highly nervous, lashed out. He accused Henry, Earl of Lancaster, of being involved in fresh plots against him. Lancaster, now going blind, protested his innocence. Mortimer insisted, and Lancaster had no choice but to move his entire household from the city to what Mortimer considered a safe distance of three miles from Nottingham.

Mortimer then went on the attack: regular Council sessions constantly reaffirmed his own authority. This proved too much for young Montague, an outspoken, hot-headed young man. He shouted abuse at Mortimer: for the first time ever the Marcher Lord was openly and formally accused of being directly responsible for Edward II's death.[9] This proved to be the last straw for Mortimer and Isabella. A court of inquiry was set up, with Mortimer acting as prosecutor and judge. Early on Friday, 19 October, the inquiry, headed by Mortimer and Isabella, and supported by the Bishops of Salisbury and London, summoned Montague and his companions, individually, for close interrogation.

The adherents of Edward III stoutly protested their innocence, except Montague who, loyal to the last, cleverly asserted that he would do nothing inconsistent in his duty to the King.[10] The depth of Mortimer's arrogance, and his true intentions, are revealed in the Marcher Lord's reply. He made the startling declaration that, if anything the King said or did conflicted with what Mortimer wanted, then the King was not to be obeyed.[11] Montague, delighted by this, immediately returned to the King and reported the entire proceedings. He depicted Mortimer as greater than the Crown, urging Edward to act, summing up the situation pithily: 'It would be better to eat the dog than let the dog eat us.' Edward, probably fearful for his mother, was reluctant to act. Moreover, Isabella and Mortimer had commandeered the castle and it would be very difficult to effect a *coup*.[12]

According to Swynbroke and local legend, Montague offered the King a way of staging his successful *coup* through a secret entrance into the castle, still called 'Mortimer's Cavern or Tunnel'. Although a secret entrance would get the plotters into the castle, it would still be thronged with Mortimer's henchmen. Accordingly, Edward summoned the Constable Robert Eland and, through a mixture of threats and promises, brought him into the conspiracy against Mortimer. The Constable agreed to force a postern gate open so that Montague and a group of knights could enter.[13] Just before dark on 19 October 1330, Montague and his band of conspirators appeared to panic and flee from Nottingham. Under the cover of darkness, they reassembled, armed to the teeth, in the park outside the castle. They stayed there for a while. Others were supposed to join them but later claimed they'd got lost. In reality they had panicked and decided to stay on the sidelines to watch developments.[14]

Montague decided to strike. He and twenty-three companions stole through the unbarred postern gate and crossed the outer and inner baileys to the door of the keep where Isabella and Mortimer were lodged. Here they were joined by the King. The door to the keep was opened and they crept up the steps.[15] High in the keep, in a room adjoining Isabella's, Mortimer had assembled a meeting of his clique, which included the Queen, the Bishop of Lincoln and others, to discuss measures to arrest Montague and the other suspects. The noise of the attacking force brought this council meeting to an abrupt end.

Sir Hugh Turplington, one of Mortimer's henchmen, raised the alarm and with others rushed down to attack the King's party, screaming 'Treason! Treason!'. A short but very violent dagger and sword fight broke out on the stairs. Turplington had his brains dashed out; another, Richard Monmouth, was cut down. The rest surrendered. Mortimer had barred the door and was busy arming himself when the King, Montague and their party burst in. Mortimer and Beresford put up a short struggle but were arrested immediately. Henry Burghesh, Bishop of Lincoln, made a vain and inglorious attempt to escape down a privy but got stuck and was hauled out. Isabella threw herself at her son's feet, screaming: '*Ayez pitie! Ayez pitie à gentil Mortimer!*'.[16]

The *coup* had been brilliantly successful. News of Mortimer's arrest created panic: the castle was now thronged with the young King's knights and the adherents of Mortimer and Isabella made themselves scarce. Edward immediately sent messages to Lancaster, inviting him to bring his troops back into the city. Lancaster hurried to obey, overjoyed at Mortimer's fall. Edward wished to carry out a summary execution there and then but Lancaster persuaded him not to act like a tyrant but to have the Welsh lord tried by his peers.[17] Mortimer, together with Beresford and a few others, was brought to Leicester and then sent south under a guard of a hundred men to be lodged in the Tower. Isabella, beside herself with grief, was treated with more consideration and placed under house arrest at Berkhampsted.[18]

On the morning of 20 October a proclamation was issued, announcing the downfall of Isabella and Mortimer and summoning a Parliament to meet at Westminster on 26 November, where the King could hear grievances against Mortimer and his cohorts.[19] The administration was purged, but no real punitive action was taken except against Mortimer and a few others. The Westminster Parliament reconvened at the end of November. Mortimer was brought from the Tower and summoned to the bar of the House. He was dressed appropriately in a mantle with the words: '*QUID GLORIARIS?*' ('Where is your glory?') inscribed on it. He was bound, gagged and given no chance to speak during his trial.

Justice was swift. Mortimer was charged on fourteen counts: he was held directly responsible for the murder of Edward II, the death of Edmund of Kent and of creating discord between Edward II and Queen Isabella. Parliament and the kingdom were given the general drift of the King's intentions. Mortimer was the source of all wickedness and Edward's parents, especially his 'Dearest Mother' Isabella, were simply casualties of this. Mortimer was judged guilty, sentenced to be hanged and handed over to the Earl Marshal to carry out the sentence.[20]

On 29 November 1330, the disgraced Earl, dressed in

the same black mantle he had worn at Edward II's funeral, a potent jibe at his hypocrisy, was dragged at the tail of a horse from the Lion Gate of the Tower to the Elms at Tyburn.[21] Alongside him rode some of his fiercest opponents, chanting verses from Psalm 51.[22] At Tyburn, Mortimer, probably in return for the King's leniency in not sentencing him to be quartered and disembowelled, addressed the crowds. He mentioned nothing about the Queen or the death of Edward II, but openly confessed that the Earl of Kent had been the victim of a cruel conspiracy.[23] Sentence was then carried out. Mortimer's body was left to hang naked for two days and nights before being handed over to the Friars Minor for burial in their church at Grey Friars near St Paul's.[24] Parliament also passed sentence on Simon Beresford, who was found guilty 'by common repute' of a number of crimes, chief of which was being Mortimer's principal accomplice. Beresford was executed on 21 December. He was the only adherent of Mortimer to suffer the full rigour of the law. Maltravers, Bayouse, Deverel, Ockle and Gurney had all fled, so sentence of death was passed upon them 'in absentia' and rewards fixed for their capture, dead or alive.[25]

These summary sentences provide an insight into who was held responsible for which crimes. Maltravers, Bayouse and Deverel were not accused of being involved in the murder of Edward II but of enticing the Earl of Kent to his death. The only two singled out as regicides were Thomas Gurney and William Ockle: 'For the death of King Edward, father of Our Lord the King who is now, that they falsely and traitorously murdered him.' Even then a distinction was made: £100 for Gurney captured alive, for his head only, 100 marks; and for Ockle, 100 marks alive and whoever brought in his head, £40.[26] The rewards were enticing enough for those who wished to make a quick profit, but the sly, versatile and mendacious Thomas, Lord of Berkeley, played a decisive hand in the escape of these wanted men.[27] Berkeley, too, should have expected to suffer the full rigours of the law. After all, he was Mortimer's henchman, related to him by marriage, and he had been directly responsible for the custody of Edward II.

Lord Thomas was not at Nottingham when Mortimer was arrested but at Berkeley. He made no attempt to flee and, when summoned to answer before the November Parliament, came to London to present his defence. By then the King must have guessed what had happened to his father. Mortimer had been arrested on 19 October but he was not executed until 29 November. The condemnations of Beresford, Maltravers, Gurney and Ockle and the rest were not drawn up until the same date. It is curious that Edward III waited over five weeks before ordering the arrest of his father's killers. Indeed, it was not until 3 December that the warrants were sworn out for the arrest of those who had enticed Kent to his death, as well as of the two regicides, Gurney and Ockle. Beresford also spent almost two months in the Tower before execution was carried out. It is likely that the King's agents used this delay to interrogate prisoners but it also gave the other condemned men at least six weeks to escape from the kingdom and flee abroad.[28] Possibly Edward III was keener to see the back of these people rather than their heads on poles over London Bridge.

But Berkeley's conduct was audacious in the extreme. He turned up in Parliament, heard the allegations levelled against him and was asked for an explanation. Berkeley's reply was as follows: 'He said that he had never been consenting to the King's death nor had he assisted the murderers or done anything to procure that death. Indeed, he never even knew about that death until the present Parliament.'[29] While conceding he was Lord of Berkeley Castle, and that the old King had been imprisoned there, but under the direct supervision of Thomas Gurney and John Maltravers, he, Berkeley, denied any responsibility for what had happened when the old King had been killed. Moreover, he had not been in Berkeley Castle at the time, but so ill he had been recuperating at his nearby manor of Bradley. He then took an oath on this and a whole troop of his friends turned up to swear a similar oath that Thomas Berkeley could not have been guilty of the old King's death and that the real culprits were Thomas Gurney and William Ockle.[30]

This, surely, must be one of the most surprising defences in law ever made. Here was a man who had been responsible for the custody of the captive King and paid £5 a day for it. When he submitted his account he made no mention of any absence. He had supervised the dressing of the royal corpse for burial and taken it to Gloucester where it was handed over to the clerk Hugh Glanville. There is no evidence of Berkeley being ill and according to his own accounts, he was in the prime of health when Edward II died, indulging in a spot of hunting and generally administering his estates. Even those who stood bail for him could not get their stories straight. In his declaration Berkeley cheerfully passes the blame to John Maltravers and Thomas Gurney. When his guarantors turned up, Maltravers' name was dropped and replaced with William Ockle.[31]

The most surprising line in Berkeley's defence was his bald, almost mocking statement: 'That he didn't even know Edward II was dead until this present parliament' – i.e. November 1330. The only thing more surprising than this is that the King, council and Parliament accepted this farrago of nonsense in its entirety. Nothing happened to Berkeley. He was released on bail and returned to the West Country unscathed. Finally in March 1337 Berkeley was cleared of all allegations that he had been involved in the murder of Edward II.[32] Maltravers was less fortunate but also escaped unscathed. He had to spend a great deal of time abroad. In 1342 the King allowed his wife, Agnes Maltravers, to travel to Flanders to be with him, which proves that although Edward III knew where Maltravers was he made no attempt to have him arrested and extradited. In fact, the exile was quietly acting as the King's agent abroad. In 1345 Maltravers was eventually granted protection to come and go, travel to and from England, without fear of arrest.[33]

The only exception to Edward III's lenient treatment of his father's murderers was Thomas Gurney. Ockle seems to have disappeared but Gurney became a refugee in Europe, hotly pursued by Edward III's agents. By 20 May 1331, Gurney had turned up in Castile. Edward successfully asked King Alphonso to secure Gurney's arrest and issued warrants and letters of protection for Gurney's safe passage. A huge reward of £300 was also given to John Martin de Lyne of Spain for the arrest of Thomas Gurney, whilst the Spanish messenger who brought the news of Gurney's capture was given the very princely sum of £50. The principal agent in Gurney's pursuit was a shadowy character known as Giles of Spain. He landed at

Dover on 17 June 1331 and put in his account for 372 days spent in pursuing Gurney, but failed to bring the prisoner back with him. Gurney had escaped from gaol. Giles had, however, managed to secure one of the smaller fry, an accomplice of Gurney, John Tilley, and incarcerated him in a Gascon prison.

Giles of Spain was a professional bounty hunter. Once he returned to England, he went looking for others who, like Tilley, had never been openly accused of being party to Edward's death: men such as William of Kingsclere, whom he arrested in Rochester; Sir Richard Durell at Northampton and John de Spicer of London. None of these men is mentioned by the chronicles, or other documents, as being involved in Edward II's murder. Nor is there any reference to them being brought to trial. The logical conclusion is that they were probably members of the garrison at Berkeley whom the King brought in for questioning and were later released.

The hunt for Gurney, however, was not given up. In January 1333, a royal agent in Naples spotted Gurney and arrested him. Sir William Tweng, a household knight, was despatched to bring the prisoner to England. According to the chroniclers, Swynbroke and Walsingham, Gurney was decapitated at sea lest he implicate other great ones of the land. Conspiracy theorists would love the story of Gurney being hustled on board ship and then executed lest, when he returned to England, he used that defence beloved of many, 'I was simply carrying out orders', before naming those really responsible. This does not fit the facts. If Edward wanted Gurney dead, professional assassins in England and Europe would have jumped at the chance to carry out the contract and fetch Gurney's head back in a barrel of salt. Sir William Tweng's account, indeed, tells a different story. He seems to have taken great care with his prisoner. Gurney was in poor condition: Tweng had to buy him clothing, linen, shoes and even a special bed for him in prison.

Gurney fell ill on the overland journey from southern Italy and thirty-nine florins were paid to physicians to treat him. Gurney, a refugee, exhausted in mind and body, and terrified of what would happen to him in England, only grew worse. Two physicians at Bayonne in Gascony were paid to tend him but their ministrations were futile and he died. Tweng, determined to carry out his task of bringing the prisoner back, dead or alive, had the body embalmed and put on board ship, which docked at Sandwich. We have no idea of what happened to the corpse afterwards but Tweng immediately travelled to the King at Berwick with his retinue of thirty men, as well as sailors from the ship, and stayed there thirteen days. Tweng probably took along his escort, as well as the sailors, to prove to the King that he had done his best for Gurney and his death had been due to natural causes rather than ill-treatment.[34]

Edward III's pursuit of his father's murderers is perplexing – none of them were arrested, whilst Berkeley, a principal player in the events of September 1327, appears to have been allowed to act with a cool arrogance. Only Gurney was singled out, not so much for punishment, but rather because the King was determined to interrogate him and discover what had really happened in the autumn of 1327. Perhaps Tweng reported what he'd learnt: after 20 July 1333, there was no further attempt to hunt down any of the regicides.

Edward III's pursuit of Gurney in particular is mystifying.

The King had Berkeley and Maltravers close at hand, not to mention his own mother, who could tell him exactly what had happened to his father. Instead he spent quite considerable sums pursuing Gurney. Was it because Gurney had to be punished for the ill-treatment and murder of an anointed one? Or was it something only Gurney could tell him?

The Purbeck marble sarcophagus in Gloucester Cathedral, with its alabaster effigy of Edward II, is one of the finest royal tombs from the medieval period. Edward II is depicted crowned, holding in one hand an orb and, in the other, his staff or sceptre. His feet rest on a crouching lion, his head lies on a single cushion supported by angels holding censers. Apparently jewels were once set in the crown and elsewhere, and, after its construction, the whole shrine was a blaze of colour, illuminated by votive candles and flickering lamps. Such light would have given the alabaster face a striking flesh-like hue. Around the tomb were twenty-eight statues of weeping angels standing on pedestals and parts of its stone canopy were painted a dark red. The whole effect would have created an aura of spiritual mystery and sanctity. No wonder that pilgrims came to regard Edward II as a saint and his tomb as a place of pilgrimage where miracles could be wrought.

Richard II (who died in 1399), visited the tomb and had his own emblem of the White Hart placed above it. Richard also tried to persuade the papacy to canonize his great-grandfather. Of course, there is little evidence of Edward II's life to regard him as a saint or a martyr. Richard II had his own political agenda: it made sense to have a saint in the family, a powerful warning to his own dissident baronage that the King's person was sacred in life and in death.

Richard II's grandfather, Edward III, however, harboured no such aspirations for his own father. Nor was he responsible for the beautiful awe-inspiring tomb. This was due more to the good business acumen of succeeding abbots of the monastery of St Peter's at Gloucester. In the Middle Ages relics, tombs and shrines were big business. Sacred objects, or alleged sacred objects, exchanged hands for vast amounts of money. Every cathedral and abbey dreamed of following Canterbury with its shrine of St Thomas à Becket as a magnet for pilgrims and visitors. Religion was good for trade. Pilgrims would throng into the town, generating work for shop-owners, taverners, hoteliers, who all profited, and still profit, from the pilgrims who flock to holy places. The Abbey itself would also be assured of a regular source of income. It is not surprising that a great deal of the refurbishment of St Peter's, Gloucester, took place after Edward II's death when his tomb became a shrine which had to be visited. Edward III may have tolerated this, even encouraged it, but there is very little evidence to show that he personally favoured or paid for the lavish shrine.

More importantly, there is no evidence of Isabella ever patronizing her husband's tomb, or promoting it as a place of pilgrimage or reparation. Henry II of England walked barefoot through the cobbled streets of Canterbury as an act of public contrition for his involvement in the murder of Becket. Isabella may have taken Edward's heart but there is little sign that she felt any compassion either for his remains or his soul.

Isabella herself *was* the recipient of much compassion and

clemency even though many viewed her as being as guilty as Mortimer of regicide and thought she should suffer the full rigour of the law. The northern chronicler of Lanercost Priory reported that Isabella herself feared some drastic punishment.[35] She had been taken from Nottingham to the royal manor at Berkhamsted, her last cry being for her son to have mercy on gentle Mortimer. Bearing in mind that Edward had wanted to execute her lover on the spot, the delay in the Welsh Marcher's eventual execution might have been due to the influence of Isabella. That Mortimer suffered none of the mutilation, the excruciating torments inflicted on de Spencer the Younger, may also have been the work of the Queen, as well as a quid pro quo for Mortimer not mentioning the Queen on the scaffold.

Isabella was a remarkable queen, a woman of outstanding ability, flawed by her infatuation with Mortimer. She certainly commanded the affection of her children and particularly her eldest son. Even at Nottingham, when Montague was urging him 'To eat the dog lest the dog eat them', Edward III betrayed a reluctance to move, rooted in fears for his mother. After Mortimer's fall, Edward III continued to show Isabella every affection and screened her from all attacks and criticism, until her death in 1358.

Just before Christmas 1330 Isabella was moved to Windsor Castle where she stayed for the next two years under comfortable house arrest.[36] The documents of the Chancery, Exchequer and Parliament are extensive and, after every *coup*, the administration was choked with petitions against those who'd held power. Yet no petitions were lodged against Isabella, nor were any references made to her scandalous private life. A whole series of crimes, the callous treatment of Edward II, the murder of Kent, whose death she had sworn by her father's soul, the appropriation of treasure and lands as well as the many oppressions the country suffered under her rule, were all squarely blamed on the scapegoat Mortimer. Isabella, of course, lost her vast estates but this was a voluntary surrender, made of 'her own free will' and no mention was made of her fall from grace.[37]

As early as November 1330, Edward III openly proclaimed the official attitude to be adopted towards his mother: any crimes committed during those years were the responsibility of Mortimer; no reference was to be made to Isabella's adulterous relationship with him.

Edward III had very little to gain by concentrating on what had happened while his mother had held the reins of power. After all, in 1327 Edward III had become King, albeit a young man of fifteen, but he had done very little, according to the evidence, to save his father, his uncle, Edmund of Kent, his cousin Henry of Lancaster and many others from Mortimer's vindictiveness. Edward III must have been highly embarrassed by what had happened between 1326 and 1330: accordingly, he adopted the attitude 'the least said, soonest mended'. The country caught his mood and this might explain the relatively low numbers of petitions presented against Mortimer after 1330.

In the country at large there was undoubtedly relief, and some considerable glee at Mortimer's downfall, particularly among those expert propagandists and adherents of Edward II, the preaching friars of the Dominican Order. In his 'Commentary on the Prophets', written shortly after December 1330, the Dominican Robert Holcott found it almost impossible to hide his pleasure at Mortimer's disgrace, drawing a veiled comparison between Mortimer and those false kings of the Old Testament who had eventually faced the justice and wrath of God.[38] There must have been some pressure on the King and his council to survey and analyse events before Mortimer's fall but this was muted. It was eventually brought to an end by a proclamation in January 1332, in which Edward III declared the official attitude towards the years of his minority. He and his council proclaimed that the validity of any grants was never to be questioned on the grounds that they had been made under the rule of evil councillors.[39] It seems that Edward did not want his conscience pricked by what had happened during the reign of Isabella and Mortimer, and this was an attitude which prevailed for the rest of Edward's reign.

The Queen's followers lost some of their property but Isabella herself was no beggar queen. In January 1331 she was given the comfortable sum of £3000 a year which, by 1337, had risen to £4000.[40] Isabella stayed at Windsor until March 1332. During this period of house arrest, her son must have questioned her closely about the proceedings at Berkeley Castle. Isabella must have known something: she, or Mortimer, may well have been the source of the King's ruthless pursuit of Thomas Gurney. But at first, the Queen Mother may have been of little help. According to Agnes Strickland, Isabella was also confined at Windsor because she was afflicted with occasional fits of madness. Strickland mentions a legend that this derangement was brought about by Mortimer's execution and mentions a groundless rumour, which prevailed for some months, that Isabella actually died at the time Mortimer's corpse was cut down. Such hysteria is more than probable. Generous payments were made to a doctor to attend upon the Queen, who may have suffered a nervous breakdown following Mortimer's execution. In the end, whatever the morality of the relationship, Isabella apparently loved the Welsh Marcher with great passion and his sudden and brutal death could, for a time, have unhinged her mind.[41] In March 1332, the Constable of Windsor secured repayment of 'expenses incurred by him in safe keeping Queen Isabella in that castle for some time by the King's order'. This very stark entry hints at confinement and detention, though this may have been due to illness rather than punishment. It also served the King well, that for almost sixteen months following Mortimer's fall, Isabella was kept out of the public eye but close enough to London for her son to visit her.

After 1332 Isabella was allowed to lead her own life. She spent some time at Castle Rising in Norfolk and there resumed a life of luxurious ease, as the local inhabitants found to their cost. The Queen Mother cheerfully returned to her old ways, ordering supplies from local merchants and never being too eager to pay her bills.[42] She also attended court and was at Pontefract with the King in June 1338. When Edward III returned from France, she stayed at the royal apartments in the Tower to celebrate the King's birthday. Four years later, during the peace negotiations with France, the French asked that Isabella be sent to Paris to negotiate on Edward III's behalf. Whether this was serious or not we don't know. The French could have seen the ageing Queen as a possible aid to the peace process, but they could also have been poking quiet fun at Edward by trying to provoke memories of Isabella's last visit to France in 1325. In the end she did not go, and the Earl of Lancaster travelled to Calais to seal the treaty in her stead.[43]

Isabella's role was now that of spectator. Her daughter

Joanna, nicknamed 'Make Peace', married David Bruce but the marriage never brought a lasting peace between England and Scotland. David did not have the martial qualities of his father: he invaded England only to be roundly defeated and captured at the battle of Neville's Cross. Joanna, who had won a reputation for saintliness and kindness, followed her imprisoned husband to England. Isabella's eldest daughter, Eleanor, was married off to a nobleman in the Low Countries as part of Edward III's attempt to build up a great alliance encircling France. John of Eltham, Isabella's second son, died in 1336 and was buried in Westminster Abbey. Others who had been involved in the great drama of Isabella's life also died during those reclusive years including, Thomas Brotherton, Earl of Norfolk, and the gaggle of bishops who had either supported or opposed her.

Isabella's war-like grandson, the Black Prince, turned France, Spain and Northern Europe into a battleground, ravaging her home country and destroying the massed might of French chivalry at the battles of Crecy and Poitiers. She, the last Capet, saw her father's great dream crumble into dust. Isabella must have wondered about the curse of Jacques de Molay, screamed from the flames as he burnt to death on an island in the Seine. After all, Isabella was supposed to have brought a lasting peace between England and France by her marriage to Edward II. Instead, her brothers had all died without male issue, leaving Edward III with a claim to the French throne. Isabella had, in effect, brought about a war that would last one hundred years.

The older she grew, the more pious Isabella became, in the spirit of the times, visiting shrines at Walsingham or entertaining visitors. She was addressed as 'Madame the Queen Mother' or sometimes 'Our Lady Queen Isabella'. She continued to live in some style: she went hunting, employed minstrels, was partial to a barrel of sturgeon, and generally acted as the lady of the manor. Her last household accounts book amply illustrates her life as a 'Grande Dame'.[44] Isabella wrote, and received letters from, her son the King, the Earl Marshal, the Duke of Lancaster, the Chancellor, her daughter the Queen of Scotland, Queen Philippa and the King of France. They brought her presents at New Year as well as a constant stream of gifts: casks of Bordeaux, boars' heads, quadrants of copper and barrels of bream. The Queen Mother also loved music. She had her own small orchestra of minstrels and paid thirteen shillings and four pence to Walter Hert, one of her viola players, to go to the school of minstrelsy in London to receive a better education. She had eight ladies of her chamber, thirty-three clerks and squires, Master Lawrence her surgeon, as well as huntsmen and grooms for the stable. She enjoyed falconry, and had caskets full of jewels with which she bedecked herself to attend the great St George's Day celebrations at Windsor in April 1358: girdles of silk studded with silver, 300 rubies, 1800 pearls and a circlet of gold.

Song birds trilled in her chambers, which were decorated with black carpets and coloured cloths. She subsidized poor scholars at Oxford and made sure that 150 poor people were given alms on the principal feasts and Holy Days of the year. In addition to this, thirteen poor people were fed at her expense every day of the year, an extra three poor people every Monday and a further three every Friday and Saturday. Only one entry indicates any memory of her husband. Isabella gave a donation of forty shillings to the Abbess of the Minoresses outside Aldgate in London to purchase food, etc. on the anniversaries of the deaths of Edward, 'late King of England', and of her second son, John of Eltham. Apart from that, the record is silent on any memory of or regret for Edward of Caernarvon.

The Queen was constantly visited by her son, her daughter, Joanna of Scotland, her grandson, the Black Prince, and notables from France. Some entries, however, show that she had not forgotten her past. At least three times in one month Roger Mortimer, the Earl of March, came to dinner. He was the grandson of her lover and was specially favoured by the old Queen. Even more regular in attendance was Agnes, the widow of the Earl of Pembroke and one of Mortimer's daughters. She and Isabella became close friends and hardly ever separated. Isabella was still a great romantic. There are many entries in her household book for parchment and vellum being prepared for her library and she still revelled in the stories of Arthur and Lancelot and sent copies of these chivalrous deeds to the King of France.

Her list of visitors average about two or three every day for the year 1357–8. Perhaps they came at the behest of her son, suggesting that Isabella was lonely or even depressed. Or did they really come to visit a Queen, who had become a legend in her lifetime, who had taken up arms and destroyed her enemies? The entries in her visitors' book do afford signs of genuine affection, even deep love for this ageing Queen. Joanna of Scotland, who followed her husband into captivity, was clothed and fed by her mother. Isabella also entertained the Earl of Douglas, and they must have laughed about how, many lifetimes ago, his ancestor had tried to capture her outside York.

In the end, death came quickly. The household accounts show no prolonged illness and record that Isabella fell ill in the course of a single day, under the effect of a too-powerful medicine which she insisted on taking. This gave rise to rumours that her mind was unbalanced, that she had sunk into a deep depression and almost willed her own death. But the household accounts for 1357–8 contradict this. She had been slightly unwell in the February of her last year but, by spring, she was better. On 1 August payments were made to Nicholas Thomason, a London apothecary, for certain spices and ointments, but these may have been for her perfumery or kitchen. However, on 12 August 1358, messengers were again despatched to London for medicines. Eight days later, a leading London physician was summoned and a messenger despatched 'with the greatest haste' to Canterbury to bring back Master Lawrence, the surgeon, to see the Queen. She died, however, on 22 August. Her corpse was dressed for burial and remained in the chapel of Hertford Castle until 23 November, with payment being made to fourteen poor persons to watch and pray by the Queen's corpse day and night. The Prior of Coventry, the Bishop of Lincoln and the Abbot of Waltham Abbey came to celebrate the funeral masses.

Isabella's corpse was taken by solemn procession into London. On 22 November 1358, King Edward III ordered the sheriffs of London and Middlesex to cleanse the city streets of dirt and all impurities, then to lay down gravel along Bishopsgate and Aldgate in preparation for his mother's corpse being brought into the city.[45] Isabella had chosen Greyfriars, the Franciscan Church at Newgate, for her last resting place. There is a legend that, before her death, she had joined the Third Order of St Francis, an organization of lay penitents, not bound by vows, who supported the spirit and religious life of St Francis of Assisi.[46] She was buried near the high altar,[47] and the Archbishop of Canterbury officiated at the ceremony. The funeral took place on 27 November and the following day her entourage travelled back to Castle Rising.

In death, as in her life, Isabella was as enigmatic and mysterious as ever. Princesses of the blood supervised their own funeral arrangements. Isabella was interred, according to legend, with her husband's heart still in the silver casket which she had been given some thirty-one years previously.[48] She was also buried in her wedding dress.[49] It would be fascinating to conclude that, in her last few weeks of life, Isabella's memory drifted back to that cold January day, some fifty years earlier, when she had met her prince at the door of Notre Dame Cathedral in Boulogne to enter into a marriage which, all of Europe thought, would bring a lasting peace to the continent.

Nevertheless, that enigmatic smile on Isabella's face on her statue above John of Eltham's tomb in Westminster Abbey is striking, as if she knows something we do not. She may have been buried in her wedding dress, with her husband's heart beside her, but she chose Greyfriars in Newgate, the same church which had received the hanged corpse of her beloved Roger Mortimer. Indeed, although she died on 22 August, her funeral took place almost on the anniversary of the day that Mortimer died on the scaffold at Tyburn. Mortimer's remains were later removed to Wigmore. Isabella's marble sarcophagus was a casualty of Henry VIII's dissolution of the monasteries, and what remained of Greyfriars was destroyed by the German air force in the Second World War. Greyfriars is now a simple park in a bustling part of London, although, according to folklore, Isabella's ghost still haunts the ruins of the monastery.

Maybe Isabella did not choose to be buried in Gloucester because, as we shall see, in her heart of hearts, she knew that her husband's corpse was not buried there. Why should she lie next to the remains of some commoner, whose body had been used to disguise the fact that her husband had not died at Berkeley but had escaped to live out life obscurely? Is that why Isabella cared very little for Gloucester or bothered to pray for her husband's soul or confess to a crime she may have liked to have committed but did not? Perhaps that explains her enigmatic smile and rather mysterious funeral arrangements.

Isabella's death marked the end of an era. From now on, English kings would wage war against France and not give up their claim to the French throne for centuries. Isabella's war against the de Spencers, their destruction and her husband's fall from grace, had also marked the beginning of an era. Other English kings had been brought to book, faced rebellion, forced to sign charters, swear oaths and bow before the opposition. Isabella, however, brought about the first formal deposition of an English king, even though it was for her own selfish motives. She began a process which, over the next few hundred years, would bring the Crown under the rule of Parliament. Forty-one years after her death, her great-grandson, Richard II, would also be deposed and imprisoned. In the fifteenth century the Crown became locked in a fierce struggle with the barons and great lords over who should sit on the throne at Westminster and how that king should rule. The Tudors later reacted against this, emphasizing their own glory and power, but the first legal deposition by Parliament of a reigning monarch in 1327 was then cited by those who constructed the process for Charles I's deposition and public execution over 300 years later.

SEVEN

The Immortal King

'. . . William Le Galeys . . . qui asserit se patrem domini regis nunc.'

'. . . William the Welshman . . . who claims that he is the father of our present Lord the King.'

'The King is dead, long live the King!' Deep in the folklore of many cultures lies the idea of the immortal king – or the king who dies, but rises again. The concept plays a central part in religious belief, and even in our own constitution, where it is recognized that the wearer of the crown may die but the sacred office always continues. It is understandable, therefore, that throughout the medieval period, kings and princes, who died in mysterious circumstances, were said to have survived. After the battle of Hastings, William of Normandy was unable to find the corpse of Harold and had to ask the latter's mistress, Edith 'Swan Neck', for her help in combing the battlefield for his body. Richard II is supposed to have starved to death at Pontefract in 1399. Rumours grew that he had escaped and the hostile Scottish court was only too willing to produce a look-alike, although the English dismissed him as a 'mammet', a puppet of their enemies. The prime examples, of course, are the young Edward V and his brother Richard Duke of York, the Princes in the Tower. For years after his victory at Bosworth in 1485, Henry VII was dogged by the likes of Lambert Simnel, Perkin Warbeck and others, who claimed to be one of the lost princes.

In France, there was a similar trend. Did Joan of Arc die at Rouen in 1431, or was she allowed to escape to Lorraine where she married and raised a family? Did little Dauphin Louis, who disappeared into the Bastille, the heir apparent of Louis XVI and Marie Antoinette, survive in hiding? Well into the nineteenth century, the French government was harassed by various claimants who put forward well-documented evidence that they were Louis XVII, a prince of the blood and the rightful heir to the French throne. A similar mystery surrounds Marshal Ney, Napoleon's general, who first abandoned his master when he was exiled to Elba but then rejoined him and fought at the battle of Waterloo. Ney was court-martialled for treason and shot, but legend persisted that he had really escaped to live out a secret life in America.

In the twentieth century, an impostor claimed to be Anastasia Romanov, the daughter of Tsar Nicholas II of Russia, the only survivor of the massacre of her family. Following the Second World War, the western allies and the newly founded Israeli government investigated stories that leading Nazis, such as Martin Borman and others, had cheated the hangman's noose and were hiding in the cities of South America.

Accordingly, stories that Edward II did not die at Berkeley must, at first, be regarded as highly suspect.

Even during his own lifetime Edward had had to face pretenders, such as the Oxford scholar who elaborated his incredible story about the sow and his missing ear. The *Brut Chronicle*, which had a reputation for instigating rumour and gossip, clearly states that one of the reasons Edmund of Kent believed his brother had not been killed at Berkeley were the constant rumours, throughout the length and breadth of the kingdom, that Edward of Caernarvon had survived. After Kent's execution, Isabella and Mortimer had been forced to issue proclamations stridently condemning both the Earl of Kent and the allegations that Edward II had not died and been buried in Gloucester Cathedral. However, in this case there was one piece of written testimony which cannot be overlooked.

Around 1340 a letter was written by Manuel Fieschi, claiming to have met and talked to the deposed Edward II.[1] Fieschi was not a rumour-monger, but an Italian priest, a high-ranking papal notary, provided with an English benefice at Salisbury as early as 1319. On the 18 June 1329 Fieschi was given another benefice at Ampleforth in Yorkshire and a few months later he was made a Canon of Liege. By the fourteenth century, the practice whereby high-ranking clerics collected benefices or prebends was fast becoming one of the leading abuses of the western Church. On 20 December 1329, Fieschi was made Archdeacon of Nottingham as well as a Canon of Salisbury Cathedral. By 26 August 1330, Fieschi was resident at the Papal Curia and must have known about Kent's conspiracy as well as the consequent fall of Isabella and Mortimer. On 10 December 1331, Fieschi gave up the archdeaconry of Nottingham in return for a benefice at Luton Manor in the diocese of Lincoln. On 3 December 1333, Fieschi must have returned to England as it is recorded that he swore out letters of attorney on that date. Two years later he was given fresh letters of attorney to return to Italy. On 28 April 1342, Edward III ratified Fieschi's retention of the benefices at Salisbury and Ampleforth. The Pope created Fieschi Bishop of Vercelli the following year and he died in 1348.

Fieschi was a distant cousin of the English royal family, and consequently must have been acquainted with Edward II during his visits to England. He was an ambitious cleric, recognized and respected by the English Crown and its Church, as well as the papacy. His letter to Edward III reads as follows:

In the name of the Lord, Amen. These things which I heard from the confession of your father, I have written down with my own hand and for this reason I have taken care to communicate them to your lordship. First of all he said that, feeling that England was in insurrection against him because of the threat from your mother, he departed from his followers in the castle of the Earl Marshal by the sea which is called Gesota [Usk]. Later, driven by fear, he boarded a vessel, together with Lord Hugh de Spencer, the Earl of Arundel and a few others and landed in Glomorgom [Glamorgan] on the coast. There he was captured together with the said Lord Hugh and Master Robert de Baldoli [Baldock] and they were taken by Lord Henry de Longo Castello [Lancaster] and they led him to Chilongurda [Kenilworth] castle and others were taken elsewhere to other places and there, many people demanding it, he lost his crown. Subsequently you were crowned at the feast of Candelmas next. Finally they sent him to the castle of Berchele [Berkeley]. Later the attendant who guarded him, after a time, said to your father: 'Sire, Lord Thomas de Gornay and Lord Simon d'Esberfoit [Beresford] knights have come to kill you. If it pleases you I shall give you my clothes so that you can escape more easily.' Then, dressed in these clothes, he came out of prison by night and managed to reach the last door without opposition because he was not recognized. He found the porter sleeping and straight away killed him. Once he had taken the keys of the door, he opened it and left together with the man who had guarded him. The said knights, who had come to kill him, seeing that he had escaped, and fearing the Queen's anger, for fear of their lives decided to put the porter in a chest, having first cut out the heart. The heart and the body of the said porter they presented to the wicked queen as if it were the body of your father and the body of the porter was buried in Glocestart [Gloucester] as the body of the King. After he had escaped the prison of the aforesaid castle he was received at Corf [Corfe] castle together with his companion, who had guarded him in prison, by Lord Thomas, castellan of the said castle without the knowledge of Lord John Maltraverse, the lord of the said Thomas, in which castle he remained secretly for a year and a half. Later on, hearing that the Earl of Kent, who had maintained that he was alive, had been beheaded, he embarked on a ship with his aforesaid custodian and by the will and counsel of the said Thomas, who had received him, had crossed to

Ireland where he remained eight months. Afterwards, because he was afraid that he might be recognized there, donning the habit of a hermit, he returned to England and came to the port of Sandvic [Sandwich] and in the same disguise he crossed the sea to Scluss [Sluys], travelled to Normandy and, from Normandy, as many do crossing Languedoc, he came to Avignon, where he gave a florin to a papal servant and sent, by the same servant, a note to Pope John [John XXII]. The Pope summoned him and kept him secretly and honourably, for more than fifteen days. Finally, after various deliberations covering a wide range of subjects, after receiving permission to depart [licencia] he went to Paris, from Paris to Brabant and from Brabant to Cologne to see the [supposed relics of the] Three Kings and offer his devotions. After leaving Cologne, he crossed Germany and reached Milan in Lombardy and in Milan he entered a certain hermitage of the castle Milasci [Melazzo] where he remained for two and a half years. Because this castle became involved in a war he moved to the castle of Cecime in another hermitage in the diocese of Pavia in Lombardy. And he remained in this last hermitage for two years or thereabouts, remaining confined and carrying out prayers and penitence for you and other sinners. In testimony of these things I have appended a seal for your lordship's consideration. Your Manuel Fieschi, notary of the Lord Pope, Your devoted servant.

Fieschi's letter was found in the departmental archives at Montpellier in a cartulary, compiled in 1368, of Gaucelm de Deaux, Bishop of Maguelonne, treasurer of Urban V. It was published in a transcription by Alexandre Germain in 1878 and again in 1881.[2] William Stubbs, the great nineteenth-century English editor of medieval manuscripts, published it in the second volume of his edition of *The Chronicles of Edward II*. Commenting on the letter, Stubbs says; 'It must have been the work of someone sufficiently well acquainted with the circumstances of the King's imprisonment.' Nevertheless he dismissed it as improbable because of inconsistencies in matters of detail. Stubbs' spiritual successor, the great Manchester historian. T. F. Tout, was not so definitive: 'It is a remarkable document, so specious and detailed, and bearing none of those marks by which the gross medieval forgery can genuinely be detected. Yet who can believe it if it is true? Was it simply a fairy tale? The confession of a madman? Was it a cunning effort of Edward III's enemies to discredit the conqueror of Crecy?'

In 1901, an Italian scholar, Constantino Nigra, published the letter with a detailed scholarly analysis. He assigned it to around 1336–7, the earliest possible date. Nigra laid great emphasis on the fact that the Genoese family of Fieschi, especially Manuel and his brother Carlo, were well known in Avignon and England and that the two Italian towns mentioned in his letter – Milasci and Cecime – were also very familiar to Fieschi. Nigra stresses the status and knowledge of Fieschi and maintains that his letter should be taken seriously. Finally, he points out that the letter is signed as 'Your Manuel Fieschi, notary of the Lord Pope', not 'Fieschi Bishop, or Bishop-elect, of Vercelli', dating its contents before January 1343.

In 1924, Anna Benedetti, professor of English Language

and Literature at Palermo, published her work, *Eduardo II*. Benedetti, following Nigra and the English writer H. D. Rawnsley, identified the castle of 'Milasci' as Melazzo de Acqui. Melazzo is a small castle, which stands on a hill top overlooking a river some forty-five miles north of Genoa. The castle has now been turned into a tourist attraction with renovated buildings and shady courtyards above well laid-out gardens. On the walls of one of the castle corridors are two huge plaques regarding 'Edward II, Plantaganet King of England'. The first plaque recounts how the English King was deposed from the throne in 1327, escaped from the murderous Thomas Gurney in Berkeley Castle, visited Pope John XXII in Avignon and later travelled to Melazzo. A second plaque commemorates Fieschi's letter, pointing out how he was a contemporary of both Edward II and Edward III, and where the letter could be found. Of course, both plaques were put up long after Professor Germain published the letter and after the Italian historian Nigra had identified 'Milasci' as Melazzo.

Benedetti also identified the castle of Cecime as Cecime Sopra Voghera. There is no castle at Cecime, only a small fortified mountain village, with walls enclosing an area of no more than nine acres. The village is built on a promontory overlooking the river Staffora, about fifty miles north-east of Genoa. Benedetti argued, quite rightly, that a hermit like Edward II could not live in such an enclosed area without provoking considerable interest. She does point out that near Cecime, high in the Appenines, is the monastery of St Alberto of Butrio, which can only be approached by country trackways and is often referred to as being at Cecime. This then must be the 'hermitage' referred to in Fieschi's letter. St Alberto's, even today, is solitary and isolated. In the fourteenth century it could only have been reached by narrow paths, virtually impassable in winter, a suitable hiding place for a fugitive king. Its flourishing Benedictine monastery was abandoned in the sixteenth century and most of its records have now disappeared. However, it is still used today by a religious confraternity, and the monastery owns three Romanesque churches. In one of these, Benedetti and others argue, lies the tomb of the 'hermit king', Edward II.

On the west side of this church stands an open cloister with a row of pillars, behind which lies an empty tomb, probably pillaged over the centuries, which has been carved out of rock. It is over two yards long, about a yard wide and two feet high. The tomb itself has no decoration or motifs, only two places for candle-holders. Benedetti has pointed out that the Museum of Art at Turin possesses two large candlesticks, which are said to have come from St Alberto's. The candlesticks were fashioned in Limoges, and on the base of each are two lions rampant. Benedetti claimed these candlesticks could have been a votive offering to the monastery by Edward III as, during his reign, Limoges was in the English-occupied duchy of Gascony.

Benedetti has also argued that some of the sculpture and architecture around the cloisters is a secret chronicle of Edward II's and Edward III's reigns. G. P. Cuttino and Thomas W. Lyman, however, in their very scholarly article on Edward II, published in *Speculum* (1978), clearly demonstrate that the sculpture is much older than the fourteenth century and can be interpreted in many ways. The empty tomb itself probably dates from the eleventh century, although, of course, it could have been used in the fourteenth to hold the remains of Edward II. Cuttino's principal criticism of Benedetti's and Nigra's theories was that their research at Melazzo and Cecime came after the publication of Germain's transcription of the letter and its subsequent publicity. However, in 1958 another Italian historian, Dominicoe Sparpaglione, interrogated a local elder, one Zerba Stefano, aged eighty-eight, who faithfully declared that the tomb at St Alberto's of Butrio had been the focus of local ritual in his grandfather's era, well before 1900, and that his grandfather and other locals had talked of an English king who had taken refuge in the hermitage. Germain's discovery of the Fieschi letter in 1878 was not published in Italy until 1901 but local legend had existed long before then, of an English king who had been hidden and was later buried in the Hermitage of St Alberto.[3]

Of course, Nigra and Benedetti's commentaries are based on the famous letter, and the crucial question remains, is Fieschi's letter true? Does it reflect what really happened? A critical analysis of its contents is essential and is best done taking each relevant section in turn.

> In the name of the Lord, Amen. These things which I heard from the confession of your father, I have written down with my own hand and for this reason I have taken care to communicate them to your lordship.

This opening sentence is highly ambiguous. It hints that Fieschi might have already written a letter to Edward III and this was a second missive. Fieschi declares he had met Edward III's father and talks unambiguously about the confession 'of your father'. Such a statement can be challenged. Fieschi was a Catholic priest. This hermit, claiming to be Edward II, apparently went to him and made his confession. In the Catholic Church the role of the confessor is sacrosanct: to break the secrecy of the confessional warrants the harshest ecclesiastical penalties. Some might argue that the hermit claiming to be Edward II did not make a sacramental confession but a simple narration of what had happened to him since his escape from Berkeley Castle. However, Fieschi uses the word 'confession', then skillfully circumvents it by declaring that he's only going to mention 'these things which I have heard from the confession', namely, matters not covered by the sacrament.

Fieschi, a papal lawyer, could draw a clever distinction between what was told to him under the seal of confession and those matters peripheral to it. Nevertheless, Fieschi was playing with fire. Moreover, he gives no reason why he accepted the hermit to be Edward II or why he believed him. He provides no description, and the hermit, apart from his story, apparently offered no proof. Nor does Fieschi give any reason why he should communicate these matters to Edward III or why this hermit, who had been wandering Europe for almost ten years, should decide to turn up and tell Fieschi everything. Perhaps the hermit thought he was protected by the seal of confession or that Fieschi, his distant kinsman, would not communicate his findings to the English court. Yet this seems illogical. Most refugees and exiles are only too happy to hide in obscurity. Why should the former King of England suddenly decide to break his silence and put his trust in a man only too eager to betray him? If this hermit was Edward II, he was courting danger. Edward III had clearly demonstrated, by his pursuit of Gurney, that he was both ruthless and relentless. What hope did the hermit have that Fieschi wouldn't betray him? Within months of his confession, English agents might be dogging his footsteps. The opening sentence lays Fieschi's own motives open to question.

> First of all he said that, feeling that England was in insurrection against him because of the threat from your mother, he departed from his followers in the castle of the Earl Marshal by the sea which is called Gesota [Wye].

Fieschi is now providing accurate detail of the events of 1326. Edward II, fearful of his wife's invasion, fled west and did cross the Severn/Bristol Channel to the castle of Chepstow. This information would have been known to many, but again Fieschi is clever. He says Chepstow Castle was held by the Earl Marshal and this is accurate. Thomas Brotherton, Earl of Norfolk, half-brother of Edward II, had been created Earl Marshal in 1313 and the castle given to him.[4] Edward II did flee there for a short while during his fruitless escape from the invading forces of Isabella and Mortimer.

Many people would have known of Edward II's flight from his kingdom in 1326 but only a few were aware of his arrival at Chepstow and that this castle was held and maintained by the Earl of Norfolk. The second sentence clearly reinforces Fieschi's assertion that he had heard the confession of Edward II, especially when he talks of 'your father' and 'your mother'.

> Later, driven by fear, he boarded a vessel, together

with Lord Hugh de Spencer, the Earl of Arundel and a few others and landed in Glomorgom [Glamorgan] on the coast. There he was captured together with the said Lord Hugh and Master Robert de Baldoli [Baldock] and they were taken by Lord Henry de Longo Castello [Lancaster] and they led him to Chilongurda [Kenilworth] castle and others were taken elsewhere to other places and there, many people demanding it, he lost his crown.

Again, Fieschi's factual accuracy cannot be questioned. He demonstrates an inside knowledge of those last frantic days of Edward II. Edward II did take ship with de Spencer and Arundel and landed in Glamorgan where he was captured along with de Spencer and another adherent called Baldock. Edward II was taken by Lancaster to Kenilworth whilst the others, as has been noted, were brought to Hereford for execution. The writer only makes one omission: Edward II was not immediately taken to Kenilworth by Lancaster but, as noted above, to Monmouth, where he surrendered the Great Seal to Isabella's envoys.

Finally, they sent him to the castle of Berkeley.

If this sentence is studied in connection with the previous one, it seems a *non sequitur*, as if Fieschi had been talking of where the imprisoned Edward II had been after Kenilworth and before he was taken to Berkeley. Fieschi then apparently changed his mind, deleted this entry and decided to concentrate on Edward II's imprisonment at Berkeley in April 1327. This *non sequitur* actually enhances his story. Edward II had been imprisoned at Kenilworth under the custody of Henry of Lancaster but then transferred, by indenture, to the care of Sir John Maltravers and Lord Thomas Berkeley. To throw off pursuers like the Dunheveds and others, the deposed King was not taken immediately to Berkeley but to other castles in the kingdom before being transferred to Berkeley. The phrase 'Finally, they sent him to the castle at Berkeley' proves this. This would certainly have provoked the interest of Edward III and enhanced the value of the letter: very few people knew about Edward II's peregrinations before his final incarceration at Berkeley. At the least, Fieschi had listened to someone closely involved in Edward II's downfall and imprisonment.

> Later the attendant who guarded him, after a time, said to your father: 'Sire, Lord Thomas de Gornay and Lord Simon d'Esberfoit [Beresford] knights have come to kill you.

Again, this is an accurate reflection of what happened. Simon de Beresford had been Mortimer's lieutenant and was hanged at Tyburn in 1330 as his accomplice 'in many crimes'. Thomas Gurney was held directly responsible for the murder of Edward II, which explains his flight from England in 1330 and Edward III's later pursuit of him through Europe. At the same time, however, this section sits uncomfortably. Both Beresford and Gurney were dead and unable to corroborate or deny Fieschi's story. The statement also makes no reference to the other man specifically accused of Edward II's murder, William Ockle. Moreover, this anonymous attendant is highly suspect. Undoubtedly Edward II had people who guarded him, but Fieschi specifically names 'an attendant' as if he was the only one, more of a servant than a gaoler.

Furthermore, Mortimer, 'with his tribe of wild Welsh-men', would hardly have entrusted the custody of his enemy to one attendant. How did the attendant know that Simon de Beresford and Thomas Gurney were going to kill the King? Mortimer and Isabella didn't advertise whom they had chosen for this horrific and grisly task. Moreover, there is no evidence that Beresford was involved in the actual murder. True, he may have been with Mortimer at Abergavenny. Beresford was regarded as the accomplice of Mortimer 'in all his crimes', but the Parliament of 1330 did not name him as a regicide and Lord Berkeley never mentions Beresford as being directly associated with Edward II's murder.

'. . . If it pleases you then I shall give you my clothes then you may escape more easily.'

This assertion is highly questionable. Berkeley was a for-midable fortress and Edward II would have been closely confined. It would have needed more than a change of clothes to effect an escape. If Swynbroke's assertion is correct, Edward was stripped of all royal attire and, as a prisoner, would have hardly worn distinctive dress. Fieschi's statement also implies that, by mere chance, Edward's attendant had the same strong and striking phy-sique as his royal prisoner. In this matter, Fieschi's tale borders on the incredible.

Then, dressed in these clothes, he came out of prison

by night and managed to reach the last door without opposition because he was not recognized. He found the porter sleeping and straight away killed him. Once he had taken the keys of the door, he opened it and left together with the man who had guarded him.

Fieschi depicts a lack of security at Berkeley difficult to accept. According to the Italian priest, Edward changed his clothes, managed to get out of his prison, walked along corridors, across baileys in the dead of night and reached some postern gate in the castle. He then killed the porter, opened the door and escaped. No other guards were on duty either around the prison itself or in the castle grounds and so Edward II escaped 'because he was not recognized'. The castle in fact would have been swarming with Mortimer's henchmen. Gates would have been guarded, all entrances heavily defended. What's more, such an escape would need careful planning. Berkeley was surrounded by a moat. If anyone left by a postern gate they would have to swim this and then thread their way through treacherous marshy grounds. Once they were clear of the castle they would need horses. Even if the security had been as light as Fieschi's letter describes, the escape would have been noticed, the hue and cry raised and a full pursuit organized.

> The said knights, who had come to kill him, seeing that he had escaped, and fearing the Queen's anger, for fear of their lives decided to put the porter in a chest, having first cut out the heart. The heart and the body of the said porter they presented to the wicked queen as if it were the body of your father

and the body of the porter was buried in Glocestart [Gloucester] as the body of the King.

The reaction of Beresford and Gurney to the escape beggars belief. They are not bothered about an escaped king wandering the highways and byways of Gloucestershire but about what Queen Isabella might do or say. If indeed they did replace the King's body with the porter's, they would have needed the connivance and co-operation of others in Berkeley Castle, including Lord Thomas, John Maltravers and other knights and guards. They would also have needed to be extremely fortunate in managing to secure a corpse which, by sheer luck, resembled the dead King. This part of the story can be dismissed out of hand except for one fascinating detail: the business of the King's heart. The clerk Hugh Glanville supervised the funeral arrangements of Edward of Caernarvon. He had to pay a woman, probably from the locality, for embalming the body, removing the heart and then taking it to Isabella. Nevertheless, as shall be shown later, this was done under great secrecy, and Glanville even tried to 'doctor' his account to hide what this woman had done – it only came to light because of some scrupulous clerk at the Exchequer. The only other source of the story of the heart are the Berkeley accounts, which describe how Lord Thomas bought the special casket for the heart to be taken to the Queen. Fieschi, amidst his farrago of possible untruths, has specified one correct factual detail to strengthen his credibility in the eyes of Edward III. True, the story of the heart being removed may have eventually become public knowledge, but Fieschi was writing during Isabella's lifetime when such details were still a matter of secrecy. Glanville did not present his account until 1335, eight years after the murder.

> After he had escaped the prison of the aforesaid castle he was received at Corf [Corfe] castle together with his companion, who had guarded him in prison, by Lord Thomas, castellan of the said castle without the knowledge of Lord John Maltraverse, the lord of the said Thomas, in which castle he remained secretly for a year and a half.

Corfe Castle in Dorset has figured prominently in the captivity of Edward II. The deposed King was taken there before he was placed in Berkeley. Edmund of Kent truly believed that Corfe was his half-brother's hiding-place. This part of Fieschi's story, however, must be taken with more than a pinch of salt. In his account there is no reference to the Dunheved gang or to the other conspiracies and covens being formed in Buckinghamshire or Wales. Instead, we are presented with a picture of the liberated king, not pursued by horsemen or Mortimer's hordes, but travelling through the English countryside, arriving at Corfe, disguised as a hermit, and staying there eighteen months. It could be argued, if the story were true, that Edward might well have chosen a place his pursuers would least suspect, under their very noses, but it was a highly dangerous ruse and very unlikely. The deposed Edward II had friends and partisans all over England. He could have called on men like Rhys Ap Griffith to hide him in the fastness of Wales and spirit him abroad to France, Spain, or wherever else he wished to go. Or there was the Dominican Order, with its international network of houses, which would have provided a marvellous chain of escape for the deposed King. Others, too, would have helped but Edward apparently ignored them, according to Fieschi's account. He arrived at Corfe and was able to shelter there unnoticed for eighteen months.

Of course, Edward II might have changed his appearance, and people saw what they expected to. But someone's memory would have been jogged. The keepers at Berkeley would have instituted some form of search, circulated the description of both the escaped King and his mysterious attendant. Fieschi might have replied that if the story was being put about that Edward II had died at Berkeley, there would be no search for him. Gurney and Beresford arranged the funeral of the supposedly dead King, so why should anyone suspect that a lonely hermit and his companion were the deposed King of England and his liberator? This is a tenuous argument. Corfe Castle was under the direct command of Edward of Caernarvon's gaoler, John Maltravers. The castle also contained Mortimer's agents, Bayouse and Deveril, who were later to play such a key role in the destruction of Edmund, Earl of Kent. Nor do we have any idea who Fieschi is referring to when he talks of the castellan of Corfe 'Lord Thomas': no record exists. Fieschi probably got his facts mixed up and is alluding to Lord Thomas Berkeley.

Fieschi does not explain why Edward stayed from September 1327 to February/March 1330 in the one place, and in fact, cleverly links the story of Corfe to the conspiracy of the Earl of Kent, which he refers to in the next section of his letter.

Later on, hearing that the Earl of Kent, who had

maintained that he was alive, had been beheaded,
he embarked on a ship with his aforesaid custodian
and by the will and counsel of the said Thomas, who
had received him, had crossed to Ireland where he
remained eight months.

Fieschi is implying that the liberated Edward probably
stayed at Corfe, hoping that his half-brother Edmund
of Kent would come to his assistance. When Kent was
executed outside the gates of Winchester, Edward and
his attendant, with the aid of the even more mysterious
'Lord Thomas', took ship to Ireland, where he stayed until
late autumn 1330, around the same time that Mortimer
and Isabella fell from power. Fieschi suggests that Kent's
conspiracy was based on the truth, but he ignores all the
contradictions. Corfe Castle was not a large place, and at
the time it was crawling with Mortimer's agents, intent
on drawing the Earl of Kent to his death. Moreover, all of
them failed to notice the hermit and his mysterious friend.
A castle community was self-enclosed, with everybody
knowing everybody else's business. Yet this mysterious
hermit was allowed to come and go as he wished at a time
when Corfe was at the centre of a bizarre conspiracy. Nor
does Fieschi explain why Edward should sail to Ireland,
where he would receive little support. The only part of
that country directly under the English Crown was the
city of Dublin, and the area around it called the Pale: this
was dominated by James Butler, Mortimer's close ally and
henchman. Isabella elevated Butler to the status of Earl
Ormonde in return for his help and support of her lover.

Afterwards, because he was afraid that he might be

recognized there, donning the habit of a hermit, he returned to England and came to the port of Sandvic [Sandwich] and in the same disguise he crossed the sea to Sclusa [Sluys], travelled to Normandy and, from Normandy, as many do crossing Languedoc, he came to Avignon, where he gave a florin to a papal servant and sent, by the same servant, a note to Pope John [John XXII].

Further inconsistencies in Fieschi's letter now become apparent. Edward supposedly escaped from Berkeley, walked through the English countryside, stayed in a royal castle controlled by Mortimer's men for eighteen months and then coolly took ship to Ireland. He only stayed there for eight months and returned because he was frightened of being recognized. Why Edward II, who had no fear of such recognition in England, should panic about being noticed in the streets of Dublin or in the wild remote countryside beyond, is never explained. True, Mortimer's henchmen were in Dublin. English traders called there, but it was safer than Corfe. Moreover, Edward II had never been to Ireland or surrounded himself with Irish princes, noblemen or merchants. So who would recognize the deposed King, who was supposed to be dead and buried in Gloucester?

Edward II's supposed flight back to the very busy English port of Sandwich, a place frequented by diplomatic envoys from the English court, merchants, burgesses, was even more improbable. The route he was then reported to have followed is also highly suspicious. Edward landed at the French port of Sluys and travelled through Normandy, the only other part of France, as well as Gascony, where

Edward might have been recognized. English influence was particularly strong in Normandy because of its possession of the neighbouring counties of Ponthieu and Montreuil. Edward II had been married at Boulogne sur Mer in Normandy and there were certainly other less dangerous routes he could have taken: he had visited northern France and journeyed to Paris on at least two other occasions, in 1313 and 1320.

According to Fieschi, Edward reached the papal court of Avignon during the late autumn of 1331, but this time he was alone. His mysterious liberator, the man to whom he owed his life has abruptly disappeared, without any reference to his fate. The last mention of this hero of the hour was when he accompanied Edward to Ireland. The deposed King chose a place where rumours about his supposed escape were rife, thanks to Kent's conspiracy and the exchange of sharply worded letters between Isabella and Pope John XXII. This cunning old pope had died in 1334 so he, too, like all the others mentioned in this letter, had gone to the grave supposedly carrying the secret with them. Edward III would therefore be unable to verify Fieschi's story. Moreover, the Italian priest cunningly depicts Pope John XXII as acting in great secrecy, meeting the deposed King 'in camera' and acting as host for a mere fifteen days. If Edward III had made inquiries at Avignon about the veracity of Fieschi's story, the papal court would have been unable to answer, whilst Fieschi could point to the secrecy Pope John XXII had thrown over this matter.

Finally, after various deliberations covering a wide range of subjects, after receiving permission to depart [licencia] he went to Paris, from Paris to Brabant and from Brabant to Cologne to see the Three Kings and offer his devotions.

Fieschi describes Edward leaving Avignon and, once again, placing himself in great danger. He journeyed to Paris, then on to Brabant and across into Germany to visit the famous shrine of the Three Kings at Cologne. Why the deposed King should do this is not explained. If Edward was frightened of being recognized in Ireland then Paris and Brabant were very dangerous places. He could have been recognized in the French capital by his wife's kinsmen, and in Brabant English influence was dominant through the marriage alliances of his kinswomen as well as trade links. In those dangerous years of 1331 to 1336, England and France teetered on the verge of outright war: an Englishman, disguised as a hermit, would have certainly excited suspicion and attracted the attention of the authorities. Nor, in Edward II's life, is there any indication of any special devotion on his part to the shrine of the Three Kings at Cologne. His visit there is not explained nor why the supposedly royal hermit was travelling across northern Europe at the very time his own son and English troops were there.

After leaving Cologne, he crossed Germany and reached Milan in Lombardy and in Milan he entered a certain hermitage of the castle Milasci [Melazzo] where he remained for two and a half years.

If Edward II had left Ireland in December 1330 and travelled through France and Germany, his peregrinations through northern Europe, before he reached Melazzo, took about four years. This would place him in the hermitage at Melazzo sometime in 1334 so he might have left it in the summer of 1336. Fieschi is now on home territory. The area of Italy he pinpoints is the desolate region of north-east Lombardy: a very difficult place to carry out an investigation, if Edward III had been so inclined. Mountainous, served only by narrow trackways, cut off during late autumn, winter and early spring by snow and rain, English bounty hunters such as Giles of Spain could have spent months, if not years, trying to track down this elusive English hermit.

> Because this castle became involved in a war he moved to the castle of Cecime in another hermitage in the diocese of Pavia in Lombardy.

Again Edward III could not dispute the accuracy of this statement. Italy, particularly the north, was riven by internecine petty wars, where local lords waged blood feuds and constant disputes over boundaries with neighbours or nearby towns. Fieschi, being very astute, names 'Milasci' and 'Cecime' but there are a number of places in northern Italy which bear both these names. He calls Cecime a castle but no trace of a castle has been found there, only a fortified village with the Abbey of St Alberto of Butrio nearby. Did he quote these names to justify his story? Fieschi had acted as a papal tax collector in that area and could set himself up as an expert on the local geography.

> And he remained in this last hermitage for two years

or thereabouts, remaining confined and carrying out
prayers and penitence for you and other sinners.

Fieschi is now being deliberately ingenuous. Is he claiming
that the deposed English King stayed at Cecime for the
rest of his life? Or that he moved elsewhere? If the latter,
he could be alluding to Edward II's move to the nearby
monastery of St Alberto of Butrio. Fieschi gives no further
details about the deposed King, except that he appeared to
have undergone some form of religious conversion, spending his time in prayer and reparation. He provides no details
of where and when the confession was taken or really why
he was writing this letter in the first place. Instead he says
that he will append his seal to the letter to establish its
veracity and ends by terming himself Edward III's 'devoted
servant' as well as notary, legal advisor to the papal curia.

What should we make of this letter? First, if we study the
chronology carefully, we have one firm date, March 1330,
when Kent was executed and the 'hermit king' was supposed
to have left Corfe and travelled to Ireland where he stayed
for eight months. This would bring the chain of events to
the December of 1330 when Edward may have returned to
England. He would have then travelled to France and would
have arrived in Avignon sometime towards the end of 1331
or the beginning of 1332. He would have then travelled back
across France, through the Low Countries to Cologne and
from there into the area around Milan and Lombardy. A fair
reckoning would be about two years for such travel, would
bring the chronology to the spring of 1334. If Edward stayed
at Melazzo for two and a half years, and Cecime for another
two, that takes us to the year 1338. If another year is added
for Fieschi to write his letter, and receive whatever reply he

wanted, then his letter was known at the English court by 1339 or early 1340.

Secondly, the letter is a clever compound of factual details, for example, the dead King's heart being handed to Isabella, intermingled with some highly suspect assertions, such as that Edward II stayed quite safely at Corfe Castle for eighteen months without being detected. It would have been difficult for Edward III to confirm or deny Fieschi's assertions, except to repeat the accounts Isabella had written to Pope John XXII: that a public funeral had taken place and Edward II was buried under a marble sarcophagus in Gloucester Cathedral.

The real clue to understanding this letter is the writer Fieschi and his motives for despatching it. After all, he was a papal notary, a distant kinsman of the English royal family, a visitor to England, who knew Edward II by sight, and a holder, albeit an absentee one, of benefices in the English Church. As Chaucer remarked: '*Cacullus non facit monachum*' ('The cowl doesn't make the monk'). This could certainly be applied to Fieschi. He was a papal tax collector, and such men were not famous for their generosity of spirit or adherence to the law of Christ. He was also an absentee landlord, drawing revenues from Church positions for which he did very little work. Priests like Fieschi were often castigated by critics as shepherds more interested in the fleece rather than the flock.

In 1319 Fieschi had been given a prosperous benefice in Salisbury, in itself a minor holding, but he did better under Isabella. Between 1319 and the fall of Edward II, Fieschi received nothing else. During Mortimer's and Isabella's rule, however, he was given the benefices of Ampleforth in June 1329, the archdeaconry of Nottingham six months later, as well as being made a Canon of Salisbury Cathedral. In addition to this he also managed to pick up the canonry and prebend of Liege in October 1329, and this may well have been at the behest of Isabella and Mortimer. Fieschi was also in England at that time, which would provide him with some insight into the political turmoil. Isabella and Mortimer were bribing this venal priest and they had the true measure of the man: Fieschi would be of use at the papal court and could exercise influence to win papal support, if not its blessing, for Isabella's rule.

Such generosity to a foreign cleric was quite exceptional, particularly one who, apparently, had little to do with the English government or court. Clergy in England rightly objected to such home-grown plums being given to foreigners. Fieschi, therefore, must be regarded as Isabella's man, both body and soul, at least during her regime. He was back at the papal curia by August 1330, a significant date for it was at the beginning of September that Pope John XXII wrote to Isabella and her son, expressing his deep surprise at Edmund of Kent's story about Edward of Caernarvon having escaped from Berkeley and sheltering at Corfe Castle. Isabella's case was presented to the papal curia by her envoy John Walwayn,[5] the same clerk who had been responsible for informing the government about the Dunheved attack in July 1327. Thus Walwayn was a man in the know, closely associated with the deposed King's imprisonment, and able to brief the papacy in considerable detail. If Fieschi had been resident at the papal court at the same time, Walwayn could count on his support to reinforce the official story and reject Kent's claims. After all, Isabella and Mortimer had paid the piper and they would certainly expect him to dance to their tune.

Yet even after Isabella and Mortimer's fall from power the generosity towards Fieschi continued. He was provided with another prebend in Lincolnshire, more prosperous than the archdeaconry of Nottingham. At the same time Fieschi was made Provost of Arnhem and, a year later, appointed to the canonry and prebend of Renaix. In 1333 and 1335 letters of attorney were granted to Fieschi because of his absence from England; after this, all further grants end.[6] The reason for this might have been the storm of protest Edward III had to face over the appointment of foreigners to prosperous benefices in the 1330s. The constant absenteeism of these nominees, as well as the need to raise cash, forced Edward to give way to demands that such appointments be limited. Edward III even began to charge 'aliens' for the benefices and property they held in England. Fieschi, a foreigner and an absentee cleric, would certainly have felt the effect of this shift in policy. Revenues would have dried up and his income cut. This, then, could well have been the true reason for his letter: a very clever way of stirring memories that Edward III wanted forgotten. Fieschi was using information, not to mention his status at the papal court, to put a shot across Edward III's bows. He had been rewarded by Isabella and Mortimer for supporting them at the papal court over Kent's conspiracy; now he was serving notice that he was changing his mind. It was no idle threat. Fieschi had inside knowledge of Edward II's death and burial as well as of Kent's conspiracy. The Italian priest might prove to be a serious nuisance at a time when Edward III was not only committed to an all-out war against France but involved in a fierce fight with both the papacy and his own Archbishop of Canterbury, John Stratford. The years 1339–41 were difficult ones for Edward III and not the time for old scandals to surface.[7] Indeed, Fieschi might have written more than one letter; this one, certainly, is a model of deceit. Some of the assertions are surprising, but it contains just enough facts to arouse suspicions.

The personal animosity of Fieschi towards the English court is also noticeable. His letter must have arrived in England sometime around 1339–40. Isabella still had another eighteen years to live and, thanks to Edward III's propaganda, she was being treated with all the honour and dignity of 'a dear mother and queen dowager'. Fieschi's letter does not recognize this. Gurney, Maltravers, Beresford, Baldock, de Spencer and the others are described in bland, objective terms. The Earl of Kent is dismissed in a few phrases. However, when Fieschi comes to talk of Isabella, he describes her as *'maliciosae'*, malicious or wicked. This is hardly the way an Italian priest would describe the King of England's mother, especially when Isabella had been so generous and open-handed with Fieschi. The adjective 'malicious' or 'wicked' was a subtle dig at Edward III. If Fieschi didn't get his way, and his father's possible escape became public knowledge, it would be the King's 'dear mother' who would bear the brunt. Questions would be asked, memories stirred. Isabella's reputation, so carefully protected by her loving son would, once again, be the staple conversation in the courts of Europe.

Towards the end of the letter Fieschi has another sly dig at the English crown when he describes Edward of Caernarvon's role as a hermit at Cecime. Fieschi depicts the deposed king as leading a life of reparation and prayer and piously adds: 'for you and other sinners'. The actual Latin is *'vobis et peccatoribus aliis'*. It would have been more diplomatic to have said *'pro nobis et aliis peccatoribus'* ('for us and other sinners'). Fieschi is thus drawing a fine distinction between himself and the King of England. By using the plural 'for you', '*vobis*' and not the singular '*tibi*', he's also including Isabella in this. In this parting shot, Fieschi is reminding Edward III that not only does Isabella have to answer for what happened at Berkeley in 1327 but so will her son.

Finally, the way the letter ends reinforces the sly threat: Fieschi guarantees its veracity with his seal, but he also cleverly juxtaposes his title of papal notary with 'your devoted servant'. Fieschi presents himself to the English king as either the papal lawyer *or* Edward's 'devoted servant'. The English King must decide which.

Fieschi's letter is finely balanced – a clever concoction, mixing fact with fiction. It can be read as a secret message to Edward to be more careful in his dealings with Fieschi. It seems this clever piece of blackmail had the desired effect: on 28 April 1342, Edward III ratified Manuel Fieschi as prebendary of Netheravon in the diocese of Salisbury and as a prebendary of Ampleforth in the diocese of York. Fifteen months later Fieschi was promoted even higher, when he was appointed Bishop of Vercelli in North Italy, the very diocese of which Melazzo and Cecime were a part. Did Edward III, to silence this clever Italian priest, bribe Avignon to win papal approval for such a nomination, or so that Fieschi could control this mysterious 'king'?[8] After 1342–3 Edward III received no further communications from Fieschi or his family.

Fieschi, it appears, deliberately exploited Edward III's fears. He may also have learnt of a certain incident which took place in 1338 when Edward III, commanding his armies in the Low Countries, met a man claiming to be his father. In 1329 Fieschi had been appointed by the papacy, probably at the behest of Isabella and Mortimer, to the canonry of Liege in the Low Countries. In 1332, he was made Provost of Arnhem and in 1334 he was endowed with a canonry at Lilles, also in the Low Countries. He was well placed to hear the chatter about how Edward III, when his forces were based outside Antwerp in 1338, had despatched two men-at-arms to bring one 'William Le Galeys' or 'William the Welshman', '*qui asserit se patrem domini regis nunc*' ('who claims to be the father of our present King'), from Cologne to Koblenz and then to Antwerp, where he stayed three weeks.

The incident took place at the end of 1338.[9] It is perhaps no coincidence that William the Welshman was taken near Cologne, one of the places mentioned in Fieschi's letter. The Italian priest may have heard about this and spun his story around it. But who was this 'William the Welshman' on whom Edward III spent the quite princely sum of almost £2 for three weeks in December 1338? Is it possible that Fieschi met this lunatic, or very cunning man, wandering Europe pretending to be Edward II and that he was inspired by him to fabricate his story?

'William the Welshman' would have been a good alias for Edward II. He was often called Edward of Caernarvon, the first Prince of Wales. Even after his deposition, a great deal of sympathy existed for him throughout the principality. We have no record of what happened after Edward III met this person. Was he allowed to go free? My theory is that 'William the Welshman' was not Edward II but someone closely involved in his imprisonment, someone who knew enough about Edward II to excite royal interest. Indeed, what better person than Mortimer's elusive William Ockle?

William Ockle was one of Mortimer's adherents. Unlike

Gurney, he was not of knightly rank but a commoner, promoted for his good service to the rank of 'scutifer' or squire. According to the November Parliament of 1330, Ockle was judged guilty of being involved in Edward II's death. Unlike Gurney, he was not the object of any search and appears to have been allowed to disappear because he was a commoner, with Gurney being portrayed as the principal regicide. Parliament placed a reward of £100 on Gurney alive and one hundred marks if he was brought in dead. A much smaller sum was awarded for William Ockle: one hundred marks alive, £40 dead.

Ockle probably escaped, following Maltravers to the Low Countries but then might have decided to earn his living by pretending to be the King in whose death he was allegedly involved. He would certainly have known enough facts to elicit interest and perhaps sympathy. The story spread through Europe and eventually came under the scrutiny of the English Crown. Ockle would have kept his first name, but to protect himself, changed his surname, or had it changed for him, to denote his nationality: 'Galeys' or 'the Welshman'. Another possibility is that Ockle went mad as he wandered through Europe, becoming more worthy of pity than royal justice. What happened to him after December 1338 is a matter for conjecture. He may have been harmless enough and released – Edward III was only too eager to keep such matters as secret as possible.

In conclusion, a close scrutiny of the evidence suggests that Fieschi's letter was a clever attempt at blackmail which, in the end, succeeded, and it should be dismissed as such. It contains some interesting detail mixed with a tissue of lies. What is fascinating about Fieschi's letter, as well as the incident of 'William the Welshman', is that it provides deep insight into Edward III's own attitude to his father's death. If Edward III truly believed, and had the evidence to hand, that his father had been killed at Berkeley and buried at Gloucester, he would have rejected Fieschi's letter out of hand and not spent time and energy on the wandering 'William the Welshman'. Fieschi must have known this. The fact that his letter was written in the first place, rather than what it actually says, provides telling proof that the accepted story of Edward II's death and burial at Gloucester was highly suspect in his son's mind. Fieschi was exploiting Edward III's fears and nightmares, fully confident that his barbed comments would find their mark. Great lies, as Machiavelli has said, are those based on a truth. Fieschi's letter is a fine example. He decided to exploit a great secret for his own private purposes, peppering it with teasing facts and half truths. Fieschi might not even have met the deposed Edward II, but his letter or, more importantly, the reasons he wrote it, are compelling enough to reassess the events of September 1327 and pose the question: did Edward II die at Berkeley? I think not. He escaped and a look-alike lies buried beneath that marble sarcophagus in Gloucester Cathedral.

EIGHT

The King is Dead, Long Live the King

'Edmund, Earl of Kent . . . you have been, many a
day, working to deliver Sir Edward, some time King
of England . . .'

Brut Chronicle

O n reflection, the evidence that Edward II did escape
from Berkeley is not conclusive but of sufficient
strength to question seriously the accepted story. The idea,
described in Fieschi's letter, that Edward was guarded at
Berkeley by one keeper and found it easy to leave his gaol,
kill a porter and then walk off into the English countryside,
is laughable. Dunheved was probably the one who freed
him. Despite the high security in Berkeley, the Dominican
probably collected a gang in the woods around the fortress
and, with inside help as well as assistance from great lords,
managed to get into the castle sometime around 19–20
July 1327.

John Walwayn, a leading clerk, was immediately despatched to Berkeley to assess the damage. His letter,
printed from the Ancient Correspondence in the Public

Records Office, manifests his panic. The letter is a plea to the Chancellor, begging for greater powers to pursue the conspirators. Walwayn, in his panic, also let slip vital information, saying 'that the rebels had forced the castle of Berkeley, taken the father of Our Lord the King out of our guard and feloniously plundered the said castle'. Thus, the Dunheved attack would not have been some petty assault. The rebels did not simply remove the King and flee for their lives. They got into the castle, overcame the garrison, probably driving them back into the towers or part of the keep, and then plundered the castle at their will. This would have included the stables, storerooms and armouries, and they had the time, as well as the resources, to collect their booty and cart it away.

Walwayn lists twenty-one names in his letter: these are to be regarded as the leaders rather than the entire gang. The Dunheveds would have recruited outlaws, poachers, men desperate for money or whatever plunder they could take.

Isabella and Mortimer reacted vigorously. Commissions were issued to track down the rebel gang but the government kept the reason as secret as possible. On 1 August 1327, letters were issued naming the leaders of the attack but the charge was 'for coming with an armed force to Berkeley Castle to plunder it' (the letter omits any reference to them getting in) 'and refusing to join the King in his expedition against the Scots.' Isabella and Mortimer were desperately trying to hide something. Dunheved and his gang had no more intention of joining the royal levies in Scotland than of flying to the moon, but desertion from the royal army was a general accusation and would ensure that the sheriffs and other royal officials would hunt them down. Isabella and Mortimer were in a quandary. If they, like Walwayn, panicked or instituted special measures, everyone would know what had happened at Berkeley, and Isabella and Mortimer would have to face the consequences. The hunt had to be conducted in secret: members of the Dunheved gang who were arrested disappeared, whilst a leading adherent of Hugh de Spencer, William Aylmer, was offered a pardon and freedom, probably for turning King's evidence and betraying his comrades.

Isabella and Mortimer would have had to consider where the escaped King would flee. Edward of Caernarvon's supporters were not in Dorset or Corfe Castle but in Wales. Isabella would remember how, in 1326, Edward and de Spencer had fled to Wales to raise troops against her, whilst Howel Ap Griffith's allegations against William of Shalford in 1331 insinuated that the King's greatest support was to be found in the principality. If the escaped King had reached there, it would take an army to track him down through the woods and mist-filled valleys where he might find shelter and succour amongst his own supporters and those who resented Mortimer. That medieval chatter-box, Walsingham, sums up Welsh loyalty towards Edward of Caernarvon: 'When Scotland would openly rebel against him and all England wanted rid of him, then the Welsh in a wonderful manner loved and esteemed him. As far as they were able, they stood by him, grieving over his adversities both in life and in his death, composing mournful songs about him in the language of their country. His memory remains to the present day which neither the fear of punishment nor the passage of time can destroy.'[1]

According to Howel Ap Griffith's letter, Mortimer had moved his headquarters to Abergavenny just across the Severn from Berkeley. On 4 September 1327, he had been confirmed as Justice of all Wales with power to arrest those breaking the peace in Wales. He did not join the court again until 4 October at Nottingham where again he witnessed charters. Why should Mortimer, the Queen's lover, this sinister *éminence gris* behind the throne, deliberately absent himself for almost six weeks, not only from his beloved paramour, but from the centre of power? If there were malefactors in Wales, they posed no real threat. Wales was constantly in turmoil and Mortimer had lieutenants like William Shalford to keep an eye on things.

It is more likely that Mortimer moved to Abergavenny to supervise discreetly the search for the escaped King. A pragmatist, Mortimer realized that Edward of Caernarvon would head directly for Wales. Agents like William Ockle would be used in the search but with little success. It must have been like looking for the proverbial needle in the haystack. Isabella was now faced with a dilemma. Edward II would have been free for almost six weeks. Isabella and Mortimer could not publicize their search so they continued the pretence that the deposed King was still safely housed at Berkeley. The logical next step was to claim that Edward II had died of a '*fatalis casus*', a fatal accident at Berkeley, but a corpse had to be produced, exhibited and buried. This would remove two problems at one stroke. First, if Edward of Caernarvon emerged into the public eye, he could be dismissed as an impostor, a look-alike, and not a focus for treasonable rebellion. Secondly, his death would put an end to all conspiracies and agitation, as well as removing a potential embarrassment, not only to the government but to the Queen. She could now act the role of the grieving widow, free to do anything she liked.

The two men responsible for this possible deception were probably Gurney and Ockle, with Berkeley as a passive observer. A suitable look-alike had to be found and killed. This probably took place in the middle of September 1327, after which the news was secretly despatched to Lincoln where Isabella was waiting. The date of 21 September, the beginning of the autumn Equinox, was chosen for two possible reasons. First, it was the feast of St Matthew the Evangelist. Edward II's birthday was on 25 April, the feast of an Evangelist (Mark), so placing his death on the feast of another saint was a clever touch of irony. Secondly, and more appropriately, 21 September 1327 marked the anniversary, to the day, of the beginning of Isabella's invasion, when her fleet left Dordrecht: this, perhaps, was a subtle way of honouring that anniversary.

A messenger reached the Queen at Lincoln on the night of 23 September to give details of what was being prepared, but a full week would pass before Thomas Gurney reached the court of Nottingham, where the young King was about to hold a Parliament, with the official news that Edward of Caernarvon was dead, a task which earned Gurney 31s. 1d. Isabella and Mortimer, of course, would wonder where their prisoner had escaped to, but for now they deliberately played the matter down. No great fuss, no proclamations, the body would stay at Berkeley for a month before being transferred to Gloucester for burial. Doubtless Thomas of Berkeley was in on the conspiracy. The corpse Gurney and Ockle produced would have had more than a passing resemblance to the former King: the hair would have been cropped, the face shaved and, of course, the body embalmed for burial. The *Brut Chronicle*'s assertion that 'friends and kin of the dead King were kept well away' certainly seems true. Even Hugh Glanville, the clerk responsible for the burial arrangements of the dead King, did not assume his duties until 22 October 1327. What happened in the previous month? An old woman was hired to embalm the corpse for burial, probably within a week of Edward II's supposed death. By 28 September the corpse would have been ready for display in the small chapel of St John at Berkeley Castle. The chronicler Adam of Murimouth, whose testimony is fairly reliable, says: 'Berkeley invited leading notables from the area to view the corpse but, this was done superficially, and they stood far off.'

Mortimer, too, supervised affairs from afar. Smyth of Nibley, the official Berkeley historian, remarks: 'What secret intelligence passed between father-in-law and son-in-law [Mortimer and Berkeley] I can only conjecture.'[2] By the time Mortimer had left the area, at the beginning of October 1327, the corpse was already sealed in the lead coffin (glimpsed in 1855, when the tomb was hurriedly opened and closed).

Apart from Thomas Berkeley and the woman who dressed the corpse, the only other person allowed near the alleged deceased King was the sergeant-at-arms, William Beaukaire, paid for staying at Berkeley '*Iuxta Corpus Regis*' from 21 September to the day of the funeral. In the literally hundreds of thousands of entries on the Calendars of Close, Patent rolls and other official records between 1327 and 1333, there is no trace of this Beaukaire. This is very surprising. Surely a sergeant-at-arms, deputed to guard the corpse of a King, would be someone well known? Wouldn't he, too, be questioned after 1330? Perhaps Glanville had been ordered to insert this item to show the clerks of the Exchequer that someone did actually stand by the corpse, see it and protect it.

Glanville's expenses are, in essence, a piece of creative accounting, which gives the impression that his responsibility for the burial arrangements for the dead King was a routine task. This was not the case: Glanville did not take over the custody of the corpse until 22 October 1327 when it was safely sealed in its lead casket. He finished his duties at the end of December 1327 but his accounts were not formally enrolled at the Exchequer until years later when Mortimer was long dead, Isabella in retirement and public curiosity had abated. Even then, the barons of the Exchequer questioned Glanville's account. He had claimed expenses for travelling for seven days from Gloucester to York after Edward II's funeral was over. The Exchequer clerks queried this and Glanville confessed that he hadn't gone directly to York. Instead, he had escorted a certain woman 'who'd disembowelled the King' to the Queen at Worcester.

The role of this woman is crucial in proving that the official story of what happened at Berkeley is highly suspect. The corpse was dressed, not by a physician or even a local doctor or leech, but by a local 'wise woman'. If Edward II had died a violent death, the effects of this violence, be it poison or the famous story about a red-hot poker being inserted up into the bowels, could be explained away. A royal physician could be bribed, sworn to silence. But if the corpse was not a king's? A physician might draw the line at that, and Mortimer and Isabella would have to take a relative stranger into their confidence. As it was, this woman was carefully watched. The embalming must have been finished by the beginning of October 1327. Three days later Mortimer joined the court but, according to Glanville's account, this mysterious woman was kept in some form of confinement from 1 October 1327, right through the period during which the alleged royal corpse was lying in state at both Berkeley and Gloucester. The Queen left Gloucester on 21 December 1327 and travelled, via Tewkesbury, to Worcester, where she celebrated Christmas before moving north to Nottingham at the beginning of January 1328. Glanville took the woman 'who disembowelled the King' to the Queen. The journey lasted two days, after which Glanville left Worcester for York. So, it seems possible that this 'wise woman' was closely confined under house arrest from the end of September to almost the end of December 1327, and then secretly taken to the Queen, a fact Glanville tried to hide through false accounting. Such secrecy does provoke deep suspicion. Was this woman closely interrogated by Isabella and Mortimer on what she had seen as well as what she had done? Did she hand over the heart she had taken from the corpse which Thomas Berkeley had placed in a silver cup or casket? And what happened to her afterwards? Mortimer was ruthless, why should he, or Isabella, have scruples about silencing the chatter of some old woman?

According to my theory, this is what happened to Edward II in 1327. He escaped from Berkeley in July 1327 and fled. Mortimer moved from Abergavenny to supervise the hunt. This proved unsuccessful so, to block any attempt by the deposed King to re-emerge onto the political scene, as well as to end all conspiracies, Mortimer and Isabella changed tack. A corpse, a look-alike, was produced and taken secretly to Berkeley. Gurney and Ockle, under Berkeley's supervision, kept it secret while a local 'wise woman' prepared the corpse for burial: the hair, moustache and beard were shaved, it was clothed in a shroud and open to a quick and superficial view by local notables, hand-picked by Berkeley. A date was chosen for the death, and Isabella secretly informed within two days, but the news was not officially proclaimed until 1 October 1327. By then, the lead coffin had been sealed, the 'wise woman' safely detained, and Glanville despatched to take over the proceedings. He, too, was under strict instructions: his accounts should not provoke suspicion and were withheld from public scrutiny.

The funeral was celebrated in an open and ostentatious way, with all due honours being shown, although it was held shortly before Christmas at the height of winter to ensure it did not become a public attraction. Pope John XXII, in his letter to Isabella of 1330, emphasizes, with great irony, the way the funeral was celebrated. He accepts Isabella's assertion that Kent was at the funeral, but both he – and Lancaster two years earlier in 1328, when he staged his rebellion against Isabella – made the same important point: that once Edward II had been transferred to Berkeley, both before and after his death, *no one* was allowed to see him. Certainly none of his kith and kin, be it his half-brothers or the great magnates of the land.

By January 1328 Isabella and Mortimer were able to relax. Edward II had not emerged: a royal death had been announced and a royal funeral had taken place. The real threat to their regime had been removed. Isabella was now free to act the genuinely sorrowful widow. No Pope, magnate or bishop could declare, or even hint, that perhaps it was time she left Mortimer and rejoined her husband. All the evidence indicates that at least for a while their plan worked. No objections were raised, no protest voiced until 1328 when Edmund, Earl of Kent began to voice growing suspicions.

Kent had been executed for his conspiracy to free Edward II from Corfe Castle in March 1330. This was the end of a search which had begun in 1328, when Henry of Lancaster had despatched a letter to the mayor and citizens of London, saying he had certain news from Kent but dared not communicate it in writing. Kent then went to Avignon to visit Pope John XXII in the autumn of 1329 where he informed John XXII of his suspicions that his half-brother was still alive and that he intended to free him. According to Kent, Pope John XXII gave him his blessing and promised moral and financial support. Naturally, when the conspiracy failed and the Earl was executed, Pope John XXII publicly rejected his story – but did so in a highly ironic manner.

Kent had been a leading magnate of the country. Stories about devil-raising friars aside, why did this important noble believe that his half-brother was alive? What proof did he possess? Isabella rejected his conspiracy, pointing out that Kent, like others, had attended the funeral but, as Pope John XXII replied, all Kent saw was a coffin, not what it contained. True, it would be easy to depict Kent, not noted for his constancy, as being prompted by guilt, remorse, even hatred towards Isabella and Mortimer but he did not act alone. His conspiracy included remnants of the de Spencer faction but also two leading churchmen, William Melton, Archbishop of York, and Stephen Gravesend, Bishop of London. Both these prelates were a cut above the court bishops of Isabella and Mortimer; they were saintly men, dedicated to their dioceses. Melton, in particular, had tried to defend his flock from the depredations of the Scots and was generous in lending money, without interest and with little expectation of repayment, to those in need. At the same time they were politicians, astute men, responsible for the management of far-flung dioceses, with more than a finger on the political pulse. Both these bishops supported the Earl of Kent. Melton even furnished the conspiracy with the stupendous sum of £5000 and sent one of his leading clerks, Taunton, to accompany Kent on his mission to Avignon. Melton and Gravesend would not have been convinced, or pleased, by stories about devils appearing to friars. Kent, therefore, must have had more precise details in order to elicit their support.

The *Brut Chronicle*, extremely well informed on this matter, published the letter Kent allegedly wrote to his brother who, he thought, was hiding in Corfe. It reads as follows:

Sir knight, worshipful and dear brother, if it pleases you, I pray heartily that ye be of good comfort. For I shall so ordain for you that you soon shall come out of prison and be well delivered of the distress that you be in. And understand, your great worship, that I have assisting me all the great lords of England with their force that is to say, with armour, with treasure, and without number they will maintain and help your quarrel so that you shall soon be King again as you were before. And this they have all sworn to me upon a book, prelates as well as earls and barons.[3]

This letter rings true. It also shows the depth and extent of Kent's following. Men like William of Melton and

Stephen Gravesend would not have entered into such a conspiracy, taking oaths on the Bible, unless Kent had furnished proof. So what was this? Undoubtedly, some of the evidence mentioned above provided some proof, possibly reinforced with rumour and gossip from Berkeley Castle and the principality of Wales. But in the end Kent failed because, like Mortimer, he did not know where his half-brother truly was. At this point, Mortimer intervened: Kent had to be caught and shut up as quickly as possible. If he was looking for his half-brother, then why not bring the matter swiftly to an end and furnish him with a false lead?

Kent rose to the bait. He was lured to Corfe Castle and trapped. When he was arrested at Winchester, according to the *Brut Chronicle*, Mortimer confronted him.

> Sir Edmund Earl of Kent, you shall understand . . . that ye be his [King Edward III's] deadly enemy and traitor and also a common enemy unto this realm for you have been, many a day, working to deliver Sir Edward, some time King of England, your brother, who was put out of his rule by common assent of all the lords of England, in conspiracy against our Lord the King's estates and also of his realm:

This same declaration was repeated when Kent was formally interrogated by the coroner of the King's household.[4] Neither statement actually states that King Edward II was dead, only in that in trying to deliver him from prison, Kent had committed high treason. The repetition of the same passage in a chronicle, a direct quotation of the charges made against the Earl, only increases suspicion that Edward II was not actually dead. Queen Isabella, in particular, was furious at Kent for putting her husband back in the centre of the political arena. She visited her son 'and bade him with her blessing that he [Edward III] should be avenged upon him [Edmund Earl of Kent] as upon his deadly enemy'. She swore an oath 'by her father's soul' that she would be avenged on Kent and refused the disgraced Earl both compassion and a fair trial: Kent was dragged out and executed, at the Queen's express command, to silence him quickly and quietly.[5]

Isabella and Mortimer did their level best to quell all rumours about Edward II's possible survival. In doing so, they also pinpointed the real source of Kent's story: – Dunheved's assault on Berkeley Castle. John Walwayn was the clerk sent to Berkeley to clear up the chaos after the attack: Walwayn, by no coincidence, was also Isabella's emissary to Pope John XXII to scotch Kent's story. If Walwayn's panic alerted historians over 660 years later, it must have had the same effect in the hurly-burly days of 1327. Did Kent discover this? And did Isabella send Walwayn to 'purge' his mistake before the Pope?[6]

The Earl of Kent's execution proved the last straw for the young Edward III. The *coup* which toppled Mortimer and Isabella in the autumn of 1330 at Nottingham Castle provided him with a heaven-sent opportunity to discover the truth about his father's death. At this point Isabella may have been questioned; Mortimer and Beresford certainly would have been. The Marcher lord was held for at least a month, Beresford for two months, before execution was carried out. Mortimer was not allowed to speak at his trial in 1330. On the scaffold he expressed, or was forced to express, deep contrition at the way Kent had been trapped and executed. But was he really admitting that Kent's plot had been a tissue of lies, not really justifying his summary execution? Or was he openly proclaiming, in a highly ambiguous way, that Kent's death was unjust, that the Earl had been executed for discovering the truth?

Edward III was certainly in no great hurry to arrest the others involved in his father's death. Mortimer fell from power on 19 October 1330. Parliament did not pass sentence on Gurney and Ockle until 26 November, posting rewards on their heads, dead or alive. Another week passed before the general warrants of arrest were issued. Edward III apparently wanted to give these men a good headstart and, apart from Gurney, little evidence exists that his pursuit of them was ruthless or relentless.

The only person who didn't flee was Lord Thomas Berkeley. Berkeley had weathered many a crisis during a long and complex life. An astute, wily man, he must have known that Mortimer was set for a fall. Nevertheless, he still had to be brought before the bar of Parliament and face very serious charges. Friends in high places are one thing but treason and regicide tend to cut across them. Berkeley must have had some assurances that he wouldn't be following the same path as Beresford or Mortimer, especially as his replies to charges were both blunt and shrewd (see chapter 6 pp. 158–163). When asked about the King's death, Lord Thomas coolly replied: 'That he was never consenting, provided assistance or procured his death.' This was followed by the most surprising assertion: 'And he never knew about this death until the present parliament.' This bald assertion, that he didn't even know about Edward II's death, some three years earlier, until this Parliament, at first sight beggars belief. The remark is not just a throwaway line, however, but a very clever hint to the young King. To paraphrase, it would appear that Berkeley was really saying: 'How can I be tried for the death of a man who may well still be alive? And I can produce proof that this is the case.'

Finally, Berkeley's defence is the convergent point of Fieschi's letter, Kent's story and the Dunheved attack itself. The latter was highly successful: inside help must have been provided. Did Lord Thomas Berkeley in 1330 claim, rightly or wrongly, the credit for this, a defence which could not be publicly aired but secretly put forward in some form or other? Did Berkeley claim that, all the time, he was a secret opponent of Mortimer and used the Dunheved attack as proof of this? Dunheved was certainly supported by 'great ones of the land'. Kent, a born plotter, was one of these. Berkeley, too, with his consummate skill at political survival, might have had a finger in this particular pie, or at least pretended to. Kent perhaps used this in his secret negotiations with Pope John XXII and Fieschi got to know of it.

The Italian priest's letter may be a farrago of truth and lies but it might actually support this story. Fieschi talks of a mysterious 'Lord Thomas', not a knight but a 'Seigneur', a 'Dominus' – which accurately describes Berkeley's status. This 'Lord Thomas' apparently received the escaped King, sheltered him at Corfe against Maltravers and later aided his escape to Ireland. It is my belief that Fieschi stumbled upon some aspects of the truth here. In a rather garbled way, the Italian priest is describing Lord Thomas Berkeley's secret defence of his actions at the November Parliament of 1330. Fieschi must have learnt this either from some source in England or from the papal court. Making such a defence was, on Berkeley's part, a brilliant move. Who could contradict it? Who would want it debated in public? Why should an innocent man, who'd done so much for the old King, be punished? As for the events of September to October 1327, Lord Thomas had little choice but to co-operate with Mortimer. After all, hadn't Edward III been forced to do the same?

Thomas Berkeley, it would seem, would be the last person Edward III would want to bring to trial. Indeed, considerable evidence exists that Berkeley not only protected himself and issued a subtle threat of blackmail, but even helped the other suspected murderers, especially Gurney, to leave the kingdom as speedily as possible. If this was the case, why did Edward III in the spring of 1331 begin his two-year pursuit of Gurney? The answer to this may lie in the Parliament records. Mortimer and Beresford had been condemned for being responsible for Edward II's death. The rest had fled. Berkeley had been questioned and he had adroitly side-stepped the issue: 'I don't know what really happened. I did my best but I wasn't directly responsible. Only Gurney has the answer, he might know what happened to your father.'

Gurney, then, would have been able to clarify all doubts, corroborate or disprove Berkeley's story. No wonder Lord Thomas helped Gurney and others to escape; he could pass the blame onto them whilst they were in no position to disprove his story. The Crown might have had its doubts about Berkeley, hence the seven-year delay in issuing a full pardon to him. However, in view of Berkeley's public, not to mention his private defence, what could the King do but go after the one person who might know the full truth – Thomas Gurney? The pursuit of Gurney was motivated not by revenge but by a desire to know the full facts about the fate of Edward II. Did Gurney talk before he died? Or was he too ill, too tired? Did he take his secret to the grave? Probably the latter: Edward III's arrest of 'William the Welshman', as well as Fieschi's letter, indicate that secret doubts remained.

Little wonder, therefore, that Edward III spent so much money and time on Gurney and very little on his father's grave. The abbots of Gloucester, thanks to the growing fame of their abbey church, St Peter's, with its royal tomb, transformed it with the some of the most magnificent perpendicular architecture of the Middle Ages. But there is scanty evidence that either Edward III or Isabella singled out St Peter's, Gloucester, for patronage and lavish expenditure. Edward III wanted to erase all memory of his father. Moreover, why should the Crown spend sums on a royal tomb, which could have possibly housed the remains of some unfortunate look-alike?

In conclusion, the central question still remains: if Edward II escaped, what happened to him? Why didn't he proclaim himself and become a rallying point for rebellion and dissent? A number of possibilities present themselves. First, Edward II may have been broken in body and spirit by the time he was released in July 1327. The chroniclers' description of him during the deposition process illustrates a man at the end of his tether. There is considerable evidence that once he was taken from the custody of Henry of Lancaster, he was hurriedly moved around the country and probably abused, physically and mentally, by his new gaolers. The Dunheveds may have released a man whom they could scarcely acknowledge to be their King. Perhaps there is some truth in 'William the Welshman's' story? It is possible that Edward II, a broken man, wandered through Europe, rejected by many because of his appearance and lack of wits. He was, however, accepted by the papacy, furnished Fieschi with a good story and spent his last days as a hermit in the mountains of northern Italy.

A second possibility is that Edward II, during the Dunheveds' ferocious attack upon Berkeley, was seriously injured or wounded and later died elsewhere. However, if the Dunheveds were harbouring him, some legends would have grown up, local folklore about a king dying and being buried. And it is unlikely that his liberators would have allowed his corpse to remain in an unmarked grave but would probably have converted it into a shrine, which would eventually have attracted public attention.

The third possibility is that Edward II escaped unscathed but that Mortimer's men pursued him and the Dunheveds, in what the medieval knights called, 'une lutte à l'outrance' ('a fight to the death'). Edward II and his adherents would have been massacred, killed on the spot. However, if this was the case, Mortimer would no doubt have had the corpse, wounded or not, taken back to Berkeley, dressed and embalmed for burial, then exhibited so as to stifle any protests or doubts. Moreover, if the King's corpse *had* been brought back, a great deal of the speculation stirred up by Kent, Edward III, Berkeley and others, would not have arisen.

There is one other possibility. It's not a fairy-tale ending but, knowing what we do of Edward II, a possible outcome. Edward II escaped from Berkeley towards the end of July 1327. For a while there would have been disorientation and confusion. However, within two months of his escape, Mortimer and Isabella were announcing to a full Parliament at Nottingham how Edward II had died at Berkeley, and the remaining months of 1327 taken up with staging a most elaborate funeral.

If Edward II had re-emerged he would have faced immediate imprisonment and execution as an imposter. After the events of Berkeley and the public funeral in St Peter's, what hope did he have in a country controlled by his former wife and her lover? True, he may have elicited the support of men like Kent and Lancaster, but what then? What guarantee did he have that his reappearance would automatically lead to his restoration? Would Lancaster and Kent keep faith with him, men who only a few months earlier had gleefully participated in his destruction and that of his favourites?

A further clue may lie in Edward II's own character and attitude. He had been King for almost twenty years. He had lost his wife and his crown. He had faced constant opposition from his nobles and seen his favourites seized and barbarously executed. He had been deserted by his family as well as leading magnates in both church and state. Perhaps he did not wish for a restoration. The constant complaints of chroniclers is that Edward II never really wanted to be king. He had provoked the crisis with Thomas of Lancaster and other barons by trying to abdicate his responsibilities as king and give them to someone else – at the beginning of his reign, Gaveston; at the end, the younger de Spencer. Edward II might have wished to live out the rest of his life in peace, either at home or abroad. A man born to be king, the crown had proved most hazardous to him: he not only realized the danger of a public re-emergence but fundamentally lacked the will to achieve it.

In the end, the true fate of Edward II can only be a matter of speculation. However, there is considerable evidence that the corpse in the lead coffin beneath the beautiful Purbeck marble sarcophagus in St Peter's at Gloucester is not Edward II's.

A Note on sources

The primary source material for medieval England and Europe is plentiful, and has been brought together by different individuals and organizations. Most of the chronicles of the period were written in different monasteries up and down the kingdom, often borrowing from, and interdependent on, each other. In the main they have been published either by learned societies or the great Victorian historians like William Stubbs in the Rolls Series. Some chronicles have not been published and can be found in manuscripts either at Canterbury or the University of Cambridge.

The volume of surviving administrative materials is considerable. Much has been published by the Public Record Office, e.g. the *Calendar of Patent Rolls* and *Calendar of Close Rolls*. These include hundreds of thousands of individual letters, writs, orders, etc. either issued open ('patent') or sealed ('closed'). The rest can be found in either the manuscript collection of the British Library or the Bodleian in Oxford. Others are under the care of the Historical Manuscripts Commission.

In France there are two principal sources: the National Archives or the Bibliotheque Nationale.

In the bibliography, I have cited a list of sources consulted, both principal and secondary, and the more important secondary sources are cited in the text or the footnotes. 'F' stands for folio; 'M' or 'Mem' is the abbreviation for Membrane.

Main abbrevations

Annales Lond.	*Annales Londonienses*, ed. W. Stubbs (Rolls Series, London, 1882)
Annales Paulini	*Annales Paulini*, ed. W. Stubbs (Rolls Series, London, 1882)
Arch.	*Archaeologia* series of journals
Arch. Nat.	Archives Nationales
Avesbury	*Robertus de Avesbury, De Gestis Mirabilibus Regis Edwardi Tertii*, ed. E.M. Thomson (Rolls Series, London, 1889)
Bibl. Nat.	Bibliotheque Nationale
Bodl.	Bodleian Library, Oxford
Brit. Lib.	British Library
Brut	*Brut, Chronicle* ed. F. W. D. Brie (Early English Text Society, 1906)
Bull. Inst. Hist. Research	*Bulletin of the Institute of Historical Research*
Bull. John Ryl. Lib.	*Bulletin of the John Ryland Library*
Cal. Chanc. Warr.	*Calendar of Chancery Warrants*
Cal. Ch. Rolls	*Calendar of Charter Rolls*

Cal. Cl. Rolls	*Calendar of Close Rolls*
Cal. Fine Rolls	*Calendar of Fine Rolls*
Cal. Papal Letters	*Calendar of Papal Registers*
Cal. Pat. Rolls	*Calendar of Patent Rolls*
Canon of Bridlington	*Gesta Edwardi de Caernarvon Auctore Canonico Bridlingtoniensi,* ed. W. Stubbs (Rolls Series, London 1882–3)
Dignity of a Peer	*Lords' Report on the Dignity of a Peer. IV.*
Eng. Hist. Rev.	*English Historical Review*
Foeders	T. Rymer, *Foedera, Coventiones, Litterae,* ed. A. Clarke and F. Holbrooke, I, II, (London, 1816–18)
Hist. Mss. Comm.	Historical Manuscripts Commission
The Household Book	*The Household Book of Queen Isabella,* ed. F. D. Blackley and G. Hermansen (Edmonton, 1971)
Knighton	*Chronicon Henrici Knighton,* ed. J. R. Lumby, I (Rolls Series, London, 1889)
Lanercost	*The Chronicle of Lanercost,* ed. H. Maxwell-Lyte (Glasgow, 1919)
Melsa	*Chronica Monasterii de Melsa,* ed. E. A. Bond, II (Rolls Series, London, 1867)
Murimouth	*Adae Murimouth Continuatio Chronicarum,* ed. E. M. Thompson

	(Rolls Series, London 1889)
Northern Registers	*Historical Papers and Letters from Northern Registers,* ed. J. Raine (Rolls Series, London, 1873)
Parl. Writs.	*Parliamentary Writs,* ed. F. Palgrave, II (London, 1827–34)
Polychronicon	*The Polychronicon of Ranulph Higden,* ed. C. Babington and J. R. Lumby, VIII (Rolls Series, London, 1864–86)
Rot. Parl.	*Rotuli Parliamentorum,* I
Rot. Scot.	*Rotuli Scotiae in Turri Londinenai et in Domo Capitulari Westmonasteriense Asservati,* ed. D. Macpherson, J. Caley, W. Illingworth, T. H. Horne, I (London, 1814)
'Scalacronica'	'Scalacronica', ed. H. R. Maxwell, *Scot. Hist. Rev.* III (1905–6) and IV (1906–7)
Scot. Hist. Rev.	*Scottish Historical Review*
Soc. Antiq.	Society of Antiquaries
Statutes	Statutes of the Realm, I (1812)
Swynbroke	*Chronicon Galfredi le Baker de Swynbroke,* ed. E. M. Thompson (Oxford, 1889)
Trans. Roy. Hist. Soc.	*Transactions of the Royal Historical Society*
Trin. Coll. Camb.	Trinity College, Cambridge
Trokelowe	*Johannis de Trokelowe et Henrici de Blaneford Chronica et Annales,*

ed. H. T. Riley (Rolls Series, London 1866)

Willelmi Cappellani *Willelmi Cappellani in Brederode postea Monachi et Procuratoris Egmundensis Chronicon*, ed. C. Pijnacker Hondyk, XX (Historisch Genootschap, 3rd Ser., Amsterdam, 1904)

Notes

ONE: A Fitting Marriage . . .

1. A. Strickland, *Lives of the Queens of England*, (London, 1970) Vol. I. p. 541 (1832).
2. P. C. Doherty 'The date of the birth of Isabella' *Bull Inst. Hist. Res.* XLVIII (1975), pp. 246–8. This is an edition of a papal letter from the Archives Nationales, which proves 1296 to be the year of her birth. There are a few references to her in the French royal accounts: *Les Journaux du Tresor de Philippe le Bel*, ed. J. Viard (Paris 1840), p. 700, Arch. Nat. 'J' 149. No. 30.
3. Pierre Dubois, *Summaria Brevis et Compendiosa*, ed. H. Kampf (New York, 1936) provides a clear and contemporary account of Philip IV's ambitions. R. Fawtier, *The Capetian Kings of France*, (Glasgow, 1960), pp. 60, 121 and 162.
4. *Foedera* I, p. 904 and Brit. Lib., Cottonian Ms. Julius, E.I. fos 54r–56r.
5. On Edward I and the Low Countries, See F. Bock *England's Beziehiengen zim Reich unter Adolf von Nassau* (Innsbruck, 1933), p. 199 and *Inventaires des Manuscrits concernants les Relations de Flandre et L'Angleterre*, ed. J. de St. Genois (1842), p. 162. On Philip IV, see *Rerum Gallicarum et Francicarum Scriptores: Receuil des Historiens des Gaules et de la France*, ed. P. Danou and J. Naudet (Paris, 1738–1904), Vol. XX, pp. 576, 677.
6. *Foedera* I, pp. 906–7 Arch. Nat. J. 631. No. 30, Brit. Lib., Cott Mss. Julius, EI, fos 63, 64, 66 and 67.
7. In the ensuing row, Philip accused Boniface of such treachery: Arch Nat. J. 633, No. 6. Bibl. Nat. Fr. Mss. (Nouvelles Acquisitions), 6999, fo. 235.
8. *Foedera* I, p. 951 and E/30/51a.
9. *Foedera* I, pp. 952–4. Arch. No. J. 633, 12, 13, 17–19.
10. S.C. 6/44/16.
11. Doherty, 'The date of the birth of Isabella', pp. 246–8.
12. *Letters of Edward, Prince of Wales*, ed. H. Johnstone (Roxburghe Club, 1931), pp. 144–5. References to Isabella, see Bibl. Nat., Collection Brienne, 7007, f. 1.
13. C. 47/29/5/25.
14. E/101/684/11, No. 7 and E/101/370/15, m. 15.
15. *Foedera* I, p. 1012. Brit. Lib., Add Ms. 22923, f. 4.
16. William Wallace had been captured and executed in London.
17. See Chapter 6, p. 223.
18. Geoffrey La Tour-Landry, *Book of the Knights of La Tour*, ed. T. Wright (London, 1868), pp. 26–7.
19. *Le Menagier de Paris*, ed. Jerome Pichon (Paris, 1846), Vol. I, pp. 168–9.
20. *Knighton* II, pp. 57–8.

21. Geoffrey Chaucer, *The Canterbury Tales*, ed. Nevill Coghill (Penguin, 1982), pp. 31–2.
22. Henry VIII prohibited this by Act of Parliament.
23. *The Canterbury Tales*, p. 309.
24. T. F. Tout, *Edward I* (London, 1890), p. 225.
25. *Foedera* II, 1. p. 650; R. Twysden, *Historiae Anglicanae Scriptores Decem* (London, 1652) co. 1. 2765.
26. H. Johnstone, *Letters of Edward*, p. 115. H. Johnstone, *Edward of Caernarvon 1284–1307* (Manchester, 1946), pp. 9, 17.
27. *The Register of Thomas Cobham – Bishop of Worcester*, ed. H. Pearce (Worcs. Hist. Soc., 1930), pp. 97–8.
28. H. Johnstone, *Letters of Edward*, pp. XIV–XIVI, 114.
29. H. Johnstone, *Edward of Caernarvon*, pp. 30, 86.
30. *Annales Paulini*, p. 260; *Cal. Papal Registers, Letters 1305–1352*, pp. 430–1.
31. *The Antiquarian Repository II* (1779), pp. 58–9.
32. H. Johnstone, *Letters of Edward*, p. XXXVIII.
33. H. Johnstone, *Edward of Caernarvon*, pp. 42, 43.
34. H. Johnstone, *Edward of Caernarvon*, p. 45.
35. *Chronicle of Bury St. Edmunds* ed. and translated by Gransden. (London 1964) pp. XXXIII and 157.
36. *Roll of Arms of Caerlaverock*, ed. T. Wright (Rolls Series 1864), p. 18.
37. *Calendar of Patent Rolls 1292–1301*, p. 576
38. 'Scalacronica', p. 130.
39. H. Johnstone, *Letters of Edward*, p. XXXVIII.
40. The full story is given in H. Johnstone's *Letters of Edward*, pp. XI–XIIV.
41. H. Johnstone, *Letters of Edward*, p. XXXVII.
42. Ibid., pp. XXXIX and L.
43. *Annales Lond.*, p. 143.
44. Ibid., p. 146; *Chronicle of Pierre de Langtoft*, ed. J. Wright (Rolls Series, 1867), p. 368.
45. J. Barbour *The Bruce*, ed. W. N. Mackenzie (London, 1909), pp. 71–6.
46. *The Chronicles of Walter of Guisborough*, ed. H. Rothwell (Royal Historical Soc., London, 1957), pp. 377–9.
47. Ibid., pp. 382–3.
48. Brit. Lib. Add. Mss. 22923, fo. 6.

TWO: Isabella and the King's Favourite

1. *Roll of Arms*, ed. T. Wright (Rolls Series, 1864), p. 18.
2. *Vita Edwardi* (London 1957), p. 40; *Chronica Monasterii de Melsa* II, p. 286; *Canon of Bridlington*, p. 91.
3. Brit. Lib., Stowe Ms. 553, fo. 21v. (He died during the Scottish Expedition of autumn 1322.)
4. *Vita Edwardi Secundi*, p. 41.
5. *Trokelowe*, p. 64
6. *Annales Paulini*, pp. 255, 262; *Trokelowe*, p. 64; *Flores Historiarum* III, p. 331; *Murimouth*, p. 9; *Lanercost*, p. 210; *Melsa* (Meaux) II, p. 355.
7. *Vita Edwardi*, pp. 15 and 30.
8. The Chronicle evidence for this is overwhelming: see *Vita Edwardi*, pp. 7, 17; *Annales Paulini*, p. 259; Brit. Lib., Ms. Harl. 636, fo. 232; *Lanercost*, p. 210.
9. *Murimouth*, pp. 11–12; *Annales Lond.* I, p. 156; *Lanercost*, p. 187.
10. *Annales Paulini*, p. 259; *Trokelowe*, p. 65; *Vita Edwardi*, p. 2.
11. Thomas Walsingham, *Historia Anglicana* (Rolls Series, 1863), p. 125; *Lanercost*, p. 194; *Annales Lond.*, pp. 151, 152 and 157.

12. On Edward I's death, see *Annales Paulini*, p. 256; Rothwell, *Walter of Guisborough* (1957), p. 37. The news reached London, see E/101/373/15f. 43v. for Gaveston's recall, see, ibid., fo. 21v. For the Charter, see *Foedera* II, 1. 2. For the heraldic arms, see E/101/373/15f. 9r.

13. E/101/373/15, f. 22r.

14. A. P. Stanley, *Historical Memoirs of Westminster Abbey* (London, 1882), pp. 128–30.

15. For this mixed judgement, see *Flores Historiarum* III, p. 137; *Vita Edwardi*, p. 40; *Lanercost*, p. 183; 'Scalacronica', p. 136.

16. T. H. Parker, *The Knights Templar in England* (University of Arizona Press, 1963), p. 86 et seq.

17. *Foedera* II, pp. 19, 24.

18. Arch. Nat., J. 654, No. 8; Bibl. Nat. Coll., Brienne, fos. 67–76.

19. Brit. Lib., Mss. Harl. 636, f. 32.

20. *Foedera* II, p. 23.

21. Agnes Strickland, *Lives of the Queens of England* V, p. 473.

22. *Foedera* II, p. 24; E/101/376/6 M.2.

23. Strickland, *Lives*, pp. 472–4.

24. Ibid.

25. Mss. de L'Arsenal de Paris 3346, f. 10; *Annales Paulini*, p. 258.

26. E/101/373/6, M.2.

27. C.47/29/6/3. Brit. Lib. Cottonian, Ms. Nero DX, f. 108.

28. There are three highly recommended, very scholarly works on Edward II's troubles with his baronage: John Maddicott, *Thomas of Lancaster* (Oxford, 1970), pp. 72–3; J. C. Davies, *The Baronial Opposition to Edward II* (Cambridge, 1918); and Natalie Fryde, *The Tyranny and Fall of Edward II 1321–1326* (Cambridge, 1979).

29. E/101/373/6, M.2; E/101/373/7, M.3; *Foedera* II, p. 31.

30. Strickland, *Lives*.

31. E/403/141 M.8; *Annales Paulini*, p. 260; Maddicott, *Thomas of Lancaster*, pp. 73–4.

32. E/101/325/4/M.2.

33. *Foedera* II, p. 36.

34. *Annales Paulini*, pp. 259–62, gives an eye-witness account of the Coronation débâcle.

35. E101/373/7/M.5; *Cal. Pat. Rolls 1307–1313*, pp. 55, 58, 63.

36. Arch. Nat., J. 655, No. 25.

37. *Flores Historiarum* III, p. 148; Maddicott, *Thomas of Lancaster*, pp. 83–4.

38. *Les Journaux du Tresor de Philippe le Bel*, ed. J. Viard (Paris, 1840), No. 5898.

39. Maddicott, *Thomas of Lancaster*, pp. 85–8.

40. Bodl., Ms. Lat. Hist. C.5. (R) Mems. 1, 7.

41. Hist. Mss. Comm. Report, 4 (1874), p. 394; *Annales Paulini*, pp. 264–5; *Cal. Pat. Rolls 1307–1313*, p. 186.

42. Exchequer payments to Isabella: E/403/141/M.7; E/403/144 Mems. 1, 4, 5, 8; grant of lands, see *Cal. Pat. Rolls 1307–1313*, pp. 101, 113, 156.

43. *The Household Book of Queen Isabella*, ed. F. D. Blackley and G. Hermansen (Edmonton, 1971), pp. 133, 207, 215.

44. *The Household Book of Queen Isabella* describes Isabella's lavish lifestyle in 1311. The Queen's influence on grants can be seen in *Cal. Pat. Rolls 1307–1313*, pp. 58, 69, 74, 78, 92.

45. Brit. Lib., Cott. Mss. Nero C. VIII, f. 58v. Two agents were sent to France '*pro negociis regis secretis*' ('on the secret business of the King').

46. *The Household Book of Queen Isabella*, pp. 137–8.

47. Brit. Lib., Cott. Mss. Nero C. VIII, f. 84v; Bodl., Ms. Tanner 197, f. 54.

48. *Trokelowe*, pp. 75–6.

49. *The Household Book of Queen Isabella*, pp. 103–4.

50. Gaveston's downfall is described in detail by Maddicott, *Thomas of Lancaster*, pp. 121–30.
51. E/101/375/2 Mems. 3 and 4.
52. E/159/89 Mem. 15; Brit. Lib., Add Ms. 15664, f. 174.
53. *Foedera* II, p. 178; Brit. Lib., Cott. Ms. Julius A. 1, f. 51.
54. Walsingham, *Historia Anglicana* I, p. 134.
55. Ibid., p. 135.
56. *Annales Lond.*, p. 221.
57. Desmond Seward's *The Monks of War* (Paladin, 1974), pp. 197–214, gives a clear account of this great scandal.
58. *Receuil des Historiens des Gaules, et de la France*, Vol. XXI, ed. M. de Wailly (Paris, 1855), pp. 38, 657 and Vol. XXIII, pp. 135–9.
59. E/30/1422.
60. Bibl. Nat., Lat. Mss. 8504, fos. 1–2.
61. *Receuil des Historiens des Gaules*, Vol. XXI, p. 657; E/101/375/9, f. 25; E/404/483/10.
62. J. C. Davies, *The Baronial Opposition to Edward II* (Cambridge, 1918), p. 85.
63. E/101/375/9, f.1.v.
64. Seward, *The Monks of War*, pp. 211–12.
65. E/101/375/9, f. 5v.
66. *Chronique de Pays Bas*, ed. J. Smet (Brussels, 1856), II, pp. 138–9; H. Cordier, *Annales de l'Hotel de Nesle, Memoires de L'Institut National de France* XLI (1920), p. 36; 'Scalacronica', ed. H. R. Maxwell; *Scot. Hist. Rev.* III, 1905–6, pp. 453–4.
67. E/101/375/9, fos. 19, 25, 27.
68. Soc. Antiq., Mss. 120, fos. 15, 97 v.
69. *Cal. Pat. Rolls 1313–1317*, pp. 490, 491, 518, 519.
70. Hilda Johnstone makes reference to this 'Legend' in her short monograph, 'Isabella the She-Wolf of France', *History* XXI (1936–1937), pp. 208–19.
71. Maddicott, *Thomas of Lancaster*, p. 204.
72. *Cal. Pat. Rolls 1317–1321*, pp. 112, 115, 116, 222, 223.
73. E/101/377/7, M.8.
74. *Trokelowe*, p. 103.
75. *Annales Paulini*, pp. 287–8.
76. Brit. Lib., Add. Mss. 17362, f. 49.
77. E/101/377/11.
78. W. J. Smith, 'The Revolt of William Somerton', *Eng. Hist. Rev.* LXIX (1954), pp. 76–87.
79. *Annales Paulini*, p. 297.
80. Ibid., p. 297.
81. Brit. Lib., Add. Charters 26, 684; *Cal. of Cl. Rolls 1318–1323*, p. 477.
82. Irin. Coll. Camb., Ms. R.5.41, fos. 114v.–115v.
83. Ibid.

THREE: The New Favourite and Isabella's Disgrace

1. *Vita Edwardi*, pp. 97–102, 104.
2. *Trokelowe*, p. 110; *Annales Paulini*, p. 299; Trin. Coll. Camb., Mss. R.5. 41, f. 115v.
3. *Cal. Cl. Rolls 1318–1323*, p. 478.
4. S.C.6/1090/12. M.1.
5. Brit. Lib., Cott. Mss. Nero D, f. 111b.
6. Natalie Fryde, 'John Streetford, Bishop of Winchester, and the Crown, 1323–1330', *Bull. Inst. Hist. Research* XLI (1971), pp. 54–5.

7. *Flores Historiarum* III, p. 346.
8. Maddicott, *Thomas of Lancaster*, pp. 310–12.
9. *Vita Edwardi Secundi*, pp. 124, 125, 136.
10. J. Taylor, 'The Judgement on Hugh Despencer the Younger', *Medievalia et Humanistica* XII (1958), pp. 70–7.
11. *Vita Edwardi Secundi*, p. 126.
12. Trin. Coll. Camb., Ms. R.5.41., f. 118.
13. E/101/380/5; *Cal. Pat. Rolls 1321–1324.*, p. 405.
14. Miscell. books (Duchy of Lancaster), DL.42/11, f. 66; John Taylor, '*Judgement on Hugh Despencer*', op. cit.
15. Mary McKisack, *The Fourteenth Century*, (Oxford, 1959), p. 75.
16. SC. 1/63/169.
17. *Calendar of Docs. Relating to Scotland* III, p. 146.
18. E/163/4/11 No. 15. This is a collection of draft letters and includes Edward's earlier letters (Nos. 73 and 8) to Winchester and Reynolds.
19. Brit. Lib., Stowe Mss. 553, f. 134 v.
20. *Receuil des Historiens des Gaules* XX, p. 632.
21. *Foedera* II, pp. 506, 620.
22. *Le Livere de reis de Brittanie*, ed. J. Gloves (Rolls Series, London, 1865) p. 354.
23. Trin. Coll. Camb., Mss. R.5. 41, f. 114.
24. *Foedera* II, p. 569; E/403/201. M.4.
25. C/61/35; SC.6/1125–1127; E/403/201, Mems. 14–15.
26. E/403/201, Mems. 14–15.
27. E/15/97, Mem. 187 b.
28. *Select cases in the Court of King's Bench under Edward III*. Vol. ed. G. O. Sayles (Selden Society, London, 1958) Vol. 74, p. 155.
29. *Calendar of Papal Registers, Letters II 1305–1341*, pp. 461, 468, 469, 475 and 477.
30. E. L. G. Stones, 'The Folvills of Ashby Folville', *Trans. Roy. Hist. Soc.*, 5th series (1957), Vol. 7 pp. 124 ff; Brit. Lib., Stowe Mss. 553, f. 68.
31. *The War of St. Sardos* ed. Pierre Chaplais (Camden Society, 1954), 3rd Series. Vol. LXXXVII pp. 199–201.
32. Ibid., Appendix III, p. 265.
33. Ibid., Appendix III, p. 267.
34. *Foedera* II, p. 613.
35. *Swynbroke*, p. 20; SC.I/49/100.
36. *Cal. Cl. Rolls 1323–1327*, p. 580.
37. *Chroniques de London*, ed. C. J. Aungier (Camden Society, 1844), p. 49; *Vita Edwardi Secundi*, p. 143.
38. *Cal. Cl. Rolls 1323–1327*, p. 579.
39. E. L. G. Stones, 'The date of Roger Mortimer's escape from the Tower of London', *Eng. Hist. Rev.* LXVI (1951), p. 978.
40. E/159/85, Mems. 19. 32b.
41. E/101/375/3f. 33.
42. *Cal. Pat. Rolls 1321–1324*, p. 119.
43. SC/1/37/45.
44. *Chronica Monasterii de Melsa* II, p. 348. C/81/125/6788. Edward II bitterly complained to the French. *The War of St. Sardos*, pp. 179, 193.
45. *Cal. Cl. Rolls 1323–1327*, pp. 576–7.
46. *Cal. Pat. Rolls 1324–1327*, pp. 206, 208–11.
47. *Cal. Cl. Rolls, 1323–1327*, p. 543.
48. *Cal. Papal Registers 1305–1342* II, pp. 477, 479.
49. Walsingham, *Historia Anglicana* I, p. 179.
50. This was all known in England by January 1326: see SC.1/49/91–92 and *Foedera* II, p. 617.
51. *Foedera* II, pp. 636–7.
52. E. L. G. Stones, *The Folvills*; *Cal. Pat. Rolls 1324–1329*, p. 145.

53. *Cal. Pat. Rolls 1324–1327*, p. 232.
54. Ibid., pp. 292–3.
55. 20 September 1326 is the last day Isabella and her group are mentioned in the Hainault account. See *Rekiningen Van de Herberge Van Joanna Van Valois 1319–1326*, XLVI ed. H. Smit, (Historisch Genootschap, 3rd Series, 1924), p. 261.
56. *Cal. Cl. Rolls 1323–1327*, p. 613. *Cal. Pat. Rolls 1324–1327*, pp. 315–16.
57. *Annales Paulini*, pp. 313–14.
58. Walsingham, *Historia Anglicana* I, p. 180; *Swynbroke*, p. 21; *Knighton* I, p. 435.
59. *Foedera* II, pp. 643, 644. The King could only raise four volunteers in the entire capital, see Trin. Coll. Camb., R.5.41, f. 121 V.
60. C/62/103 M.2.
61. Anthony Wood, *History and Antiquities of the University of Oxford*, ed. J. Gutch (Oxford, 1729) I, p. 411.
62. *Historiae Anglicanae Decem. Scriptores*, ed. R. Twysden (Oxford, 1652), Col. 2765.
63. *Knighton* I, p. 436.
64. *Cal. Cl. Rolls 1323–1327*, p. 652; Antiq. Soc. Ms. 122, f. 89.
65. *Historia Roffensis* (Anglia Sacra), ed. H. Wharton (London, 1691), p. 366.
66. *Annales Paulini*, p. 315; Walsingham, *Historia Anglicana* I, p. 181; G. A. Williams, *Mediaeval London, from Commune to Capital*, (University of London, 1970), pp. 295, 296.
67. Trin. Coll. Camb., Ms. R.5.41, f. 123v; J. Smyth of Nibley, *The Lives of the Berkeleys*, I (Gloucester, 1883), p. 287.
68. *Foedera* II, p. 646.
69. Soc. Antiq., Mss. 122, f. 96.
70. *Foedera* II, p. 647.
71. *Annales Paulini*, p. 319; *Murimouth*, p. 49.
72. *Chroniques de Londres*, ed. C. J. Aungier (Camden Society, 1844), p. 49; *Vita Edwardi Secundi*, p. 143.
73. *Cal. Cl. Rolls. 1323–1327*, pp. 580–1.
74. Ibid.
75. The *Lanercost Chronicle* (p. 249) says Edward II sent his Dominican confessor, Thomas Dunheved, to the Pope to obtain a divorce. Dunheved was definitely out of the country. *(Cal. Papal Registers 1305–1342)* II, p. 474. This remarkable conversation is in the *Historia Roffensis* in *Anglia Sacra*, I, ed. H. Wharton (London, 1691), pp. 365–7.
76. The gossip surrounding such sexual misconduct can be found in the *Chronographia Regum Francorum*, ed. H. Moranville (Société d'Histoire de France, Paris 1891), vol. I, p. 285 and Willelmi Cappellani in *Brederode postea Monachi et Procuratoris Egmundensis Chronicon*, ed. C. Pijnacker Hondyk (Historisch Genootschap, 3rd Series, Amsterdam, 1904), XX, p. 177.
77. *Literae Cantuarienses*, ed. J. B. Sheppard (London, 1889), p. 137, n. 46.

FOUR: The She-Wolf Triumphant

1. *Brut* Chronicle I, pp. 239–40.
2. J. Taylor, 'The Judgement on Hugh Despencer the Younger', pp. 70–7.
3. *Knighton* I, p. 436; Trin. Coll. Camb., Mss. R.5.41, f. 123 V; *Annales Paulini*, pp. 319–20; *Brut*, p. 240. All these sources provide a graphic account of the gruesome executions.
4. *Cal. Pat. Rolls 1324–1327*, pp. 339–40; C/47/3/53/7.
5. *Knighton* I, p. 444.

6. *Calendar of Plea and Memoranda Rolls of the City of London*, ed. A. H. Thomas (Cambridge, 1926), pp. 15–19.
7. *Cal. of Cl. Rolls 1323–1327*, p. 655; *Annales Paulini*, pp. 315, 316, 321, 322.
8. *Cal. Pat. Rolls 1324–1327*, pp. 343–6.
9. *Cal. of Plea and Memoranda Rolls*, pp. 42–3.
10. E/101/382/3.
11. *Cal. Fine Rolls 1319–1327*, p. 422; *Foedera* II, p. 647.
12. The source of this is the Chronicle of the Hainaulter Froissart and an 'Apologia' published by Adam Orleton in 1334. *Oeuvres de Froissart*, ed. Kervyn de Letternhove (Brussels, 1867) II, p. 85. *Winchester Cathedral Cartulary*, ed. A. W. Goodman (Winchester, 1927), pp. 104–7.
13. The source for the proceedings are two very scholarly articles: M. McKisack, 'The Fourteenth Century', pp. 90 et seq. and M. V. Clarke, 'Committees of Estates and the deposition of Edward II, *Historical Essays in honour of James Tait*, (Manchester, 1933).
14. *Historia Roffensis* (Anglia Sacra) I, p. 367.
15. Walsingham *Historia Anglicana* I, p. 186.
16. Ibid., p. 188.
17. *Swynbroke*, p. 28; *Chronique de Froissart*, ed. S. Luce (Paris, 1869), Vol. I, Part II. p. 257.
18. *Swynbroke*, p. 29; *Brut*, p. 252.
19. This poetry is ascribed to Edward II, see Fabyan: *New Chronicles of England and France*, ed. H. Ellis (London, 1811), p. 430.
20. *Winchester Cathedral Cartulary*, ed. A. W. Goodman (Winchestes, 1927), p. 107.
21. T. F. Tout, *'The Captivity and Death of Edward of Caernavon, Collected Papers of T. F. Tout* III, (Manchester, 1934), p. 157.
22. *Cal. Pat. Rolls 1327–1330*, pp. 79–81.
23. Ibid., pp. 99–100; S.C.I./29/64.
24. *Knighton* I, p. 444.
25. E/101/382/10M.6; *Knighton* I, p. 444.
26. Tout, 'The Captivity and Death of Edward', pp. 156, 157.
27. *Cal. Pat. Rolls 1327–1330*, pp. 130, 154.
28. J. Smyth *The Lives of the Berkeleys* I, p. 292.
29. This is all mentioned in the 'Compotus' or Account of the Clerk Hugh Glanville, printed with a commentary in S. A. Moore's article, 'Documents relating to the Death and Burial of Edward', *Archaeologia* (1887), Vol. 50, Pt. I, pp. 215–26.
30. T. F. Tout, 'The Captivity and Death'. *Swynbroke*, p. 31; *Annales Paulini*, p. 333; Smyth, *Lives of the Berkeleys* I, p. 293.
31. *Murimouth*, pp. 52–4.
32. Tout, 'The Captivity and Death of Edward'.
33. *Murimouth*, p. 52. J. Smyth of Nibley's account proves this, in *Lives of the Berkeleys* I, p. 293.
34. *Cal. Pat. Rolls, 1327–1330*, pp. 130, 154.
35. *Cal. Pat. Rolls 1327–1330*, p. 153.
36. The main source of evidence is F. J. Tanquerery's edition and commentary on J. Walwayn's Letter in his article: 'The Conspiracy of Thomas Dunheved, 1327', *Eng. Hist. Rev.* (1916), XXXI, pp. 119–25.
37. Smyth, *Lives of the Berkeleys*, I, p. 299.
38. *Cal. Pat. Rolls 1327–1330*, p. 154.
39. Ibid., p. 158.
40. KB/27/270 (Michaelmas/Edward II), Mem. 29; *Cal. Pat. Rolls 1327–1330*, pp. 386, 557, 572.
41. The fate of the gang is mysterious: some were arrested (Tanquerery, Conspiracy of Thomas Dunheved', p. 124). Thomas Dunheved disappeared into prison. (*Annales Paulini*, p. 337). Stephen lived

long enough to join Kent's conspiracy *(Cal. Fine Rolls 1327–1337)*, p. 169).

42. *Cal. Pat. Rolls 1327–1330*, p. 100.
43. KB/27/274. M. 10.
44. Tanquerery, 'Conspiracy of Thomas Dunheved', p. 120.
45. *Cal. Cl. Rolls 1327–1336*, pp. 217–18; *Cal. Pat. Rolls 1327–1336*, p. 207.
46. C/53/114/20 and 15.
47. For the full account and text, see Tout, 'The Captivity and Death of Edward'.
48. *Annales Paulini* p. 337; *Canon of Bridlington*, pp. 97–8; *Murimouth*, pp. 53–5; *Polychronicon* VIII, p. 324; *Knighton* I, p. 446; *Swynbroke*, pp. 33–4.
49. *Swynbroke*, pp. 31–2.
50. Tout, 'Death and Captivity of Edward II', p. 164.
51. *Winchester Cathedral Cartulary*, pp. 104–7.
52. *Chronica Monasterii de Melsa* II, Meaux version, p. 355.
53. *Murimouth*, pp. 53–4.
54. *Foedera* II, p. 718.

FIVE: The Burial of a King

1. Smyth of Nibley, *Lives of the Berkeleys*, I p. 296.
2. *Historical Papers and Letters from Northern Registers*, ed. J. Raine (Rolls Series, London, 1873), p. 355.
3. D.L. 10/253.
4. On Gurney, see *Cal. Cl. Rolls 1327–1330*, p. 59. On Ockle, see E/101/303/16, S.C.I./38/194.
5. E/101/382/10. M. 19; *Foedera* II, p. 725.
6. Tout, 'The Captivity and Death of Edward', pp. 168 n1 and 169 n1.
7. *Lanercost*, p. 259.
8. The three main (and virtually only) records for the royal burial are: *Murimouth*, pp. 53–4; Smyth of Nibley, *Lives of the Berkeleys*, pp. 293–4. S. A. Moore, 'Documents relating to the Burial of Edward II' (*Arch.*, Vol. Part 50.1, 1887) pp. 215–26 lists all the items mentioned here including Glanville's account. This evidence will be critically analysed later.
9. Brit. Lib., Add. Mss. 24, 459, f.173.
10. E/101/382/10. M.20.
11. Moore, *Documents*.
12. *Brut*, p. 254.
13. *Annales Paulini*, p. 341; *Foedera* II, pp. 740–1.
14. Mortimer was absent from 3 March 1328 until 21 April 1328. C53/115/85 – C.53/115/69. (A list of Charter witnesses.)
15. *Foedera* II, p. 743; R. Nicholson, *Edward III and the Scots* (Oxford, 1965), p. 52.
16. *Cal. of Plea and Memoranda Rolls*, p. 63.
17. Ibid., p. 65.
18. Henry of Lancaster attempted a *coup*; hostilities were avoided when Isabella and Mortimer forced him to concede: see *Knighton* I, pp. 450–1; *Cal. Cl. Rolls. 1327–1330*, pp. 528–30.
19. *Annales Paulini*, pp. 342–3.
20. *Cal. Pat. Rolls: 1327–1330*, p. 439; McKisack, *The Fourteenth Century*, p. 484.
21. The *Brut* Chronicle describes Mortimer's extravagances and his son's reaction, see pp. 261–2.
22. *Foedera* II, p. 783.
23. *Brut*, p. 266; *Swynbroke*, p. 44.
24. *Murimouth* (Appendix), pp. 255–7.
25. *Cal. of Plea and Memoranda Rolls*, p. 72.

26. C53/114/7.
27. *Cal. Papal Registers 1305–1342*, p. 499.
28. *Foedera* II, p. 783. The Government was still pursuing Stephen Dunheved in 1329, see *Cal. Fine Rolls 1327–1337*, p. 169.
29. *Cal. Fine Rolls 1327–1337*, pp. 168–9; *Cal. Pat. Rolls 1327–1330*, pp. 556–7; *Cal. Cl. Rolls 1330–1333*, p. 132.
30. *Cal. Fine Rolls 1327–1337*, p. 149; *Rot. Parl.* II, pp. 53–4.
31. *Cal. Pat. Rolls 1327–1330*, pp. 548, 549, 557.
32. *Foedera* II, p. 782.
33. *Brut*, pp. 265–6; *Chronica Monasterii de Melsa* II, p. 359; *Knighton* I, p. 452.

SIX: The Downfall of the She-Wolf

1. *Swynbroke*, p. 45.
2. C. G. Crump, 'The Arrest of Roger Mortimer and Queen Isabella', *Eng. Hist. Rev.* XXVI (1911), pp. 331–2.
3. *Murimouth*, p. 60.
4. *Cal. Fine Rolls 1327–1337*, p. 129.
5. *Brut*, p. 271 n. 31; *Rot. Parl.* II, p. 52.
6. S.C.1./38/195.
7. Entries show they were well treated after 1330. See *Cal. Cl. Rolls 1330–1333*, pp. 158–9; *Cal. Pat. Rolls 1330–1334*, pp. 10 and 22.
8. *Brut*, p. 270.
9. *Brut*, pp. 268–9.
10. *Brut*, p. 269; *Rot. Parl.* II, p. 53; 'Scalacronica' IV, p. 33.
11. *Rot. Parl.* II, p. 53.
12. 'Scalacronica' IV, p. 35; *Brut*, p. 269.
13. Ibid.
14. *Brut*, p. 270.
15. *Brut*, p. 271; 'Scalacronica' IV, p. 35; *Swynbroke*, p. 46.
16. *Brut*, p. 271.
17. 'Scalacronica' IV, pp. 157–8.
18. S.C.8/152/7583; *Swynbroke*, p. 46; E/403/255. M.2; *Cal. Pat. Rolls 1330–4*, p. 36.
19. *Cal. Cl. Rolls 1330–1333*, pp. 161–2.
20. *Rot. Parl.* I, II, pp. 52–3.
21. *Murimouth*, p. 62 n. 11.
22. *Chronica Monasterii de Melsa* II, p. 360.
23. S.C. 1/38/5.
24. *Swynbroke*, p. 47; *Murimouth*, p. 62.
25. *Rot. Parl.* II, p. 53.
26. *Rot. Parl.* II, p. 54.
27. Smyth of Nibley, *Lives of the Berkeleys* I, p. 297.
28. *Foedera* II, p. 801.
29. *Rot. Parl.* II, p. 57.
30. Ibid.
31. Smyth, *Lives of the Berkeleys* I, p. 297; *Rot. Parl.* II.
32. *Foedera* II, p. 960.
33. *Cal. Pat. Rolls 1340–1343*, p. 378; *Foedera* III, pp. 56, 146.
34. All the details of Edward III's pursuit of Gurney can be found in Joseph Hunter's article 'On the Measures taken for the Apprehension of Thomas Gurney', *Archaeologia* Vol. 27 (London, 1838), pp. 274–97.
35. *Lanercost*, p. 267.

36. Payments to the Constable, see *Cal. Cl. Rolls 1330–1333*, p. 434; E/159/108M104.
37. *Cal. Fine Rolls 1327–1337*, p. 204; E/103/4/30 M. 4v.
38. B. Smalley, *English Friars and Antiquity* (Oxford, 1960), pp. 138–9.
39. *Cal. Pat. Rolls 1330–1334*, p. 242.
40. *Cal. Pat. Rolls 1330–1334*, pp. 271, 529–30.
41. Strickland, *Lives of the Queens of England* I, pp. 535–7.
42. Hist. Mss. Comm., 11th Report: Appendix III, pp. 213–19.
43. *Murimouth*, pp. 155, 231; *Foedera* II, p. 170.
44. This last year and its household book are described by E. A. Bond 'Notices on the Last Days of Isabella, Queen of Edward II', *Archaeologia* Vol. 38 (London, 1853/4), pp. 453–9.
45. *Knighton* II, p. 100; F. Devon, *Extracts from the Issue Rolls of the Exchequer* (London, 1837), p. 172; *Foedera* II, p. 411.
46. *Monumenta Franciscana*, ed. J. S. Brewer (Rolls Series, London, 1858), I, pp. 506, 515; *Lanercost*, p. 267.
47. C. L. Kingsford, *The Grey Friars of London* (Aberdeen, 1915), pp. 70–4.
48. Ibid.
49. The Public Record Office document E/101/393/4 gives an inventory of Isabella's belongings and mentions this detail.

SEVEN: The Immortal King

1. Fieschi's career and pedigree are clearly laid out in a very scholarly article by G. P. Cuttino and Thomas W. Lyman, 'Where is Edward II?', *Speculum* Vol. 53 (1978), pp. 522–42. I disagree, however, with what they write about the letter, its dating and the evidence of *Swynbroke*. The main thrust of this article is on the architectural controversy surrounding Edward II's last reputed resting place (which they resolve brilliantly) rather than an analysis of the letter itself or the events of 1326–30.
2. M. A. Germain, *Publications de la Société Archaeologique de Montpellier* Vol. 37 (1877), pp. 118–20.
3. This summary of the evidence is based, in the main, on Cuttino's article in *Speculum* mentioned in note above.
4. *Dictionary of National Biography*, Vol. XIX (Oxford, 1993) p. 632.
5. *Foedora* II, p. 783.
6. On Fieschi's career, see *Speculum*, Vol. 53, pp. 539–40.
7. McKisack, *The Fourteenth Century*, pp. 273 et seq.
8. Cuttino, 'Where is Edward II?' *Speculum*, Vol. 53, p. 542.
9. E/36/203 fos. 178–9, 'William the Welshman who announced that he was King of England, father of the present King'.

EIGHT: The King is Dead, Long Live the King

1. Walsingham, *Historia Anglicana* I, p. 83.
2. Smyth of Nibley, *Lives of the Berkeleys*.
3. *Brut*, p. 265.
4. *Brut*, pp. 265–7.
5. Ibid.

Bibliography

I: MANUSCRIPT SOURCES

A. *Public Record Office*
   Chancery
   C.47 (Chancery Miscellanea)
   C.49 (Parliament and Council)
   C.53 (Charter Rolls)
   C.61 (Gascon Rolls)
   C.62 (Liberate Rolls)
   C.81 (Chancery Warrants)

   Duchy of Lancaster
   D.L.10 (Royal Charters)
   D.L.41 (Miscellanea)
   D.L.42 (Misc. Books)

   Exchequer
   E.30 (Diplomatic Documents)
   E.101 (King's Remembrancer, Accounts Various)
   E.159 (K. R. Memoranda Rolls)
   E.163 (Exchequer Miscellanea)
   E.199 (Sheriffs' Accounts)
   E.368 (L.T.R. Memoranda Rolls)
   E.403 (Issue Rolls)
   E.404 (Warrants for Issue)

   Ancient Deeds
   Series 'D'
   Series 'W.S.'

   King's Bench
   K.B. 27

   Special Collections
   SC.1 (Ancient Correspondence)
   SC.6 (Ministers' Accounts)
   SC.8 (Ancient Petitions)

B. *Archives Nationales*
   Series J : Cartons 356, 403, 408, 631, 633, 654, 655.

C. *Bibliothèque Nationale*
   Coll. Brienne, 7007

Coll. Moreau, vol. 255
Fr. MS. Nouvelles Acquisitions, 6999
    MS. 10132 (Chronicle of Thomas Mauberge)
Lat. MSS. 8504

D. *Bodleian Library, Oxford*
MS. Ashmole 794
MS. Douce 128 (French *Brut*)
MS. Lat. Hiat. c.5(R) (Rolls of the King's daily household expenses, 1308–9)
MS. Tanner 197 (Wardrobe Book, 1311–12)
MS. 751
MS. 956

E. *British Museum*
Add. MSS. 7967
        15664
        17362 (Wardrobe Book, 1319–20)
        22923
        24459
        35093
        35114
Add. Ch. 26684
Cottonian MSS. Julius A.I.
             Julius E.I.
             Nero C. VIII (Wardrobe Book, 1310–11
             Queen's Wardrobe Book, 1311–12)
             Nero D.II.
             Nero D.VI.
             Nero D.X.
             Vitellius A.XVI.
             Vitellius E.X.
MS. Harleian 636 (Polistoire of Christ Church, Canterbury)
Harleian MS. Royal 13.E.IX
Stowe MSS. 553

F. *Lambeth Palace Library*
MS. 242
Register of Walter Reynolds

G. *MSS. de l'Arsenal de Paris. 3346*

H. *Society of Antiquaries*
MSS. 120
      121
      122
      541

I. *Trinity College, Cambridge*
MS. R. 5.41

2: PRINTED SOURCES

A *Chronicles*

Adae Murimouth Continuatio Chronicarum, ed. E. M. Thompson (Rolls Series, London, 1889)

Annales Londonienses, ed. W. Stubbs (Rolls Series, London, 1882)

Annales Monasticii, ed. H. R. Luard, IV (Rolls Series, London, 1869)

Annales Paulini, ed. W. Stubbs (Rolls Series, London, 1882) *Brut*, ed. F. W. D. Brie (Early English Text Society, 1906)

Chronica Gentis Scotorum Johannis de Fordun, ed. W. F. Skene, I (Edinburgh, 1839)

Chronica Monasterii de Melsa, ed. E. A. Bond, II (Rolls Series, London, 1867)

The Chronicle of Lanercost, ed. H. Maxwell-Lyte (Glasgow, 1919)

'Chronicle of the Civil Wars of Edward II', ed. G. Haskins, *Speculum*, XIV (1939)

Chronicle of Walter of Guisborough, ed. H. Rothwell (Camden 3rd Series IXXXIX, 1957)

Chronicon Abbatiae Ramesiensis, ed. W. Mackay (London, Rolls Series, 1886)

Chronicon Galfredi le Baker de Swynbroke, ed. E. M. Thompson (Oxford, 1889)

Chronicon Henrici Knighton, ed. J. R. Lumby, I (Rolls Series, London, 1889)

Chronique de Froissart, ed. S. Luce, I (Paris, 1869)

Chronique de Jean le Bel, ed. J. Viard and E. Deprez, I (Société de l'Histoire de France, Paris, 1904)

Chronique de Pays Bas, ed. J. Smet, *Receuil des Chroniques de Flandre*, II (Brussels, 1856)

Chronique Parisenne Anonyme de 1316 a 1339, ed. A. Hellot, XI (Memoires de la Société d'Histoire de Paris)

Chroniques de London, ed. C. J. Aungier (Camden Society, 1844)

Chronographia Regum Francorum, ed. H. Moranville, I (Société d'Histoire de France, Paris, 1891)

Cronijke Van Nederlandt, ed. Charles Piot (Brussels, 1897)

Flores Historiarum, ed. H. R. Luard, III (Rolls Series, London, 1890)

Gesta Edwardi de Caernarvon Auctore Canonico Bridlingtoniensi, ed. W. Stubbs (Rolls Series, London, 1882–3)

Les Grandes Chroniques de la France, ed. M. Paulin, V (Paris, 1837)

Historia Dunelmensis Scriptores Tres, ed. J. Raine, I (Surtees Society, Edinburgh, 1939)

Historiae Anglicanae Decem Scriptores, ed. R. Twysden (London, 1652)

Historia Roffensis printed in Anglia Sacra, ed. H. Wharton, I. (London, 1691)

Johannis de Trokelowe et Henrici de Blandeford Chronica et Annales, ed. H. T. Riley (Rolls Series, London, 1866)

Le Livere de reis de Brittanie, ed. J. Glover (Rolls Series, London, 1865)

Nicolai Triveti Annalium Continuatio, ed. A. Hall (Oxford, 1722) *Oeuvres de Froissart*, ed. Kervyn de Lettenhove, II (Brussels, 1867)

The Polychronicon of Ranulph Higden, ed. C. Babington and J. R. Lumby, VIII (Rolls Series, London, 1865–86)

Receuil des Historiens des Gaules et de la France, ed. M. de Wailly, XX, XXI (Paris, 1855)

Receuil des Historiens des Gaules et de la France. ed. M. de Wailly, Delisle et Jourdain, XXII, XXIII (Paris, 1855–76)

Robertus de Avesbury, De Gestis Mirabilibus Regis Edwardi Tertii, ed. E. M. Thompson (Rolls Series, London, 1889)

'Scalacronica', ed. H. R. Maxwell, *Scot. Hist. Rev.* III (1905–6), IV (1906–7)

Vraves Chroniques de Jean le Bel, ed. M. L. Polain, I (Brussels, 1863)

Walsingham, Thomas, *Historia Anglicana*, ed. H. T. Riley, I (Rolls Series, 1863)
Willelmi Cappellani in Brederode postea Monachi et Procuratoris Egmundensis Chronicon, ed. C. Pijnacker Hondyk, XX (Historisch Genootschap, 3rd Series, Amsterdam, 1904)

B *Published and Calendared Documents*

Calendar of Chancery Warrants, 1244–1326
Calendar of Charter Rolls
Calendar of Close Rolls
Calendar of Documents Relating to Scotland, ed. J. Bain, III (Edinburgh, 1887)
Calendar of Fine Rolls
Calendar of Letterbooks Preserved among the Archives of the Corporation of the City of London, 1275–1498, ed. R. Sharpe, Books 'D' and 'E' (London, 1899–1912)
Calendar of Papal Registers, Letters II 1305–1341
Calendar of Patent Rolls
Calendar of Plea and Memoranda Rolls of the City of London, ed. A. H. Thomas (Cambridge, 1926)
Cole, H., *Documents Illustrative of English History in the 13th and 14th Centuries* (London, 1844)
Devon, F., *Extracts from the Issue Rolls of the Exchequer* (London, 1837)
Eulogium Historiarum, ed. F. S. Haydon (Rolls Series, London, 1863)
Gesta Abbatum Sancti Albani, ed. H. T. Riley, II (London, Rolls Series, 1867)
Groot Charterboek de Graaven Van Holland, ed. F. Mieris, II (Leyden, 1754)
Hardy, T. D., *Syllabus (in English) of the Documents Relating to England and other Kingdoms contained in the collection known as 'Rhymer's Foedera'*, I (London, 1869)
Historical Papers and Letters from Northern Registers, ed. J. Raine, (Rolls Series, London, 1873)
The Household Book of Queen Isabella, ed. F. D. Blackley and G. Hermansen (Edmonton, 1971)
Inventaires des Manuscrits concernant les Relations de Flandre et L'Angleterre, ed. J. de St Genois, (Messager des Sciences Historiques, 1842)
Les Journaux du Tresor de Charles IV, ed. J.Viard (Paris, 1840)
Les Journaux du Tresor de Philippe le Bel, ed. J. Viard (Paris, 1840)
Letters of Edward, Prince of Wales, ed. H. Johnstone (Roxburghe Club, 1931)
Literae Cantuarienses, ed. J. B. Sheppard (Rolls Series, London, 1889)
Lords' Report on the Dignity of a Peer, IV
Memorials of St. Edmund's Abbey, ed. T. Arnold, II (Rolls Series, London, 1892)
Monumenta Franciscana, ed. J. S. Brewer, I (Rolls Series, London, 1858)
Parliamentary Writs, ed. F. Palgrave II (London 1827–34)
Political Poems and Songs, ed. T. Wright, I (Rolls Series, London, 1859)
Recits d'un Bourgeois de Valenciennes, ed. Kervyn de Lettenhove (Louvain, 1877)
Recueil des Historiens de France: Documents Financiers (Comptes Royaux, 1285–1314), ed. R. Fawtier, III (Paris, 1956)
Register of Walter Stapledon, Bishop of Exeter, 1307–1326, ed. F. C. Hingeston-Randolph (London, 1892)
Registre du Tresor Des Chartes, ed. R. Fawtier, I (Paris, 1958)
Rekeningen Van de Herberge Van Joanna Van Valois, 1319–1326, ed. H. Smit, XLVI (Historisch Genootschap, 3rd Series, 1924)
Rotuli Parliamentorum, I.
Rotuli Parliamentorum Anglie Hactenus Inediti, ed. H. G. Richardson and G. O. Sayles (Camden Society 3rd Series, LX, 1935)
Rotuli Scotiae in Turri Londinensi et in Domo Capitulari Westmonasteriensi Aservati, ed. D. Macpherson, J.Caley, W. Illingworth, T. H. Horne, I (London, 1814)

BIBLIOGRAPHY

Rymer, T., *Foedera, Conventiones. Litterae*, ed. A. Clarke and F. Holbrooke, I, II
  (London 1816–18)
Select Cases in the Court of King's Bench Under Edward III, ed. G. D. Sayles, V
  (Selden Society, London, 1958)
Smyth of Nibley, J., *The Berkeley Manuscripts: The Lives of the Berkeleys*, I
  (Gloucester, 1883)
Statutes of the Realm I, (1812)
Vite Edwardi Secundi, ed. N. Denholm-Young (London, 1957)
The War of St. Sardos, ed. P. Chaplais (Camden Society 3rd Series, LXXXVII,
  1954)
Winchester Cathedral Cartulary, ed. A. W. Goodman (Winchester, 1927)

C *Secondary Sources*

Bock, F., *England's Beziehiengen zim Reich unter Adolf von* Nassau (Innsbruck,
  1933)
Bond, E. A., Notices on the Last Days of Isabella, Queen of Edward II,
  Archaeologia, Vol. 38 (London, 1853/4)
Cambridge Medieval History, VII (Cambridge, 1932)
Chaplais, P., 'English Arguments concerning the Feudal Status of Aquitaine',
  Bull. Inst. Hist. Research XXXI (1946–8)
Clarke, M. V, 'Committees of Estates and the deposition of Edward II',
  Historical Essays in Honour of James Tait, ed. J. G. Edwards, V. Galbraith, E. F.
  Jacob (Manchester, 1933)
The Complete Peerage, ed. G. E. Cokayne, revised by Vicory Gibbs, H. A.
  Doubleday and Lord Howard de Walden, VIII (London, 1910–57)
Cordier, H., 'Annales de l'Hotel de Nesle', *Memoires de l'Institut National de
  France* XLI (1920)
Crump, C. G., 'The Arrest of Roger Mortimer and Queen Isabella', *Eng. Hist.
  Rev.* XXVI (1911)
Cuttino, G. P. and Thomas W. Lyman, 'Where is Edward II? *Speculum*, Vol.
  53 (1978)
Davies, J. C., *The Baronial Opposition to Edward II* (Cambridge, 1918)
Davies, R. R., *The Bohun and Lancaster Lordships in Wales in the
  Fourteenth and Fifteenth Centuries* (Oxford University, D.Phil. thesis,
  1965)
Doherty, P.C., 'The Date of the Birth of Isabella, Queen of England
  1308–1358', *Bull. Inst. Hist. Research*, XLVIII (1975)
Dubois, Pierre, *De Recuperatione Terrae Sanctae*, ed. W. Brandt (New York,
  1956)
Dubois, Pierre, *Summaria Brevis et Compendiosa*, ed. H. Kampf (New York,
  1936)
Edwards, Kathleen, 'The Political Importance of the English Bishops during the
  reign of Edward II', *Eng. Hist. Rev.* LIX (1944)
Fawtier, R., *The Capetian Kings of France* (Glasgow, 1960)
Fryde, N., 'John Stratford, Bishop of Winchester, and the Crown, 1323–1330',
  Bull. Inst. Hist. Research XLI (1971)
Germain, M. A., *Publications de la Societe Archaeologique de Montpellier*, Vol.
  37 (1877)
Griffin, M. E., 'Cadwallader, Arthur and Brutus in the Wigmore Manuscript',
  Speculum, XVI (1941)
Holmes, G. A., 'Judgement on the Younger Despenser, 1326', *Eng. Hist. Rev.*
  LXX (1955)
Holmes, G. A., 'The Rebellion of the Earl of Lancaster, 1328–1329', *Bull. Inst.
  Hist. Research*, XXVIII (1955)

Hunter, J., 'On the Measures taken for the Apprehension of Thomas Gurney', *Archaeologia*, Vol. 27 (1838)

Hunter, J., 'The Mission of Queen Isabella to the Court of France', *Archaeologia*, XXXVI (1855)

Johnson, C., 'The Homage of Guienne in 1304', *Eng. Hist. Rev.* LIII (1938)

Johnstone, Hilda (ed.), *Letters of Edward, Prince of Wales* (Roxburghs Club, 1931)

Johnstone, Hilda, 'Isabella, The She-Wolf of France', *History*, XXI (1936–7)

Johnstone, Hilda, *The Queen's Household, The English Government at Work, 1327–1336*, ed. W. A. Morris, I (The Mediaeval Academy of America, 1940)

Johnstone, Hilda, *Edward of Caernarvon* (Manchester, 1946)

Kerling, N., *Commercial Relations of Holland and Zeeland with England* (Leyden, 1954)

Kingsford, C. L., *The Grey Friars of London* (Aberdeen, 1915)

Le Neve, John, *Fasti Ecclesiae Anglicanae*, II (Oxford, 1854)

Lizerand, G., *Clement V et Philippe le Bel* (Paris, 1906)

Maddicott, J. R., *Thomas of Lancaster, 1307–1322* (Oxford, 1970)

McKisack, M., *The Fourteenth Century*, (Oxford, 1959)

Moore, S. A., 'Documents relating to the Burial of Edward II', in *Archaeologia*, Part 50, 1887

Nicholson, R., *Edward III and the Scots: The formative years of a military career* (Oxford, 1965)

Nicholson, R., 'A Sequel to Edward Bruce's Invasion of Ireland', *Scot. Hist. Rev.* XLII (1963)

Palmer, J. N., *England, France and Christendom, 1377–1399* (London, 1972)

Parker, T. H., *The Knights Templars in England* (University of Arizona Press, 1963)

Phillips, J. R. S., *Aymer de Valence, Earl of Pembroke, 1307–1324* (Oxford, 1972)

Powicke, F., *The Thirteenth Century* (Oxford, 1953)

Round, J. H., 'The Landing of Queen Isabella', *Eng. Hist. Rev.* XIV (1899)

Seward, Desmond, *The Monks of War* (London, 1974)

Smalley, B., *English Friars and Antiquity* (Oxford, 1960)

Smit, H. J., *Bronnen Tot de Geschiedenis Van den Handel met England, Schotland, en Ierland, 1150–1450* (Gravenhage, 1928)

Smith, W. J., 'The Revolt of William Somertone', *Eng. Hist. Rev.* LXIX (1954)

Somerville, R., *The Duchy of Lancaster* I (London, 1953)

Stones, E. L. G., 'The date of Roger Mortimer's escape from the tower', *Eng. Hist. Rev.* LXVI (1951)

Strickland, A., *Lives of the Queens of England* I (new ed., London, 1970)

Tanquerery, F. J., 'The Conspiracy of Thomas Dunheved, 1327', *Eng. Hist. Rev.* XXXI (1916)

Taylor, A., *Peter Gaveston* (London University, MA Thesis, 1936)

Taylor, J., 'The Judgement on Hugh Despenser the Younger', *Medievalia et Humanistica*, XII (1958)

Tout, T. F., 'The Captivity and Death of Edward of Caernarvon', *Collected Papers of Thomas Frederick Tout*, III (Manchester, 1934)

Tout, T. F., *The Place of Edward II in English History* (2nd .ed., Manchester, 1936)

Trease, H., 'The Spicers and Apothecaries of the Royal Household in the reigns of Edward I and II', *Nottingham Mediaeval Studies* III (1959)

Waller-Zeper, S.A., *Jan Van Henegouwen, Heer Van Beaumont* (Gravenhage, 1914)

Williams, G.A., *Medieval London, from Commune to Capital* (University of London, 1970)

Wood, Anthony, *History and Antiquities of the University of Oxford*, ed. J. Gutch, I (Oxford, 1729)

Index

Adam (illegitimate child of Edward II) 35

Aldenham, Roger de 48

Annals of St Paul 128

'Anointed Ones' of Westminster 3

Arnold, Cardinal 54

Arthurian legends 20, 112, 144–5, 177

Articles of Deposition 23, 111

Arundel, Earl of 71

Aylmer, William 115, 123–5, 219

Badlesmere, Bartholomew 68, 70, 71, 74

Baldock, Robert 195

Bannockburn, Battle of 59–60

Baret, Lady 75

Baret, Stephen 75

Bayouse, Bogo 152, 163, 201

Beaukaire, William 137, 222

Beaumont, Henry 49, 79, 149

Beaumont, Louis de 61–2, 78

Bec, Anthony 40, 61

Becket's tomb, pilgrimage to 2, 25, 50, 170

Bellers, Robert 89

Benedetti, Anna 189–92

Beresford, Simon de 158, 161, 163, 164, 196, 197

Berkeley Castle 116, 118, 120–1, 122, 142, 198

Berkeley, Maurice 72, 81

Berkeley, Thomas
  after escape of Edward II 221
  carries out repairs to castle 122–3
  excuses for death of Edward II 129–30, 164–6, 230–2
  is keeper of Edward II 115–16, 137, 138

treatment after fall of Mortimer 158, 168

Betton, Richard de 86

Black Prince 175, 177

Bliton, Richard 93

Blunt, Sir Thomas 112

Bohun, Humphrey 158

Bohun, William 158

Boniface VIII, Pope 13, 17

Braose, William de 29

Bridlington Chronicle 129

Brotherton, Thomas (Earl of Norfolk) 90, 145, 175, 194

Bruce, David 142, 175

Bruce, Robert (Robert the Bruce)
  against Edward I 8, 19–20, 32
  against Edward II 51, 61, 76
  attempts to capture Isabella 62
  at Battle of Bannockburn 59
  on Edward II 40
  invades Ireland 85
  long campaign of 50
  secret agreement with Isabella 108
  victory of 142

Brut Chronicle 151, 185, 221, 227, 228

Burghesh, Henry 157, 161

Bury, Richard 157, 158

Butler, James 202

Cambridge University 5

Canterbury Tales (Chaucer) 2

Catholic Church 6–7
  see also Boniface VIII, Pope; Clement V, Pope; John XXII, Pope; Urban V, Pope Cecime Sopra Voghera 190

Celano, Thomas de 1

Charles IV, King of France (Isabella's brother) 64, 79, 80, 83, 88, 89, 97
Charnay, Geoffrey de 58
Chaucer, Geoffrey 2, 20, 21, 208
Chronicles of Edward II (Stubbs) 189
Church 6–7, 157–8
civil war (1321) 69–81, 85–6
Clement V, Pope 18, 41, 55, 58
Clinton, William 158
Corfe Castle 146, 151, 152, 200, 201–2
coronation of Edward II 45–6
Culpepper, Walter 71
Cuttino, G. P. 191–2
Cysterne, Robert de 23

Darel, Edmund 63–4
de Spencer *see* Spencer
Deaux, Gaucelm de 188–9
Deverel, John 152, 163, 201
Donald of Mar 116
Douglas, Earl of 177–8
Douglas, James 62
Dubois, Peter 12
Dunheved gang 115, 121–5, 217–19
Dunheved, Stephen 115, 124, 150
Dunheved, Thomas 88, 115, 124, 217, 231
Durell, Sir Richard 167

Eaglescliffe, John 139
Eastry, Henry 103
Eastwick, John 140
Edmund of Kent *see* Kent, Edmund Earl of
Eduardo II (Benedetti) 190
Edward I, King
    against marriage of Edward and Isabella 15–16, 17, 18–19, 32
    and the Catholic Church 7
    death of 20, 33, 38–9
    desire for united realm 3–4, 7–9
    funeral of 40
    marries Margaret 13, 15, 17, 25
    relationship with son (Edward II) 26–30
Edward II, King
    abdicates (1327) 112
    after escape from Berkeley Castle 233–6
    against marriage to Isabella 32, 42
    anniversary Mass for 131
    at Battle of Bannockburn 59–60
    becomes King 36
    becomes Prince of Wales 26–7
    betrothed to Isabella 13, 15–16, 18
    bribes French Court 88
    at Bury St Edmunds monastery 25–6
    and Catholic Church 7
    character of 23–5, 28–9, 30–1, 51, 235–6
    childhood of 23–4
    children of 35, 54, 60, 62, 67, 80, 95, 109, 120, 133, 142, 175
    coronation of 45–6
    corpse embalmed 223–4
    correspondence with Isabella 77, 78, 81, 83, 96–7
    cut off by Edward I 29–30
    death faked by Isabella and Mortimer 220–5
    death of 127–31, 133–4, 136, 138, 142
    deposed (1327) 109–12
    escapes from Berkeley Castle 122–3
    flees to Wales (1326) 91, 92, 93
    freed from Berkeley Castle by Dunheved gang 217–19, 224
    funeral 135–40
    ill-treatment during imprisonment 118–20, 133, 225, 233
    ill-treatment of Isabella (1308) 47–8
    illegitimate child of 35
    imprisonment of 107–8, 114–21, 123, 125–6
    influenced by de Spencer 65, 74, 75, 78
    Kent conspiracy and 146–53
    knighted 32
    letter to Charles IV 97–8
    loses support 89–91, 91–2
    marriage to Isabella 19, 43–4, 94
    physical appearance of 35
    popularity in Wales 219
    pursued by Isabella 92–3
    relationship with barons 36, 39, 46–7, 51–3, 59, 67–8
    relationship with father (Edward I) 26–30
    relationship with Isabella 54, 60, 63, 78–9, 82–3, 88, 94–9, 101–2
    relationship with Piers Gaveston 25, 27, 28, 33, 36–9, 43, 44, 45–8, 65, 98
    rumoured still alive 184–215
    Scottish campaign of 25–6, 30, 50, 51
    seeks divorce 88
    sexuality of 37, 98
    strategic ability of 70, 72
    support for (after imprisonment) 114
    surrenders to Henry of Lancaster 94
    and Templar Order 41–2, 43, 55
    tomb of 35, 140–1, 169–70

visits France (1313) 55–6
Edward III, King
  birth of 54–5
  blackmailed by Fieschi 210–15
  claim to French throne 175
  correspondence with Pope John
    XXII 149, 150, 157–8
  crowned (1327) 112
  diplomatic ability of 156–8
  doubts about father's death 215
  during minority 172
  goes to France (1325) 82
  increase in power of 158
  marries Philippa of Hainault 141–2
  and Mortimer 155–6, 158–62
  peace treaty with Scotland (1328) 142
  policy towards foreign clerics 210
  pursues Gurney 166–9, 196, 232–3
  relationship with Isabella 143–4, 158,
    159, 171, 172, 177
Eland, Robert 160
Eleanor of Aquitaine 22
Eleanor of Castile (Edward II's mother)
  23, 30–1
Eleanor (Edward and Isabella's daughter)
  62, 120, 175
Eltham, John of (Edward and Isabella's
  son) 11, 60, 109, 120, 175, 179
English Church 6–7

Falaise, John 49
Felton, John 93
Ferre, Sir Guy 23
Fieschi, Carlo 189
Fieschi, Manuel 185–9, 192–215, 231–2
Flanders war (1302) 17
Folvill gang 81
Foriz, Gregory 125
Froissart, John 113, 142

Gascelyn, Edmund 115
Gascony, Duchy of 8–9, 12–14, 79, 80,
  146, 191
Gaveston, Piers
  burial of 56–7
  daughter of 37, 50
  execution (1312) 53, 69
  made Earl of Cornwall 39
  made Regent in Ireland 48
  marries 37, 39
  opposed by Philip IV 47–8, 49
  relationship with Edward II 25, 27,
    28, 33, 36–9, 43, 44, 45–8, 65, 98
  relationship with Isabella 50, 94–5
Germain, Alexandre 189
Giles of Spain 166–7

Gilles, Archbishop of Narbonne 18
Gisors, John de 86
Glanville, Hugh 137, 165, 199,
  222–3, 224
Gloucester Cathedral 134, 135, 138–9,
  140, 169
  tomb of Edward II at 35, 140–1,
    169–70
Got, Bertrand de see Clement V, Pope
government see Parliament
Gravesend, Stephen 147, 226, 227, 228
Grey, Thomas de 76–7
Griffith, Howel Ap 127, 219
Gurney, Thomas
  after escape of Edward II 221, 225
  favoured by Isabella 134
  is custodian of Edward II 117
  named as assassin of Edward II
    129, 165
  on plaque at Melazzo de Acqui 190
  pursued by Edward III 166–9, 196,
    230, 232–3
  reports death of Edward II 133–4
  warrant for arrest of 163, 164

Hainault, John of 109
Hainault, Philippa of 141–2, 146
Hainault, William Count of 89
Harclay, Andrew 72, 73, 76
Hastings, Isabella 80
Hastings, John de 145
Haye, Thomas 115
Henry II, King 22
Hereford, Earl of 36, 72–3
Hert, Walter 176
Hethe, Hamo de 99, 114
Higden 129, 131
Hinkley, John 87
Holcott, Robert 172
Howell, Robert 146
Hull, William 115

Ingham, Oliver 158
Isabella, Queen
  anger at Earl of Kent 153, 228–9
  arranges Edward II's funeral
    136–7, 138–9
  arranges Gascony truce 81
  arrives in England (1308) 44–5
  betrothed to Edward 13, 15–16, 18
  character of 20, 52, 83, 102–3
  childhood of 16–17
  children of 35, 54, 60, 62, 67, 80, 95,
    109, 120, 133, 142, 175
  at coronation of Edward III 112–13
  coronation of 45–6

correspondence with Edward II 77,
78, 81, 83, 96–7
death of 178
disapproved of by Pope John XXII
145, 150, 155, 157
dresses as widow 82–3, 111, 135, 140
at execution of de Spencer 106
and Fieschi 207–9, 211
in France (1325–1326) 81–5, 88–90
funeral of 178–9
given Great Seal 71
greed of 113
at Hainault 89
health 56, 57
ill-treatment by Edward (1308) 47–8
increase in power of 48–50, 62
invades England (1326) 90–1
love of music 176
madness of 173–4
marriage to Edward 19, 43–4, 94
nearly captured by Scots 62–4, 76–8
opposes Lancaster 61–2
parents 11–12, 14, 16
physical appearance of 11
piety of 175–6
possible pregnancy by Mortimer
145, 156
pursues Edward 92–3
relationship with de Spencer the
Younger 66, 75–80, 83, 95–6,
99, 100–2
relationship with Edward II 54, 60,
63, 78–9, 82–3, 88, 94–9, 101–2
relationship with Edward III 143–4,
158, 159, 171, 172, 177
relationship with Gaveston 50, 94–5
relationship with Mortimer of
Wigmore 84–5, 87–8, 102
role after death of Mortimer
171–2, 173–8
role in civil war (1321) 72
sets up government in Paris 83
and silken purses scandal 57, 58–9
support from Pope John XXII 88–9
tomb of 179
under house arrest 162, 171, 173–4
visits France (1313) 55–6
visits France (1314) 57
withdraws from court 142–3

Johanna (Edward and Isabella's daughter)
67, 120, 142, 175, 177
John of Eltham (Edward and Isabella's
son) 11, 60, 109, 120, 175, 179
John of Nottingham 80–1
John XXII, Pope

against de Spencer 81
correspondence with Edward III 149,
150, 157–8
disapproves of Isabella and Mortimer
145, 150, 155, 157
on Edward II's funeral 149–50, 225
in Fieschi story 190, 204, 231
and Kent conspiracy 147, 148,
149–50, 209, 226, 229, 231
supports Isabella 88–9

Kedyngton 48
Kenilworth, Edward II held at 114–15,
118
Kent, Edmund Earl of
conspiracy 146–53, 163, 202, 226–30
in Fieschi's letter 202
in Isabella's Paris government 83
military role of 71, 80
Kingsclere, William of 167
Knighton 21
Knight's Tale, The (Chaucer) 20

La Tour Landry 20–1
Lancaster, Alice 75
Lancaster, Henry Earl of
against Isabella and Mortimer 143,
144, 159, 161–2
captures Edward 93
claim to throne 112
connection with Dunheved gang 125
holds Edward II in custody 107
joins Isabella's invasion 90
receives Great Seal 108
sympathy for Edward II 109, 115
tries de Spencer 106
Lancaster, Thomas Earl of 36, 49, 50, 51,
53, 59, 60, 61–2
accused of treachery 63
against Hugh de Spencer the Elder 65
against Hugh de Spencer the
Younger 70
demands exile of de Spencers 67
execution of 72–3
ignored by Edward II 36
opposed by Isabella 61–2
opposes Edward II 49, 50, 51, 59
opposes Gaveston 53
seizes power after Bannockburn 60
Lancastrians
marginalization of 143
persecution of 74, 144
Lanercost Chronicle 135
Langton, Walter 28, 29, 30, 40, 48
Launge, Jean 54, 80
Lawrence, Master 176, 178

Leeds Castle, seizure of 69, 70–1
Leygrave, Alice 23
London
   expansion of 4
   rebellion in (1326) 108–9
Louis, Count of Evreux 25, 28, 45, 54
Louis XVI, King 58
Lyman, Thomas W. 191

Maltravers, Agnes 166
Maltravers, Sir John 115, 116–17, 129,
   138, 152, 163, 164, 165, 166, 201
Margaret, Queen 13, 15, 17, 25, 47,
   48–9, 62
Marie Antoinette 58
Martin, John 166
Mathilda, Empress 22
Meaux Chronicle 37, 131
Melazzo de Acqui (castle) 190
Melton, William 114, 142, 147, 150–1,
   226–7, 227–8
millennium, medieval view of 1
Molay, Jacques de 41, 55, 57–8, 175
Monmouth, Richard 161
Montague, William 157, 159–61
Mortimer of Chirk, Roger 75
   in Wales 7, 65, 70, 72, 85–6
Mortimer, Margaret 88
Mortimer, Mathilda 30–1
Mortimer, Roger Third Earl of March
   145, 177
Mortimer of Wigmore, Roger
   bribes Fieschi 207–9
   captured at Nottingham Castle 160–1
   claim on kingdom 112
   created Earl of March 144
   on deposition of Edward II 110
   Edward II against 72
   and Edward III 155–6, 158–62
   escapes from Tower 86–7
   execution of 163
   increase in power of 144–6, 156
   invades England (1326) 90–1
   and Kent conspiracy 228, 229–30
   mourning dress of 140
   and Pope John XXII 145, 150,
      155, 157
   power in Wales 7, 65, 70, 126,
      128, 219–20
   relationship with Isabella 84–5,
      87–8, 102
   relies on Isabella's power 111
   trial of 162
   tries de Spencer 106
   withdraws from court 142–3
Morton, John 115

Murimouth, Adam 117, 129, 131, 137,
   158, 222

Neville, John 158
Nigra, Constantino 189
Norfolk, Earl of 90, 145, 175, 194
Nottingham Castle 159, 160–1

Ockle, William
   after escape of Edward II 220,
      221, 225
   favoured by Isabella 134
   and Fieschi letter 196
   flees after death of Edward II
      163, 166
   named as assassin of Edward II
      129, 165
   possible 'William the Welshman'
      213–14
   warrant for arrest of 163, 164
Orleton, Adam 86, 91, 110, 114,
   130, 157
Oxford University 5, 91

Paris, Matthew 130
Parliament
   deposes Edward II 109–12
   development of 5–6, 180
Pembroke, Agnes 177
Pembroke, Earl of 70, 71
Pessagno 57
Philip IV, King of France (Isabella's
   father) 9
   attacks Templar Order 19, 41, 55,
      57–8, 59
   death of 58
   foreign strategy of 12, 14
   at Isabella's wedding 44
   mediates in England (1312) 53–6
   opposes Gaveston 47–8, 49
   wants marriage with Edward
      14–16, 18, 42
pilgrimages, medieval 2, 25, 50, 170
Polychronicon 129, 131
Pretender, the 60–1

Rawnsley, H. D. 190
Reading, John of 129
Reading, Simon of 94, 106
Reynolds, Walter 40, 57, 64, 70, 76, 92,
   103, 111
Rhymer, Richard 24
Richard II, King 169–70, 180, 183
Richmond, Earl of 70, 71, 76, 83
Robert the Bruce *see* Bruce, Robert
Rosseleti, Ralph de 47

Rosslyn, Thomas 149
Russell, William 115

St Alberto of Butrio (monastery) 190–2
Sapy, Robert 89
Savage, Edmund 146, 151–2
Scotland
    Edward I's campaign against 7–8,
        19–20, 25, 26, 27, 32–3, 40, 50,
        51, 59, 60
    Edward II's campaign against 32–3,
        40, 50, 51, 59, 60, 76, 121
    forces attack northern England 62–3
    Isabella and Mortimer's campaign
        against 121
    peace treaty (1328) 141, 142, 149
Shalford, William 126–8, 220
Smyth of Nibley 222
Somerton, William 66–7, 87
Sparpaglione, Dominicoe 192
Spencer, de (family) 113
Spencer, Eleanor de 80, 101
Spencer, Hugh de (the Elder) 7, 54, 65,
    67, 72, 82, 92–3
Spencer, Hugh de (the Younger)
    against barons 70, 72, 74, 82
    alienates the Lords Spiritual 86
    becomes new favourite 65–8
    bribes French Court 88
    execution of 105–6
    influence over Edward II 65,
        74, 75, 78
    knighted (1306) 85
    loses support 89–91
    Orleton on 91
    and Pope John XXII 81
    price on head of 92
    relationship with Isabella 66, 75–80,
        83, 95–6, 99, 100–2
    treatment of women 75
    trial of 74, 106
    in Wales 7, 85, 94
Spicer, John de 167
Stapleton, Walter 82, 84, 86, 88, 92
Stefano, Zerba 192
Stone of Scone 143–4
Stratford, John 110, 111, 210
Strickland, Agnes 173
Stubbs, William 189
Sully, Henry de 77
Surrey, Earl of 36, 71
Swynbroke 110, 118–19, 129, 130, 131,
    156, 160, 167, 197
Swynnerton, Roger 76

Tanquerery 122
Taunton, Robert 149, 150, 227
Templar Order
    attacked by Philip IV 19, 41, 55,
        57–8, 59
    Edward II and 41–2, 43, 55
Theobald (Isabella's doctor) 80
Thomas of Brotherton 71
Thomason, Nicholas 178
Three Kings at Cologne (shrine) 205
Tilley, John 167
Tour de Nesle scandal 89
Tout, T. F. 23, 127, 189
Treaty of Paris (1259) 13
Trevisa, John 129
Trussel, William 112
Turin Museum of Art 191
Turplington, Sir Hugh 161
Tweng, Sir William 167, 168

Ufford, Robert 158
Urban V, Pope 189

Valence, Agnes de 28
Valence, Aymer de 36, 52–3
Valois, Charles de 84, 87, 147
Vescy, de (family) 89
Vescy, Isabella de 49, 61
Vita Edwardi Secundi 37

Wales
    conquered by Edward I 7
    de Spencer in 7, 85, 94
    Edward II flees to (1326) 91, 92, 93
    Edward II's popularity in 219
    Mortimer's power in 7, 65, 70, 126,
        128, 219–20
Wallace, William 8
Walsingham 167, 219
Walwayn, John 122, 125, 149, 209,
    217–18, 229
Ward, Simon 72, 73
Warwick, Earl of 36
Westminster Abbey, statue of Isabella
    179
Wife of Bath's Tale (Chaucer) 21–2
William of Nogaret 12
'William the Welshman' 213–14, 233–4
Wisham, John 158
Wishart, Archbishop 8
women, medieval view of 20–2
Wyville, Robert 158